REGIONAL DISPARITIES IN INDIA

REGIONAL DISPARITIES IN INDIA

Edited by
ATUL GOSWAMI

AKANSHA PUBLISHING HOUSE
NEW DELHI-110 059 (INDIA)

AKANSHA PUBLISHING HOUSE
4649-B/21, Ansari Road
Darya Ganj, New Delhi - 110 002

Regional Disparities in India

First Edition, 2001

Reprint Edition, 2026

ISBN 81-87606-05-3

PRINTED IN INDIA

Published by M.P. Misra for Akansha Publishing House, New Delhi and Printed at Mehra Offset Press, Delhi.

Contents

Preface

India at the time of independence, inherited from the British an economy severely afflicted by regional disparities. These disparities, looked at by the British rulers as a natural manifestation of varying resource endowments of different regions and their location hence (irreversible), were perceived differently by the social scientists and policy makers of free India. The difference in perception was fundamental in the sense that like inter-personal disparities regional disparities, it was argued by the national policy makers, could be reduced substantially, if not eliminated altogether, though appropriate government policies. The concern for growing regional disparities was reflected in the Five-Year Plan documents. An objective running though all the nine Five Year-Year Plan has been the reduction of regional disparities.

Our understanding of the problem of regional disparities has also undergone qualitative changes during the post independence period. Take for example, the issue of measuring regional disparities. It was originally believed that the most satisfactory way (if not the only way) of measuring such disparities was with the help of per capita income in real terms. States were ranked by their per capital net state domestic products (NSDP) and the ranking was taken as the index of the relative affluence (or deprivation) of the states. However, it did not take long to realise the fact that per capita income figures, besides concealing differences in intra-state inequalities in distribution, may not faithfully reflect the per capita consumption levels. A part of the income earned within the jurisdiction of a state might not be available for consumption within the state, but may get transferred to other states by way of dividend and other remittances. Conversely, income originating within a state might by supplemented by remittances of income from other states. Per capita consumption, rather than per capita income, thus came to be regarded as a more reliable measure of inter-state (regional) disparities.

Inter state (regional) disparities subsequently came to be measured in terms of availability of physical infrastructural facilities (like roads, railways, power, bank, hospitals and dispensaries, etc.) helping the growth of the three productive sector-primary, secondary and tertiary. Availability of basic minimum services like primary education, primary health care, safe drinking water supply, sanitation also came to be used as the basis for measuring regional disparities.

A significant departure from the traditional practice of measuring regional disparities on the basis of mere availability of infrastructural facilities to the access of the various social groups, particularly the depressed consisting of the SC, ST for example) to these facilities as reflected in their income levels and consumption standards, literacy rate, expectations of life at birth, infant and child morality rate, etc. forming the basis of measuring regional disparities could be noticed in more recent times. Similarly, the gender dimension of regional disparities has received the attention of the social scientist and policy makers. Other additional measures of regional disparities which are being used at present include, among others, people's participation in decision-making process in general and the participation of women in particular, environmental protection, enjoyment of human rights (i.e., the working of a vibrant civil society) and quality of governance.

The book contains papers on various dimensions of regional disparities in India authorised by some of the leading economists, social scientists and journalists, besides the keynote address by Professor K.N.Raj. The papers were presented in a national workshop organised by the Omeo Kumar Das Institute of Social Change and Development, Guwahati in the month of February, 1996. The workshop was sponsored by the National Council of Applied Economic Research, New Delhi. It deliberated on India's economic reforms, 1991 and their likely impact on regional disparities.

Professor K.N. Raj, in his Keynote Address dealt with Assam's position vis-a-vis the other states, examining the disparities in the standard of living of the people of different states by per capita consumption levels, he found Assam's standard of living in1985-86 comparing favourably only with the standard of living of Madhya Pradesh, Orissa and Bihar. However, according to him, there were no strikingly high disparities per capita consumption between states. These disparities were more pronounced between urban and rural sectors in some states. To him, while such disparities were more pronounced between urban and rural sectors in some states. To him, while such disparities 'do pose several problems and cannot be wished away, from a longer-term perspective these are not disparities that should be causing most concern'. Disparities in the levels of education and health are much more serious for future development. In this respect, Assam's performance is not very unsatisfactory. In per capita social sector expenditure, it ranked tenth among the 15 major states in 1975-76. Further, it improved its position to the eight rank by 1990-91. Professor Raj concluded that apart from the development of the social sector, the other sectors which should be accorded high priority are agriculture, irregation and soil conservation for reducing Assam's economic distance from the more advanced states.

Professor K.K. George in his paper 'Economic Reforms : What they Foretell Different States ?' examined the possible impact of reforms on regional disparities by piecing together scattered information on industrial investment decisions and investments in the pipeline. He summarised his finding thus : 'the existence of wide regional disparities in India is an inheritance from its colonial past. It was understood by the Indian planners that further widening of regional disparities would be undesirable from both economic and political angles. All Indian Five Year Plans, therefore, had emphasised the correction of regional disparities as a major objective. All policy instruments also had highlighted this regional objective. Despite all these good intentions, regional disparities only widened during the era of centralised planning. Our present study shows that the process of widening of disparities continued unimpeded during the period of liberalisation. For the poorer states in India, the difference between centralised planning and market system is only the difference between tweedledum and tweddeddee.' He cautioned that 'further polarisation among regions is bound to threaten the federal policy'.

Dr. S.C. Jha, in his paper, 'Regional disparities in India " a reappraisal' found that as a result of economic reforms, the flow of both domestic and foreign investment was directed more towards better performing regions. The low performing regions received only a small fraction of commercial bank credit and credit from all-India financial institutions. These indicate the likelihood of growing inter-regional disparities in the future. Dr. Jha contended that 'the low performing region, accounting for about 50 per cent of the nation's total population has lagged behind in almost all aspects of socio-economic development. This trend is likely to continue if no innovative strategy is adopted by the state governments in the low performing region. There is a need for drastic change in this development strategy. the central focus of this strategy has to be on human capital development, agricultural modernisation and rural industrialization. State governments will have to play the key interventionist role in infrastructure and institutional development. Market forces would not be able to make a positive contribution at this stage.

Ms. Neeraj Kaushal in her paper 'Economic Reforms and Regional Disparities', rejecting the growing disparities hypothesis, saw the possibility of both intra-state and inter-state disparities reducing in future as a result of (a) industrialists ploughing funds in less crowded and less industrialised state owing to pressure on the existing infrastructure in the relatively industrialised states : (b) more enterprising industrialists (Ambanis for example) deciding to invest in resource-rich states even through these have poor infrastructure and inefficient administration ; (c) locomotion of future development shifting to international trade, areas closer to ports, many of which are in backward states, attracting more investment ; (d) industrialists investing in states actually or potentially surplus in power ; (e) regional parties coming to power in the less developed states promising the electorate speedier regional development and (f) liberalisation scrapping policies like freight equalisation which had discriminated against less developed states.

In his paper 'Regional Imbalances in the Industrial Development of India : an Inter-temporal Study' Professor Srinath Barua found statistical evidence to the widening of industrial disparities in India both during the pre-reforms and post-reforms periods. He found the north eastern states placed at the bottom of the ranking in the composite index of industrial development despite these states being relatively rich in natural resources. He concluded as follows : Economic reforms are welcome and these can help in initiating higher rate of development only when the basic infrastructural facilities such as power, transport and communication, banking services, marketing services are adequately provided as pre-condition... Hence the centre should come forward in a big way in providing infrastructural facilities to enable the north-eastern states reap the benefits of economic reforms'.

Comparing the impacts of economic reforms on the economically backward north-eastern region with those of economically advanced western region (comprising Goa, Gujarat and Maharashtra), Dr. Jayanta Madhab, in his paper, 'New Economic Policies and Regional Disparities' argued that both foreign investors and all-India financial institutions showed a bias in favour of the more advanced western region in financing investment because of their better infrastructue and market-friendly environment resulting in what he called 'virtuous circle of prosperity'. In contrast, comparative neglect by foreign as well as domestic investors owing to lack of infrastructure, local entrepreneurs and congenial law and order, the north-eastern states, despite their rich resource base, could not come out of the 'vicious circle of poverty' already in operation there. Consequently, the disparities between the western region and the north-eastern region got widened during the post-reforms period. Taking the objective situation into account, the governments of the north-eastern states should follow a strategy of promoting investment in agriculture, horticulture and pisciculture as these states have comparative advantages in production in these fields. Besides investment in these is less susceptible to what the author termed, 'security condition'.

In their joint paper 'Impact of Growth on Access to and Change in Possession of Land, Education, Employment and Consumption and Disparities Between SC, ST and Other's Professor G. Parthasarathy, Dr. Jayashree Anand and C.V.R. Sankar sought to examine (a) the access of SC, ST and Others to land, education and employment, (b) disparities between the three social groups and (c) impact of growth on 'access' and 'disparities'. Marshalling data from the NSSO 38th and 43rd rounds, they have shown that between 1983 and 1987-88 'landlessness has grown both among SCs and STs. Disparities between 'Others' and SCs and STs also show general increase. Growth has no effect in reducing either landlessness of SCs and STs or reducing disparities'.

Dr.V.K. Ramachandran, Dr. Vikas Rawal and Dr. Madhura Swaminathan in their joint paper, 'Investment Gaps in Primary Education : a State-wise Study' attempted to provide statewise estimates of resources required to be mobilised for achieving the goal of universal primary education in India. In short, they calculated the cost of schooling of the children aged 6 to 11 years who were out of school in 1995 by applying the methodology used by Ramachandran. To them, 'the costs of getting every child in India into school in the next five years are large and vary across states, depending on current achievement's. However, they were quick to add that 'resources alone cannot transform conditions without appropriate socio-political changes and commitments from governments, teachers and parents'.

Ms. Gunilla Sterner in her paper, 'Women and Regional Development', analysing the regional development policy of Sweden, observed that, 'sustainable development can only be attained when the needs and interests of both women and men are fully recognised. One important goal for regional development policies in all countries must be to contribute to women's independence so that women, regardless of which part of the country they live, can live a worthy life measured from a female perspective. That includes equal conditions for women and men regarding education, income & properties, health and influence in society. That means that all resources of society should be equally distributed between sexes. And all unpaid work of women should be fully recognised and valued. It also means a freedom from male guardianship, sexual harassment and gender violence.'

Professor Atul Sharma examined the effect of resource flows to the states on regional disparities in his paper, 'Regional Disparities and Resources Flows across States'. Analysing the flow of resources to the states from different sources he found fiscal transfer from the central government, by and large, favouring the poorer and special category states. In contrast, financial institutions and market-oriented investment (which represents a much larger component of the total resource flows), according to him, favoured the relatively advanced states. Economic reforms which dismantled the physical control instruments like licensing, will have the effect of causing larger inflow of investment funds to the relativley more advanced states, thus widening disparities betwe n more advanced and less advanced states, thus widening disparities between more advanced and less advanced state, he argued. In order to arrest this process, he suggested an enhancement of the equity-oriented fiscal transfers so as to enable the less developed states the level and quality of infrastructure that would attract private investment, besides providing larger loan assistance with softer terms. The more advanced states with higher capacity to utilize borrowed funds more productively should be provided greater access to the capital market. However, Professor Sarma added that the mere augmenting transfer of funds to the less developed states would not ensure a quicker pace of development of these states unless an identification of the thrust areas or lead sectors was made by the government and their promotion pursued over the years.

Professor Bhanoji Rao, in his papar `A Perspective on Centre-state Relations in the context of India's Economic Reforms' argued that the present practice of resource transfer through the Planning Commission and the Finance Commission in particular with positive discrimination for less developed states had the unintended effect of providing them an incentive for not moving up the economic ladder. Further, the present arrangement of resource sharing, by making the states excessively dependent on the Centre, has made the state indifferent to their own resource mobilisation efforts, expenditure management and optimal resource allocation. He, therefore, felt an urgent need for introducing reforms in centre-state fiscal relationship. 'The need of the hour', he stated, 'is bridging the gaps in social and human development across the states in order to lay the groundwork for economic growth in line with their potentials through short-term reforms under which there would a constitutional provision for sharing all tax revenues as per a fixed proportion and the Finance Commission would be allocating grants to states for education and health in line with the state-wise targets to be achieved. 'After a desirable level of social development has been achieved in the whole country, and when international trade taxes cease to be of importance due to globalisation, the states alone would levy and collect indirect taxes (within the framework of the common market), while only direct taxes would be levied and collected by the centre. In this approach, it should be possible to do away with the Finance Commission and provide in the Constitution the sharing percentages for direct taxes'. He concluded in the following words. 'Economic autonomy, responsibility and accountability at the state level can produce India's own Indonesia, Korea and Taiwan'.

Analysing regional inequality in India with special reference to Assam, Dr. A.K. Neog, observed that 'reduction of government intervention (effected by economic reforms) is not a sufficient condition but better governance is, for the success of market. The government has a significant role in promoting market efficiency and growth, expanding public investment in infrastructure and social expenditure, reducing poverty and illiteracy and improving equity besides producing public goods. In addition, government intervention is also necessary to take counteractive measures to neutralise the gravitational and centrifugal forces associated with market in centralisation of activities, thereby reducing spatial disparities.

Dr. Neog viewed measures for opening the regional economy of the North East as a necessary condition for accelerating the pace of development. 'Low levels of farm productivity remains critical to the health of the regional economy, Particularly of the North East. Both efficiency and equity considerations demand land reforms particularly in the hill states, where land is unequally distributed.... The fact that regional inequalities are associated with regional differences in agricultural productivity also calls for development of agriculture'. At the same time 'the North East needs substantial investment in education, health and infrastructure. But the financial position of the states is so precarious that they are not in a position to meet these from their own resources. Hence government investment particularly central assistance will have to come not only for infrastructure development but also to wipe out the regional backlog, thereby enlarging the scope to catch up with the rest of the country.' To him, 'development is the best remedy to reduce regional inequality'.

Sanjoy Hazarika in his paper 'Proposals to Promote Equality and Development in India's Far East' dealt with the imbalances caused in the North East (Assam in particular) as a result of migration on a large scale from present Bangladesh during the post-independence period. He argued that 'no wall, law or police force anywhere in the world has been able to stop it (migration). People, like water, always find their level for survival'. Hence the best solution, according to him, was to be sought in 'economic development, rooted in cooperation in water and other resource sharing, multilateral trade and assisting communities at the micro level, instead of imposing centrally sponsored schemes on them'.

Professor Atul Goswami and Dr. (Ms) Archana Sharma in their joint paper, 'Inter-state Disparities in Production and Productivity of Foodgrains' looked into the trend in inter-state variations in per capita production and per hectare yield of foodgrains with the help of co-efficient of variation computed for the annual average corresponding to three triennia viz 1970-73, 1980-83 and 1991-94. They found in increasing trend in inter-state disparities and the disparities are widening over time'. For reducing the disparities, both quantitative and qualitative improvements in agricultural infrastructure, more particularly, effective water management was needed, the authors argued.

The book is expected tobe a variable addition to the existing literature on regional development in India with particular reference to the North East.

I am particularly grateful to the National Council of Applied Economic Research, New Delhi for selecting this Institute to organise the workshop.

I am also profoundly grateful to Shri L.C. Jain, the then Chairman of the Institute, for his constant guidance and advice in getting the workshop organised in a befitting manner. But for his dynamic and perceptive leadership, the workshop would not have had the participation of so many distinguished scholars belonging to different parts of the country, besides a few from other countries.

I express my heartfelt thanks to Ms. Mousumi Saikia, Assistant Research Officer of the Institute who took the pain of entering meticulously the edited manuscript into the computer. I am thankful to my colleagues for their encouraging words. I also express my sincere thanks to Mrs. M. Raghaviah, Senior Reporter, the Hindu for making her technical expertise of preparing the manuscript for publication, at my request. Thanks are also due to Shri M.P. Misra, proprietor, Akansha Publishing House, New Delhi for readily agreeing to publish the book.

Guwahati
25.09.2000

Atul Goswami
Editor

Keynote Address

K.N. Raj

I am greatly honoured by the invitation extended to me by Professor Goswami, the Director of your institute, to deliver the keynote address at this National Workshop on Regional Disparities. Professor Goswarmi's invitation was reinforced by Sri L.C. Jain, the Chairman of the Governing Council of the Institute, but since he has been a very close friend of mine for more than four decades. I take it as only a gesture of his boundless affection and loyalty to all his friends.

I must however confess that I was extremely hesitant to accept the honour, mainly for one reason. I have very little knowledge of Assam. And what would a keynote address be worth, if it is not founded on at least some familiarity with regional disparities within Assam ? Sri Jain then said that I do not have to deal with disparities within Assam and that what was really expected of me was only some observations on how such disparities should be judged in the Indian context and what kind of measures might be considered to lessen them even if not wholly eliminating them.

Let me therefore start first with disparities in the standard of living of our people in different states within India. It is important to have some idea of where Assam stands relatively to other states in the country. Fortunately, a comparable series is available from the Central Statistical Organisation for assessing inter-state disparities, and they can be used for not only ranking the different states according to the level of their per capita income at a point of time (say, in a particular year) but also the changes in ranking over a period of time (say, covering about two decades). For Assam, estimates are available only for 1977-78 and 1985-86, and so we are restricted to comparing its ranking in these two years. Among the 17 states of India. the per capita income of Assam in 1977-78 (estimated at current prices) was only Rs. 994 compared to Rs. 231 7 in Punjab; therefore it ranked 13th that year. By 1985-86 it had risen (at current prices) to Rs. 2386; in the process it took one step upward and ranked 12th in that year. I might mention in passing that, over this period of eight years, Kerala also improved its rank from the 13th to the 10th position — which suggests that Assam has ranked pretty close to Kerala and also risen along with it. From this comparison with Kerala it would seem that, though Assam ranks fairly low among the 17 states of India (about the fourth or fifth above the lowest of them, namely Bihar), its position has not declined since the closing years of the 1970s. That surely is a good enough reason for deriving some satisfaction.

However, when we are discussing disparities in the standard of living of the people in different states within India, we should be comparing not the per capita incomes in these states but the per capita consumption levels. This is because income levels reflect merely the levels of production and the income so generated, within different states; some part of the income generated within a state may however be transferred to other states (as, for instance, the dividends earned in Assam to other states like West Bengal or even Gujarat, depending on the source of the capital invested in the tea plantations of Assam) or be supplemented by transfers from other states (as, for instance, through remittances of Assamese workers in West Bengal to their families in Assam). But per capita consumption levels would reflect the net effect of such transfers.

In Kerala, the large remittances received from its workers living in the Gulf countries to their families within the state had raised the per capita consumption level in the state to the sixth position in India, even in 1977-78 when migration from Kerala to the Gulf countries had only just begun. Within a decade after that (i.e., by 1985-86), per capita consumption level in Kerala had risen to the third position in the country as a whole. However, in the case of Assam, the inclusion of income transfers does not significantly alter its ranking in terms of per capita consumption; per capita consumption in Assam ranks 12th among the 15 states for which estimates are available. If we treat per capita consumption level as an approximate measure of the standard of living in the state, Assam's standard of living in 1985-86 compares favourably only with the standard of living in Madhya Pradesh, Orissa and Bihar.

There are many qualifications which need to be made in this context. The most important of them is that, while per capita consumption level in Assam ranks as low as 12th among the 15 states for which estimates are readily available, it was only about 8 per cent lower than the level of average per capita consumption in the country as a whole, about 15 per cent lower than in Kerala, and about 37 per cent lower than in Punjab which has the highest level of per capita consumption in India. These are not really strikingly high disparities.

In fact, the widest disparities in consumption levels, and therefore in standards of living, are observed not so much as between states taken as a whole but as between urban and rural sectors within some of them. They are particularly striking in some states which have large metropolitan cities, such as Maharashtra, West Bengal, Tamil Nadu, Karnataka and Gujarat. Both income and consumption levels are even perceptibly much higher in metropolitan cities such as Bombay, Calcutta. Madras, Delhi, Bangalore and Ahmedabad.

While such disparities do pose several problems and cannot be wished away, it seems to me that, from a longer-term perspective, these are not the disparities that should be causing most concern. I consider the disparities in the levels of education and health, particularly in the facilities available at the primary level for education and health of the vast masses of our countrymen, the most serious for our future development.

Expenditures on education, medical services, public health, water supply and sanitation are generally all included in the expenditure on what is commonly referred to as social sector expenditure. A study of social sector expenditures, state-wise, undertaken by the Development Research Group in the Reserve Bank of India (and published about three years ago[1]), shows that, while Assam did not rank very high (i.e. not among the three states which had the highest rankings in India) in 1975-76, it was not among the three states with the lowest rankings either. Assam had the tenth rank among 15 states in 1975-76 and what is more, it improved its position to the eight rank by 1990-91. In fact, real per capita social sector expenditure rose in Assam by no less than 6.5 per cent per annum during this decade and a half.

However, within the social sector, the sub-sector of education did not fare as well as the sub-sector comprising medical services, public health, water supply and sanitation; while real per capita expenditure on the latter grew at nearly 7.5 per cent per annum during this decade and a half, real per capita expenditure on the former grew only by a little over 5.75 per cent per annum. I do not intend this inference to be in any sense an adverse reflection on the political and administrative leaders of Assam: the widespread prevalence of illness like malaria, their enervating and lasting effects on the victims, and above all the high mortality and morbidity rates associated with them are more than adequate reasons for according higher priority to health over education.

Apart from the development of health and education, there are also other sectors such as agriculture, irrigation and soil conservation to which it must have seemed essential to accord high priority. Between 1960-61 and 1968-69, the rate of growth of crop production in Assam was less than 1.9 per cent per annum; there was some improvement in the following 15 years, but the rate of growth of crop production was still lower than 2.4 per cent per annum between 1969-70 and 1984-85. In India as a whole, one needs to recall, agricultural production grew from the late 1960s at between 2.5 and 3 per cent per annum. For raising the rate of growth of crop output in Assam, it was necessary not only to extend irrigation and soil conservation but also introduce high-yielding varieties of rice.

High-yielding varieties did in fact get adopted from around 1969. However, the rate of growth of foodgrain output in the following decade and a half was only marginally higher than in the previous decade (being only 2.06 per cent per annum from 1969-70 to 1984-85 compared to 2.03 per cent per annum form 1960-61 to 1968-69). It was the output of non-foodgrains that recorded substantial improvement, touching over 2.75 per cent per annum between 1969-70 and 1985-86, compared to only a little over 1.5 per cent per annum between 1960-61 and 1968-69. The rate of growth of foodgrain output in Assam has in fact been very inadequate for a state in which population has been growing at a compound rate of about 3 per cent per annum over the last two to three decades.[2]

A significant increase in the rate of growth of foodgrain output in Assam, making it less dependent on imports from the rest of India, requires in the first instance some extension in the area under irrigation. Systematic data on irrigation in Assam are available only from 1980-81 onward, and even the data for 1980-81 are ad hoc estimates.

Between 1981-82 and 1987-88, the estimated "irrigation potential" is reported to have increased from 0.21 million hectares to 0.49 million hectares; however, less than 70 per cent of the potential was actually utilised in 1981-82 and slightly less than 50 per cent in 1987-88. It has been observed that "even the meagre potential created could not be utilised by the peasants because of the fact that the aspect of 'Command Area Development', which includes construction of field channels, consolidation of holdings. land levelling and shaping, and other infrastructural development had not been planned earlier."[3]

Secondly, adoption of the high-yielding varieties of rice at a faster rate is essential for achieving significant increases in output. This requires not only availability of irrigation but close contact between farmers and the agricultural extension source network. Moreover, the ability of farmers to increase the proportion of area under high-yielding varieties depends also in their cultivable land being not "very low-lying and prone to flooding and waterlogging."[4] The rate of growth of productivity of foodgrains in Assam has remained well below one per cent per annum in spite of the introduction of high-yielding varieties of rice and wheat; it is of vital importance that the factors responsible for this low rate are closely investigated and corrective action taken.

REFERENCE

1. Prabhu K. Seeta and Somnath Chatterjee, Social Sector Expenditures and Human Development - A Study of Indian States. Department of Economic Analysis and Policy, *Reserve Bank of India*, Bombay

2. Bezbaruah, M.P., *Technological Transformation of Agriculture - A Study from Assam* (Mittal Publications. New Delhi. 1994), p. 38

3. Das, Monmohan, *Structural Analysis of Peasant Agriculture in Assam*, Ch. XII, Section 12.2

4. Bezbaruah, *op. cit.* p.107.

1

Economic Reforms What they foretell different states?

K.K. George

In this paper, an attempt is made to discuss one of the most neglected aspects of economic reforms in India, viz., their impact on inter-state disparities. No doubt, it is a little too early to assess fully the impact of reforms as they are yet to gather full momentum. Besides, for evaluating the impact of reforms package on different states, we do not have reliable data on state domestic product or sectoral growth during the post reform period. Despite these problems, we have made an attempt to study the possible impact of reforms on regional disparities by piecing together scattered information on industrial investment decision and investments in the pipeline.

The key investment variables marshalled by us are:

1. The Foreign Direct Investments approved (FDIs);
2. Foreign Collaborations approved;
3. Industrial Entrepreneur Memoranda signed (IEMs);
4. Location of plants proposed to be set up by companies entering capital market;
5. The registration of new Limited Companies;
6. Investments in the pipeline that are covered by the survey of the Centre for Monitoring Indian Economy (CMIE) covering 3093 large investment projects (exceeding Rs. 5 crore) in mining,

manufacturing and infrastructure which are in various stages of approvals or implementation.

7. The investments of private corporate business sector forecast by the Reserve Bank of India annually. [1]

Our findings are presented in Tables I, II, III and IV. Table I presents the per capita amount of investments proposed. Table II presents the number of projects proposed in relation to each state's population. Table III gives an idea of the size of the investments per unit. Table IV presents the summary position.

FOREIGN DIRECT INVESTMENT (FDI)

Attracting foreign direct investment is one of the cornerstones of the new economic policy. During the period August 1991 to May 1995, 1650 Foreign Direct Investment proposals for investments aggregating Rs. 34845 crore had been approved. The data show a highly skewed distribution. In terms of per capita investment, the biggest beneficiary states were Goa, Maharashtra, Gujarat, Orissa, West Bengal, Himachal Pradesh and Tamil Nadu. All other states received less than the national average. Assam and Bihar, two of the poorest among the states attracted the smallest amounts of foreign direct investment per capita. Except for Arunachal Pradesh, none of the North Eastern States attracted any Foreign Direct Investments. On the other hand, Delhi alone accounted for as many as 235 proposals for investments amounting to Rs. 3574 crore. In fact, Delhi stood third both in number of approvals and the quantum of investments proposed. The other Union Territories like Pondicherry, and Chandigarh too received much more FDIs than some of the more populous states.

If we take the number of FDIs (as against the quantum of investment) in relation to population, only five high income states (Goa, Maharashtra, Haryana, Gujarat and Tamil Nadu) and three middle income states[2], *viz.*, Andhra Pradesh, Karnataka and Himachal Pradesh received above average number of FDIs (see Table II). Orissa's per capita amount of investment was higher despite the low number of FDIs approved because of the very large unit size of FDIs proposed in the state (see col. 2, Table III).

FOREIGN COLLABORATIONS

Foreign collaboration is yet another route envisaged under the new economic policy to attract foreign capital and technology to India. Of the total number of collaborations, the six high income states attracted 52.4 per cent, and the six middle income state 21.7 per cent of the total number. Apart from Rajasthan and Himachal Pradesh, only the high income states received above average number of collaborations in relation to their population. As in the case of FDIs, the Union Territories of Delhi, Pondicherry, Dadra and Nagar Haveli, and Damnan and Diu attracted a sizeable number of foreign collaborations. States like Assam and the other North Eastern states attracted very few collaborations. States like Arunachal Pradesh, Mizoram and Manipur attracted no foreign collaboration at all.

INDUSTRIAL ENTREPRENEURS MEMORANDA SIGNED (IEMS)

Between August 1991 and December 1994, 17064 IEMS for investment totalling Rs. 3,44,929 crore were signed. In per capita terms, only seven states received investments above the national average. Except for Himachal Pradesh and Madhya Pradesh, all these states belonged to the high income group. Among the major states, the state which received the lowest quantum of investment was Assam followed by Bihar. Per capita investments in these states were less than three per cent of that of Gujarat. The position of Madhya Pradesh comes down when the number of IEMS and employment generated are taken into account in relation to the state's large population (see Tables II and III). The size of the units proposed under the IEMS as measured by the investment per unit was comparatively larger in the states of Orissa, Madhya Pradesh and Himachal Pradesh.

CMIE SURVEY

The latest survey covers 3093 large investment projects in mining, manufacturing, electricity, railways and irrigation for which investment decisions have been taken and which are in various stages of approval or implementation. The survey covers only projects involving more than Rs. 5 crore investment. The coverage of the larger projects is relatively more comprehensive.

The combined investment outlay envisaged by the 3093 projects totals Rs. 7,76,444 crore. Of this, mining, refining and manufacturing account for 43.3 per cent, and infrastructure for 56.7 per cent.

Per capita investments in mining and manufacturing, infrastructure and aggregate investments are given separately in Table I. The position revealed is one of highly skewed distribution. In mining and manufacturing, only eight states received above average quantum of investments, of which, three each belonged to high income and middle income groups. Two were low income states. In infrastructure, seven states received above average per capita investment. Of this, three each belonged to high and middle income groups and only one belonged to the low income group.

As for aggregate investment per capita, seven states received above average quantum of investments. Of them, three each belonged to high and middle income groups and only one to low income group.

COMPANIES RAISING CAPITAL FROM THE PRIMARY MARKET

According to "Prime Issue Monitor", 1487 companies raised capital from the market during 1993-94, 1994-95 and 1995-96. State-wise location of plants of these companies shows highly uneven distribution. The six high income states accounted for 56 per cent of the number of companies raising shares. Another 24 per cent was accounted for by the six middle income states. The low income states accounted for only 14 per cent. Maharashtra and Gujarat alone accounted for 41 per cent of the total. Some of the Union Territories with tiny population like Dadra and Nagar Haveli attracted more companies than Kerala and Orissa. Daman and Diu attracted larger number of companies than Bihar, Assam and Meghalaya. Six states did not find a place in the capital market at all. In relation to population, only eight states attracted above the national average number of companies. Of these, six were high income states and two middle income states. It may be noted that no state belonging to the poorer category attracted above average number of companies.

TOTAL COSTS OF PROJECTS FINANCED BY TERM LENDING INSTITUTIONS

The Reserve Bank of India has been making annual forecasts of investments based on the phasing of projects for which term financing has been extended by term lending institutions. During the four year period (1991-92 to 1994-95), these institutions had financed 4908 projects, the total project costs of which amounted to Rs. 1,48,144 crore. The per capita project costs exceeded the national average in only five states. All of them were high income states.

NUMBER OF LIMITED COMPANIES REGISTERED

During the last three years since liberalisation, 103358 Limited Companies were registered in the country. The state-wise distribution of these companies in relation to state's population shows a very uneven pattern. The number of companies registered was above the national average only in five states, of which four were high income states and one a middle income state. The Union Territory of Delhi alone accounted for 17.7 per cent of the companies. As against this, the North Eastern States including Assam accounted for only 0.7 per cent of the number of companies registered. It is true that the location of plants of these companies may be different from those of their registered offices.

But the opportunities for employment generation provided by the location of companies' registered offices and their potential for generating further economic activities in their regions cannot be minimised.

Table IV gives the summary position giving the names of the states which are above the national average in respect of different indicators of investment. The table shows that by and large, it is either those states with higher or those with higher per capita income originating from industry and mining that attracted above average amount and or number of investment proposals in the post liberalisation period. The only exception was Orissa which did not fall in any of these categories. However, Orissa was above the national average only in respect of per capita investments in the pipeline and not in respect of the number of proposals. As noted earlier, the proposals attracted to Orissa are the relatively larger ones. And these are proposals which are aimed to take advantage of the location specific natural resources of the state. In the past too, this state as also the mineral rich Bihar had attracted huge investments. But these investments remained merely 'Cathedrals in the desert' with little spread effects in the state's economy. If the past experience is any guide, the impact of these proposed capital intensive projects on these states' economies is unlikely to be anything very big.

If we leave the above qualified exception, we find that only the six high income states and the four middle income states . Karnataka, Andhra Pradesh, Madhya Pradesh and Himachal Pradesh which have been able to attract large number of investment projects. Among the high income states, the major beneficiaries are Goa, Maharashtra, Gujarat, and Haryana. Punjab and Tamil Nadu are lagging behind the above states according to many indicators. West Bengal, though a middle income state lags behind considerably against most indicators. Kerala, another middle income state lags behind under all heads. Among the low income states, the worst appears to be Bihar followed by Assam and Uttar Pradesh. The North Eastern States do not find a place at all in the industrial investment map of India during both the pre-liberalisation and the post liberalisation era. So is Jammu and Kashmir. The geographic distribution of investments shows that they are concentrated in the Western, North Western and the Southern regions of the country. The only exceptions are Jammu and Kashmir, Kerala and to some extent Rajasthan. As seen earlier, some parts of the mineral rich Madhya Pradesh and Orissa have received large chunks of investment.

INTRA-STATE DISPARITIES

The flow of investments shows not only inter-state disparities, but also wide intra-state disparities. As may be seen from Table V, 41 districts had investments above Rs. 4,000 crore. These districts together accounted for nearly half the total volume of investments in the country according to the C.M.I.E. Survey. The concentration of investments in a few districts was pronounced in Maharashtra, Gujarat, Tamil Nadu, Himachal Pradesh, Orissa and Andhra Pradesh. In Himachal Pradesh, bulk of the investments went to two districts - Kinnaur and Kullur. In Punjab, Ludhiana alone attracted nearly one third of the investments. In Haryana, Panipat attracted nearly a quarter of the investments. In Gujarat, the four districts of Bharuch, Surat, Jamnagar and Vadodara attracted three fourths of the total investments. In Maharashtra, nearly two thirds of the total investments went to the five districts of Rajgarh, Ratnagiri, Greater Bombay, Chandrapur and Nagpur. If we take a look at the investment map of Gujarat and Maharashtra, it is found that investments are concentrated in a narrow strip running almost contiguously from the South Gujarat to the Konkan belt of Maharashtra. Similar concentration of investments in contiguous districts is found in Madhya Pradesh and Orissa. The eastern districts of Madhya Pradesh, Bilaspur and Raipur - and the western districts of Orissa - Sambalpur, Dhenkanal and Kendhujhar form another cluster of concentration of investments. In Andhra Pradesh, investments are concentrated in the three districts of Visakhapatnam, East Godavari and Nellore. In Karnataka, two districts - Dakshin Kannad and Bellary - accounted for 44 per cent of the investments, In Tamil Nadu, five districts account for nearly four fifths of the investments (South Arcot, Madras, Chidamearnar, Chenglepet, Tiruchirapally). In Kerala, more than a quarter of the investments flowed to the already developed district of Ernakulam. In West Bengal, investments were concentrated in just two districts - Hughli and Murshidabad. In Assam, Dibrugarh alone accounted for nearly one third of the investments. In Uttar Pradesh, investments were concentrated in the districts of Garwal, Shahjahanpur and Sonbhandra. In Bihar, the district of Purabi Singbhum accounted for 29 per cent of the investments.

The existence of wide regional disparities in India is an inheritance from its colonial past. It was understood by the Indian planners that further widening of regional disparities would be undesirable from both economic and political angles. All Indian Five Year Plans therefore, had emphasised the correction of regional disparities as a major objective. All policy instruments also had highlighted this regional objective. Despite all these good intentions, regional disparities only widened during the era of centralised planning. Our present study shows that the process of widening of disparities continued unimpeded during the period of liberalisation. For the poorer states in India, the difference between centralised planning and market system is only the difference between tweedledum and tweedledee.

Table VI presents the Rank correlation coefficients between the various indicators of investment and per capita SDP. The table shows that coefficients for per capita investments under all heads except those covered by the CMIE survey are positive and significant. The latter variables like per capita investment in mining and manufacturing, investment in infrastructure and aggregate investments, are also positively correlated with per capita income. But the values of coefficients are not significant. This is partly because of the huge capital intensive large volume investments which have flowed to some of the states like Orissa and Madhya Pradesh. This inference is corroborated by the high value of coefficients of correlation of even these variables when expressed in terms of number of Projects/Proposals. This is further corroborated by the negative correlation between unit size and per capita income.

What are the factors that led to the above pattern of investment under the liberalisation regime ? Apparently, the investors had been guided by the externalities provided by the existing agglomeration of industrial activities especially since the social costs of these agglomeration are not made to be borne by them. They are also attracted to some regions by their natural resource endowments.

Yet another reason for the large flow of private investments to the already developed states may lie in their higher level of per capita government investment. There is positive correlation between these investment variables. The co-relation co-efficient between per capita aggregate government investment and private sector investment in 16 states for which disaggregated data are available from the CMIE survey comes to 0.640. The coefficient between state government investment and private sector investment comes to 0.602. The correlation between central government investment and private sector investment was weak; the coefficient was only 0.288. However, there was strong correlation between central government investment and state government investment. The coefficient works out to 0.610.

The above analysis shows that the prime mover of central government investment and the private sector investment in a state is the state government's own investment. The state government's investment and the SDP are positively correlated (0.514). This is not surprising as the states' own resources are positively correlated with state domestic product (0.916). The other component that goes to finance state government's investment, *viz.*, central government's budgetary transfers was no doubt showing some progressive trends.[3] But these trends were not progressive enough to counter the strong regressive features of own resources of the states.[4] What is more, as seen above, the central government's direct investments flowed to resource rich developed states, thus offsetting the progressive impact of its budgetary transfers. Thus, weakness in India's federal financial relations is a major reason for the regressive flow of investments both before and after the economic liberalisation.

What does the prospect of widening inter-state disparities portend for the country's economy and polity ? Leave alone the question of regional equity, is it strategically wise to put all the eggs of liberalisation in very few baskets ? It may be noted that almost all the states and the union territories which attracted most of the investment projects lie on the country's borders with Pakistan. Besides, the country's industrial and financial centres are not immune to terrorism or communal tensions as the bomb blast in the Bombay Stock Exchange had shown: As the outbreak of plague in Gujarat and Maharashtra had shown, even an epidemic in one of these contiguous states can cripple the whole national economy.

In the long run, further polarisation among regions is bound to threaten the federal polity. It will be unrealistic to expect that the poorer states will continue to be contended with their "strangers at the feast" status. As for the developed states, they depend on the backward states for their supply of raw materials today. To a limited extent, the backward states also provide a market for the output of the developed states. With further impoverishment of the backward regions, the importance of these states as markets for the developed states is bound to come down especially since there is now scope for linking their economies with the global markets. The importance of backward states as source of raw materials may also come down with the opening up of the economy and the gradual shift to less input intensive industries and services. In other words with the opening up of the economy, there exists the possibility of the 'Tigers' within the country integrating their economies increasingly with those of each other as well as with the global economy rather than with those of their poorer counterparts within the country. Once the attraction of a common market is reduced, the economic rationale for federation also gets reduced. This may eventually weaken the federal polity. The threat to federal polity comes not only from the poorer constituents but also from the Canadian federation. It may be noted that the opportunity for access to the North American Free Trade Area as also to the global market is one of the driving forces behind separatism in Canada in recent years.

REFERENCES

1. I gratefully acknowledge the assistance received from Dr. P.T.Thomas in preparing this paper.

2. States whose per capita income are 10 per cent above the national average are classified as high income states. They are : (1) Goa, Punjab, Haryana, Maharashtra, Gujarat and Tamil Nadu.

   States whose per capita income ranged between 90 and 110 per cent of the national average are classified as middle income states. They are Karnataka, West Bengal, Himachal Pradesh, Kerala, Andhra Pradesh, and Madhya Pradesh.

   States whose per capita income are below 90 per cent of the national average are treated as low income states. They are : Assam, Rajasthan, Orissa, Uttar Pradesh and Bihar.

   Data for Jammu and Kashmir and the North Eastern States are not available against most investment indicators.

   States are classified on the basis of the per capita State Domestic Product (average of 87-88, 1988-89 and 1989-90). See Report of the Tenth Finance Commission. 1994.

3. See George, K.K., *Centre-State Financial Flows and Inter State Disparities in India.* Criterion Books, Delhi, 1988.

4. *ibid.*

NOTES AND REFERENCES : (TABLE I)

States are ranked according to the Per Capita Net State Domestic Product (Average of 1987-88, 1988-89 and 1989-90) - See Report of the Tenth Finance Commission, 1994.

Col. 1 Refers to Foreign Direct Investment approvals between August 1991 and May 1995; Source : SIA News Letter, Ministry of Industry Government of India, quoted in *Economic and Political Weekly* September, 1995.

Col. 2 — Refers to Industrial Entrepreneurs Memoranda (IEMS) field from August, 1991 to December 1994; Source *Economic and Political Weekly*, March 18, 1995.

Col. 3,4,5, — Refers to large investment projects for which investment decisions have been taken and which are in various stages of implementation. For the content and coverage of this data, see Centre for Monitoring Indian Economy (CMIE), *Shape of Things to Come*, December, 1994

Col. 6 — Annual Forecasts of Corporate Investments by the Reserve Bank of India for the years 1991-92 to 1994-95 - *Reserve Bank of India Bulletin*, Various Issues.

NOTES AND REFERENCES : (TABLE II)

For Col. 1 to 3 and 6 See footnotes to Table I.

Col. 4 — *Source :* New Limited Companies Registered during 1992-93, 1993-94 and 1994-95. *Answer to Parliament question* dated 9/8/1995.

Col. 5 — Reference to the location of plants of companies that went public during 1993-94, and 1995-96
Source : Prime Issue Monitor, New Delhi

Col. 7 — Refers to Foreign collaboration approvals during the period, August, 1991 to June 1993.
Source : Answer to Parliament Question - 26/8/1993.

Table 1
Economy After Liberalisation – Selected State-Wise Indicators of Investment
Investment Per Capita (Rs.)

States	*Foreign Direct Investment*	*Investment as per IEMS filed*	*Proposed Investment as per CMIE Survey*			*Total cost of projects sanctioned by term lending institutions*
			Investment in mining and manufacturing	*Investment in infrastructure*	*Aggregate Investment*	
Goa	776	18547	NA	NA	NA	6709
Punjab	252	6241	4941	4168	9110	1814
Maharashtra	726	8612	6467	5928	12395	3379
Haryana	255	7968	4083	6370	10453	1399
Gujarat	584	14454	1388	9217	22605	8278
Tamil Nadu	437	3294	3885	3957	7842	2255
Karnataka	173	3048	5134	5363	10498	1717
West Bengal	543	1303	1732	2638	4371	1564
Himachal Pradesh	535	9352	3769	42840	46609	5494
Kerala	29	1219	1769	3387	5156	271
Andhra Pradesh	192	3964	4782	3936	8719	1490
Madhya Pradesh	148	5166	4551	8289	12841	1193
Assam	1	436	4519	1980	6499	NA
Rajasthan	103	3655	1629	2625	4254	1331
Orissa	550	974	8409	17470	25880	1043
Uttar Pradesh	57	2765	1442	2675	4117	754
Bihar	9	470	968	1322	2291	481
All India	411	4070	3968	5206	9174	1750

Table 2
Economy After Liberalisation – Selected State-wise Indicators Number of Proposals Per Crore of Population

State	*IEMS*	*FDI*	*Aggregate Investment*	*New Companies getting registered*	*Location of plants of companies raising capital from the market*	*Projects sanctioned loans by term lending institutions*	*Foreign collaboration*
Goa	888	188	NA	NA	51	376	418
Punjab	476	17	41	1287	22	88	338
Maharashtra	432	59	61	2628	35	117	214
Haryana	671	86	51	593	43	137	430
Gujarat	592	35	78	1880	80	132	341
Tamil Nadu	237	49	33	1864	19	149	115
Karnataka	136	46	48	989	12	54	81
West Bengal	85	15	12	2295	5	26	52
Himachal Pradesh	327	27	101	524	21	128	186
Kerala	50	12	24	817	7	26	24
Andhra Pradesh	145	25	44	870	22	63	85
Madhya Pradesh	158	9	38	327	14	38	105
Assam	17	2	19	270	2	NA	12
Rajasthan	227	19	30	706	15	57	150
Orissa	33	8	33	284	5	17	22
Uttar Pradesh	128	9	16	253	8	27	88
Bihar	18	1	12	180	1	49	12
All India	202	19	37	1221	15	58	117

Table 3
Economy After Liberalisation – Selected State-Wise Indicators Investment Per Proposal (Amounts in Lakh Rs.)

States	*IEMS*	*FDI*	*Aggregate Investment (CMIE)*	*Projects sanctioned loans by term lending institutions*
	(1)	(2)	(3)	(4)
Goa	2106	413	NA	1784
Punjab	1311	1506	22261	2056
Maharashtra	1994	1236	20427	2887
Haryana	1187	296	20489	1019
Gujarat	2441	1688	29001	6263
Tamil Nadu	1389	888	23553	1511
Karnataka	2247	380	21659	3165
West Bengal	1540	3664	36289	9035
Himachal Pradesh	2861	1979	46350	4305
Kerala	2446	237	21437	1027
Andhra Pradesh	2740	786	19725	2366
Madhya Pradesh	3262	1665	33993	3110
Assam	2661	37	34688	NA
Rajasthan	1613	534	14183	2325
Orissa	2938	7264	77299	6005
Uttar Pradesh	2161	665	25459	2776
Bihar	2567	660	19593	9738
All India	2021	2111	25103	3122

For Notes and References, See Table I and II.

Table 4
States Which Are Above the National Average

a)	**Amount per capita**	
1.	Foreign Direct Investment	1. Goa 2. Maharashtra 3. Gujarat 4. Tamil Nadu 5. Orissa 6. West Bengal 7. Himachal Pradesh
2.	Investment proposed under IEMS	1. Punjab 2. Goa 3. Maharashtra 4. Haryana 5. Gujarat 6. Madhya Pradesh 7. Himachal Pradesh
3.	Investment in Mining and Manufacturing (CMIE)	1. Punjab 2. Maharashtra 3. Haryana 4. Karnataka 5. Andhra Pradesh 6. Madhya Pradesh 7. Orissa 8. Assam
4.	Investment in Infrastructure (CMIE)	1. Maharashtra 2. Haryana 3. Gujarat 4. Karnataka 5. Himachal Pradesh 6. Madhya Pradesh 7. Orissa
5.	Aggregate Investment (CMIE)	1. Maharashtra 2. Haryana 3. Gujarat 4. Karnataka 5. Madhya Pradesh 6. Himachal Pradesh 7. Orissa
6.	Total cost of projects financed by Term Lending	1. Goa 2. Punjab 3. Maharashtra 4. Gujarat 5. Tamil Nadu

(*Contd.*)

Table 4 (*Contd.*)

b) Number of Proposals per Crore of Population	
1. Number of FDIs	1. Goa 2. Maharashtra 3. Haryana 4. Gujarat 5. Tamil Nadu 6. Karnataka 7. Himachal Pradesh 8. Andhra Pradesh
2. Number of IEMS	1. Goa 2. Punjab 3. Maharashtra 4. Haryana 5. Gujarat 6. Tamil Nadu 7. Himachal Pradesh 8. Rajasthan
3. No. of aggregate investment proposals (CMIE)	1. Punjab 2. Maharashtra 3. Haryana 4. Gujarat 5. Karnataka 6. Andhra Pradesh 7. Himachal Pradesh 8. Madhya Pradesh
4. No. of new companies registering	1. Punjab 2. Maharashtra 3. Gujarat 4. Tamil Nadu 5. West Bengal
5. No. of companies raising capital	1. Goa 2. Punjab 3. Maharashtra 4. Haryana 5. Gujarat 6. Tamil Nadu 7. Andhra Pradesh 8. Himachal Pradesh
6. No. of foreign collaboration	1. Punjab 2. Maharashtra 3. Haryana 4. Gujarat 5. Tamil Nadu 6. Rajasthan

(*Contd.*)

Table 4 (*Contd.*)

7.	No. of projects financed by Term Lending Institutions	1. Punjab 2. Maharashtra 3. Haryana 4. Gujarat 5. Tamil Nadu 6. Himachal Pradesh 7. Andhra Pradesh

Note : Derived from Table I and II

Table 5
Districts With More Than Rs. 4000 Crore Investment

States	*Number of Districts*	*Share in State's total investment*
Punjab	1	30.1
Maharashtra	5	64.6
Haryana	1	23.8
Gujarat	4	75.1
Tamil Nadu	5	79.5
Karnataka	2	43.6
West Bengal	2	40.3
Himachal Pradesh	2	66.0
Kerala	1	27.7
Andhra Pradesh	3	52.9
Madhya Pradesh	4	30.1
Assam	1	32.2
Orissa	6	65.9
Uttar Pradesh	3	29.1
Bihar	1	29.2
All India	41	47.9

Source : CMIE, *Shape of Things to Come*, December 1994

Table 6
Rank Correlation with Per Capita SDP

1.	Per capita investment under IEMS	0.729
2.	No. of IEMS per crore of population	0.802
3.	Size of investment per project under IEMS	0.415
4.	Per capita Foreign Direct Investment (FDI)	0.665
5.	No. of FDIs per crore population	0.820
6.	FDI investment per project	0.020
7.	No. of foreign collaboration per lakh of population	0.750
8.	Per capita proposed investment in mining and manufacturing (CMIE)	0.317
9.	Per capita investment in infrastructure (CMIE)	0.432
10.	Per capita aggregate investment proposed (CMIE)	0.429
11.	No. of aggregate investment proposals per crore of population (CMIE)	0.651
12.	Investment per project (CMIE)	(-) 0.050
13.	No. of companies issuing shares per crore of population	0.780
14.	Per capita project cost of companies financed by financial institutions	0.780
15.	No. of projects financed by financial institutions per crore of population	0.726
16.	Investment per project financed by term lending institutions	(-) 0.390
17.	No. of companies registered per crore of population	0.802

Note : *. Values above 0.482 are significant at 5 % level
Source : Refer Table I

Table 7
Distribution of Investment : State by Ownership

(Rs. per capita)

State	*Government Sector*		*Total*	*Joint Sector*	*Private*	*Total*
	Central	*State*				
Punjab	334	2522	2858	4152	2099	9110
Maharashtra	1856	2807	4663	557	7174	12395
Haryana	3731	3250	6981	301	3170	10453
Gujarat	3284	4529	2789	120	1263	4166
Tamil Nadu	1650	1814	3464	1182	3195	7842
Karnataka	222	2046	2269	1290	6937	10498
West Bengal	672	910	1583	543	2244	4371
Himachal Pradesh	5996	2427	30268	1257	15084	46609
Kerala	1947	1572	3520	82	1554	5156
Andhra Pradesh	661	1589	2251	47	6420	8719
Madhya Pradesh	2495	2622	5117	423	7300	12841
Assam	1441	468	1914	3807	782	6499
Rajasthan	818	1731	2549	21	1683	4254
Orissa	5881	3148	9030	317	16532	25880
Uttar Pradesh	666	1190	1856	497	1763	4117
Bihar	1044	675	1720	18	552	2291
All India	1767	2038	383	683	4672	9161

Source : CMIE, *Shape of Things to Come*, December 1994.

2

Regional Disparities in India : A Reappraisal

Satish C. Jha

I. INTRODUCTION

It is generally believed that India's successive Five Year Plans focused on balanced regional development. A review of plan documents, however, does not confirm this. It appears that regional dimensions of development were not explicitly built into the development plans formulated and implemented during the successive plans over the decades, In actual practice, measures adopted for correcting regional imbalance were rather ad hoc and influenced by political pressure groups. The ultimate result was non-achievement of the goal of balanced regional development and massive wastage of resources. After the implementation of eight Five Year Plans, the concern for regional disparity remains as serious as ever.

There was a general expectation that India's economic reform programme, with its focus on liberalization by means of market forces, would tend to gradually narrow down the disparity. However, available facts reveal that so far there has been no impact of liberalization on the growth performance of the poorer region. Tentative estimates suggest that growth level has gone down in such regions. This could be due to market forces tilting more in favor of better performing regions, reflected particularly in terms of the level of private sector resource flow, including foreign investment in favour of better off states.

II. REASONS AND DIMENSIONS OF DISPARITY

A. *Basic Reasons*

The basic cause for regional disparity is to be sought in India's planned development strategy itself. This strategy centered on faster industrialization, with a focus on heavy industries. These were considered the 'temples' of modern India which would uplift the living conditions of the entire Indian population. This strategy gave rise to a number of problems, some of which the country is facing even today. These industries which were set up with borrowed funds from abroad, involved large investment with high capital-output ratios, long gestation periods and needed large imports of capital goods and services. The country was deprived of resource allocation in areas/ sectors where growth momentum could have been faster. The gestation period, unfortunately, turned out to be much longer due to inadequate infrastructure, unskilled labor and lack of management experience. All these factors increased the cost in almost all heavy industries, which went on adding to the government's debt burden. Even today, the high level of fiscal deficits could be very safely attributed to the heavy losses incurred by the public sector heavy industries.

On the top of these problems, macroeconomic policies and bureau-cratic intervention added further dimension to the poor performance of these industries. In order to protect such high cost of heavy industries against foreign imports, trade was restricted and protection was provided through high tariff and quotas. To stimulate investment in spite of high costs of domestically produced capital goods, capital was subsidized, resulting in distorted factor prices. This led to an adoption of technology which proved to be more capital intensive, Public sector involvement in industrialization grew more and more and as a result about 50 per cent of capital formation in the Indian economy since 1965-66 took place in the public sector. This also accounted for two-thirds of employment in the organized sector.

With a long gestation period and high costs, this sector continuously incurred losses. Some estimates[1] show that public sector's gross savings have been less than 40 per cent of the investment from 1950 to 1985. This poor performance of the public sector has

[1] Dev, S.M., Suryanarayan, M.H. and Parikh, K.S. "Rural Poverty in India : Incidence, Issues and Policies, *"Asian Development Review"*, Vol. 10, No. 1, 1992.

been responsible for India's stagnancy in economic growth performance and with high level of unemployment and incidence of poverty.

There was a general belief that with heavy industrialization, the Indian economy would attain a higher rate of economic growth which would generate trickle down effects throughout the country. Implicitly, various regions of the country would then experience covergence in per capita income growth rates, even though the level of per capita income may differ across regions in the long run. This turned out to be fallacious. India's overall economic growth performance remained poor, with the exception of the 1980s. During 1950-1980, the average level of economic growth was estimated at 3.5 per cent. As a result convergence of any form did not arise across the regions, as can be seen from Tables 1 and 2.

Economic history suggests that trickle down effects on the economy and region take place only within the framework of sustained high economic growth over a period of time complemented by sound macro-economic policies and selective state intervention. It is not purely the market forces which help attain the goal of high economic growth and its dispersal over the regions and various segments of the population. The experience of East and Southeast Asia and China bears witness to this fact[2]. China's sustained growth rate of 10-12 per cent and East Asia and Southeast Asia's average growth rate of 7-8 per cent have been the major factor towards reduction of poverty incidence and reduction of regional imbalance.

Another perceived lacuna in the Indian planning process appears to be in selection of location for the heavy industries and implicit promotion of the associated area. Apart from political pressure to locate a particular heavy industry, the consideration was to distribute the location in various parts of the country in order to bring balanced regional development. This was primarily done on an ad hoc basis, with very poor project feasibility studies. Location was determined without consideration of the resource endowment of the area, the available institutional framework, the quality of labour force, the infrastructure and above all, the partnership role of the State Government in order to help

---

[2] Jha, S.C., "Intra-Regional Trade in Asia: Current Trends and Prospects," *Financial Times Conference on Asian Capital Markets*, London, April 1994.

develop the expansion and impact in the hinterland of the industry. The emergence of linkage between the industrial setup and the rural environment did not draw adequate attention of the Indian planners[3]. For example, a few heavy industries were located in Bihar but these do not seem to have stimulated development of other industries in the state either by the public sector or the private sector. The rural hinterland of the heavy industries remains as underdeveloped as without any industry. This raises a question on the impact of industrialization as related to economic growth and balanced regional development.

Indian experience suggests that selection and location of public sector industries added an effective constraint in maximizing social welfare and economic growth. Whatever was done so far during the last 3-4 decades was based more on socio-political considerations than on the yardstick of economic efficiency. The question of dispersal and distribution from the point of view of equity is better answered at a stage of economic development when the national wealth is considered to have grown sufficiently and this can be more widely shared without damaging the process of economic growth[4]. No doubt, in the early stage if high growth momentum picks up, regional disparity might widen. But at a later stage of sustained economic growth, there remains a possibility of convergence in inter-regional growth rates.[5] Unfortunately, in the Indian case, there has been no realization of such convergence. This could be primarily attributed to continuous low national economic growth performance.

B. Dimensions of Disparity

There can be various ways to classify a region. In this paper, an attempt has been made to introduce classification based on economic performance. Coincidentally, it so emerged that the low performing region consisted of the Hindi speaking states, with the exception of Assam. Then, these states are all consequently located in the northeastern part of the country, and comprising

3. Rothermund, Dietmar and Saha, S.K. (Eds.), *Regional Disparities in India: Rural and Industrial Dimensions*, New Delhi, Manohar Press, 1991.

4. A recent theoretical study by Perotti (1993), where the level of redistribution is endogenous, generates this outcome. Empirical studies by Campano and Salvatore (1988), Jha (1996), Kuznets (1955), and Ram (1988) confirm this proposition.

5. Mishra, G.P. (Ed.), *Regional Structure of Development and Growth in India*, New Delhi, Ashish Publishing House, 1985, p.103.

Table 1
Real Per Capita Net State Domestic Product (PNSDP) in Rs.

Regions	*1980-81*	*1985-86*	*1990-91*	*1992-93*
High Performing				
Gujarat	1948	2204	2559	2719
Haryana	2370	2893	3466	3540
Maharashtra	2427	2703	3442	3469
Punjab	2674	3249	3571	3950
Medium Performing				
A.P.	1380	1549	1779	1721
Karnataka	1527	1659	2048	2275
Kerala	1508	1507	1818	2023
Tamil Nadu	1498	1798	2219	2349
West Bengal	1612	1692	1946	2056
Low Performing				
Assam	1200	1483	1805	1945
Bihar	917	1074	1195	1091
M.P.	1349	1399	1726	1509
Orissa	1231	1390	1383	1442
Rajasthan	1222	1338	1943	1897
U.P.	1278	1375	1612	1591
Mean	1609	1821	2167	2242
Standard Deviation	513.7	643.5	756.8	834.5

Source: Indian Public Finance Statistics, 1994, p.72, Ministry of Finance, Government of India. The base year for PNSDP is 1980-81.

Assam[6], Bihar, M.P., Orissa, Rajasthan and U.P. In consideration of that classification, the high performing region consists of the states of Gujarat, Haryana, Maharashtra and Punjab, and these geographically form the northwestern belt. The third category basically comprises the southern belt, which includes the states of A.P., Karnataka, Kerala, Tamil Nadu and West Bengal. Table 1 indicates the general level of economic performance of per capita net State domestic product.

For the economic growth performance, which is shown in Table 2, the regional patterns closely mirror those of per capita domestic product.

[6]. Reliable social indicators statistics could not be obtained for Assam.

Table 2
Growth Rate of PNSDP (%)

Regions	*1980-85*	*1985-90*	*1990-92*
High Performing			
Gujarat	3.07	4.25	3.08
Haryana	3.36	4.50	1.00
Maharashtra	2.08	5.79	0.39
Punjab	3.45	3.25	2.63
Medium Performing			
A.P.	1.45	4.38	- 1.64
Karnataka	1.75	4.63	5.40
Kerala	0.004	4.39	5.49
Tamil Nadu	3.36	4.86	2.89
West Bengal	2.33	3.02	2.79
Low Performing			
Bihar	4.3	1.55	- 4.45
M.P.	0.34	4.31	- 4.66
Orissa	2.12	1.54	2.11
Rajasthan	2.44	8.15	· 1.19
U.P.	1.50	3.47	- 0.65

Growth rates are computed by regressing the natural log of per capital GDP on a time trend variable and are obtained from Jha (1996). See Watson (1992) for the details of this calculation.

Source: *Indian Public Finance Statistics,* various years, Ministry of Finance, Government of India.

During the period 1985-90, the growth rate of per capita State domestic product varied from 4.25 per cent in Gujarat to 3.25 per cent in Punjab in the high performing region. In the low performing region, the level ranged between 1.55 per cent in Bihar and 8.5 per cent in Rajasthan, which seems to be an exception. For the medium performing region, the growth rate varied between 3.02 per cent in West Bengal and 4.8 per cent in Tamil Nadu. Interestingly, during 1990-92, all the regions showed declining growth rate performance. The low performing region experienced growth rates between (-)4.66 per cent in M.P. and (-)0.65 per cent in U.P., with only Orissa performing at a positive level of 2.11 per cent. For the high performing region, the economic growth rate varied between 0.39 per cent in Maharashtra and 3.08 per cent in Gujarat. In the medium performing region, interestingly Kerala appeared to be attaining a high level of 5.49 per cent against the high negative growth level of (-) 1.64 per cent in A.P.

A recent study[7] by the Indian Council for Research on International Economic Relations more or less also confirms the trend in states' growth performance for pre-reform and post-reform periods.

Table 3
Growth of Net State Domestic Product (%)

Regions	*Pre-Reform 1985-86 to 1990-91*	*Post-Reform 1991-92 to 1993-94*
High Performing		
Gujarat	4.7	5.4
Haryana	6.5	3.4
Maharashtra	7.7	2.7
Punjab	6.3	4.5
Medium Performing		
A.P.	5.5	0.2
Karnataka	4.5	7.2
Kerala	5.0	5.9
Tamil Nadu	5.4	4.1
West Bengal	5.4	5.1
Low Performing		
Assam	4.1	6.2
Bihar	4.4	- 2.3
M.P.	7.5	- 2.5
Orissa	4.6	4.3
Rajasthan	9.5	1.5
U.P.	5.3	1.2

Source: Indian Council for Research on International Economic Relations, *Mid-term Review of the Economy 1995-96,* New Delhi, 1995.

Table 3 suggests that not only has the overall economic growth rate during the post reform period declined in comparison to the pre-reform period, but with a few exceptions, there has been further widening of the disparity. The low performing region's rate of growth has declined with some states even attaining negative rate of growth.

7. Indian Council for Research on International Economic Relations, *Mid-term Review of the Economy 1995-96,* New Delhi, 1995.

In general, economic growth performance is directly related to the level of investment in the process of development.[8] In order to enhance the level of productivity, investment in infrastructure development (i.e. roads, power, railways, irrigation and development of the human capital in terms of education and health) is the engine for growth. One major factor responsible for a comparatively high rate of economic growth and per capita income in the high performing region is due to the high level of investment in the area of infrastructure and human capital development. This is interlinked with high per capita net domestic product of the state, which can arguably serve as a proxy for the level of endowments. Table 4 reflects the performance on various aspects of infrastructure and human capital development.

Table 4
CMIE's Index of Relative Development of Infrastructure: 1980-81 to 1992-93

Regions	*1980-81*	*1985-86*	*1988-89*	*1990-91*	*1991-92*	*1992-93*
High Performing						
Gujarat	125	132	128	124	122	125
Haryana	154	150	148	156	153	152
Maharashtra	118	119	113	111	110	111
Punjab	215	218	210	211	210	205
Medium Performing						
A.P.	98	105	100	98	103	103
Karnataka	101	100	95	93	99	97
Kerala	137	140	137	138	139	140
Tamil Nadu	153	142	137	139	138	138
West Bengal	132	123	116	115	115	113
Low Performing						
Assam	93	87	91	95	94	93
Bihar	97	98	96	97	96	96
M.P.	62	71	72	72	72	75
Orissa	82	81	82	86	88	89
Rajasthan	77	79	76	85	81	80
U.P.	107	108	106	111	109	109

Source: Center for Monitoring Indian Economy, Sept. 1994.

8. De Long and Summers (1993) present evidence from developing countries on the relationship between investment and economic growth. Barro (1990), Lucas (1988), and Romer (1987) construct theoretical models wherein investment in physical and human capital generates ongoing growth.

Table 5
Social Indicators

Regions	*Female Literacy > 15 yrs (%)*	*School Attendance, 10-14 yrs (%)*	*Female Married at 15 yrs (%)*	*Birth Rate / 1000*	*Infant Mortality Rate per 1000 births*
High Performing					
Gujarat	33	51	27	34	116
Haryana	22	36	47	36	101
Maharashtra	35	51	38	30	81
Punjab	32	56	14	30	81
Medium Performing					
A.P.	20	30	56	31	86
Karnataka	28	38	36	29	69
Kerala	71	84	14	25	37
Tamil Nadu	35	45	23	28	91
West Bengal	33	45	32	32	91
Low Performing					
Bihar	13	25	64	37	118
M.P.	16	25	63	38	142
Orissa	21	30	31	33	135
Rajasthan	12	19	64	40	108
U.P.	14	25	60	38	150

Source: Rothermund Dietmar and Saha, S.K., *Regional Disparities in India: Rural and Industrial Dimensions,* 1991, p. 9.

During the period 1980-81, the index of infrastructure development varied from 118 in Maharashtra to 215 in Punjab in the high performing region. For the low performing region, this index varied from 62 in M.P. to 107 in U.P. The range was between 98 in A.P. and 153 in Tamil Nadu in the medium performing region. More or less same applies for the year 1992-93. The high performing region showed an index ranging from 111 in Maharashtra to 205 in Punjab, whereas this indicator ranged between 75 in M.P. and 109 in U.P. in the low performing region. This variation occurred in spite of several planned allocation of resources for infrastructure development in all the regions. Considering the large size of the population (50 per cent or so of the total population living in this region), the per capita investment from centrally planned allocation appeared to be very low, with marginal impact on economic growth aspects. This was further complicated by low level of savings and state domestic product.

The impact of such a pattern of investment was on the quality of human factor which contributes towards its participation in develop-ment and in the rate of productivity growth.

On various scores of social development, one can observe the variation between the regions. High performing regions showed compa-ratively better performance in terms of social indicators than the low performing regions. For example, female literacy rate above 15 years was, on an average, at the level of 30 per cent against 12-21 per cent in the low performing regions. Similarly, infant mortality rate per 1000 births was in the range of 81-116, against the range of 118-150 in the low performing region. The best performer appeared to be Kerala in the medium performing region. It is interesting to note that Kerala leads all the states in social performance. Table 6 provides another set of insights into the comparative performance based on social indicators.

Table 6 shows that in general, high performing region had a better life expectancy score (at the level of more than 60 years for males). Kerala showed the highest level of life expectancy (66 years). Similarly, the rate of literacy was highest in the high performing region, with Kerala indicating the maximum of 91 per cent. The poorest score went to the low performing region, with a range between 39 and 59 per cent. The population growth level appeared to be rather mixed, with the lowest level of 1.31 per cent in Kerala. The low performing region showed the range between 0.78 per cent (Orissa) and 2.47 per cent in Rajasthan, which had the highest rate in all the regions.

Table 6
Some Social Indicators

Regions	*Life expectancy– Male (yrs.)*	*Growth of Population (%)*	*Infant Mortality / 1000 live Births*	*Literacy Rate Above 7 yrs (%)*
High Performing				
Gujarat	58.34	1.89	72	60.91
Haryana	63.41	2.33	69	55.33
Maharashtra	61.90	2.26	58	63.05
Punjab	65.61	1.85	55	57.14
Medium Performing				
A.P.	59.10	2.14	70	45.11
Karnataka	62.15	1.88	71	55.98
Kerala	66.23	1.31	17	90.59
Tamil Nadu	60.85	1.39	67	63.72
West Bengal	58.10	2.20	63	57.72
Low Performing				
Bihar	55.74	2.11	75	58.54
M.P.	56.24	2.37	111	43.45
Orissa	57.13	1.78	123	48.55
Rajasthan	57.80	2.47	83	38.81
U.P.	59.95	2.24	98	41.71

Source: Chebbi, R.K,, "Rating People's Development," *The Economic Times*, New Delhi, 6 October 1995.

With a low level of performance on the social front and low per capita state domestic product in the low performing region, the incidence of poverty was high. The low performing region had continuously higher incidence of poverty in comparison to the high and medium performing region. This is confirmed by Table 7. Recent estimates do not show any better results.

With a low level of performance on the social front and low per capita state domestic product in the low performing region, the incidence of poverty was high. The low performing region had consistently higher incidence of poverty in comparison to the high and medium performing region. This is confirmed by Table 7. Recent estimates do not show any better results.

Table 7
Proportion of Rural Population Below the Poverty Line (%)

Regions	*1970-71*	*1986-87*
High Performing		
Gujarat	41	22
Haryana	27	12
Maharashtra	44	32
Punjab	16	7
Medium Performing		
A.P.	40	16
Karnataka	45	30
Kerala	61	20
Tamil Nadu	57	31
West Bengal		
Low Performing		
Assam	31	22
Bihar	58	41
M.P.	52	33
Orissa	60	40
Rajasthan	39	16
U.P.	40	28

Source: Dev, S.M.. Suryanarayana, M.K. and Parikh, S.P., "Rural Poverty in India: Incidence, Issues and Policies, *Asian Development Review,* Vol. 10, No.1, 1992, p.41.

Amongst the various factors explainable for different rates of growth performance, available facts also show that all India financial institutions had comparatively higher level of credit allocations to the better performing regions. This could also have accelerated the process of growth in different ways.

The credit sanction, on an average, varied between Rs. 750 crore (Haryana) and Rs. 8982 crore (Maharashtra) in the high performing region during 1991-95. In contrast, the level of sanction was much lower in the low performing region during the same period. Assam had the lowest level of sanction of Rs. 114 crore, whereas UP received Rs. 1991 crore. This level of variation in financial allocation is difficult to justify on other considerations such as population, need for enterprise development and productivity growth. There are no statistics available to confirm that credit rating and rates of return in the high performing region were better than in the low performing region, which could have encouraged the financial institutions to inject a significant variation in the allocation of credit. One probable reasoning could be that the level of infrastructure and bank administrative mechanism was much better for efficient credit operation in the high performing region than in the low performing regions. If this contention is true, then policy makers and planners would have to reexamine the entire credit strategy which occupies a vital role in enterprise development.

Table 8
Sanction and Disbursement of Credit by All India Financial Institutions (Rs. Crore)

Regions	*April 1987 to March 1991*		*April 1991 to March 1995*	
	Sanctions	*Disbursements*	*Sanctions*	*Disbursements*
High Performing				
Gujarat	1576	969	5844	2756
Haryana	306	215	745	322
Maharashtra	2468	1513	8982	5628
Punjab	354	280	750	319
Medium Performing				
A.P.	1311	915	2760	1918
Karnataka	738	525	2971	1628
Kerala	285	212	558	358
Tamil Nadu	1423	972	3936	2358
West Bengal	472	378	1593	714
Low Performing				
Assam	95	51	114	101
Bihar	227	140	386	303
M.P.	710	434	1615	1037
Orissa	292	190	579	357
Rajasthan	574	271	1272	819
U.P.	1078	755	1991	817
Mean	793.9	521.3	2273.1	1429.0
Standard Deviation	636.3	401.0	2336.9	1401.1

Source: Government of India, Ministry of Finance, *Economic Survey,* 1995.

In an agriculturally predominated economy like that of India, it is generally perceived that agriculture sector provides the engine for growth. Therefore, there is a need for more investment in agriculture. This contention is confirmed in Table 9.

Table 9 indicates the rising trend in revenue expenditures across the region over the period 1974-91, but very low allocation on capital expenditures. As a result, Indian agriculture has continuously lacked the required level of capital formation, which is the key for

Table 9
State Per Capita Expenditure on Agriculture and Allied Activities
(Rs. In 1981-82 Prices)

Regions	*Revenue Expenditure*			*Capital Expenditure*		
	1974-80	*1980-85*	*1985-90*	*1974-80*	*1980-85*	*1985-90*
High Performing	24.8	31.0	40.6	1.6	1.6	3.6
Gujarat	13.6	16.5	28.1	2.7	5.6	6.3
Haryana	22.4	30.4	38.5	0.0	- 0.9	0.1
Maharashtra	39.0	52.4	64.8	3.0	3.0	5.3
Punjab	24.0	24.7	30.8	0.8	- 1.5	2.7
Medium Performing	15.3	18.5	24.9	2.4	2.0	1.8
A.P.	12.5	14.0	19.5	2.7	0.2	0.9
Karnataka	18.9	22.9	29.7	1.0	1.1	0.4
Kerala	16.2	19.7	30.7	1.4	3.4	3.2
Tamil Nadu	14.9	19.5	30.7	1.4	3.4	3.2
West Bengal	14.2	16.4	20.2	3.9	1.6	1.2
Low Performing	15.1	18.3	23.9	0.9	0.5	1.0
Bihar	8.3	11.2	11.9	0.3	0.3	0.8
M.P.	28.9	35.5	42.1	1.5	0.9	1.2
Orissa	17.4	21.0	27.5	1.5	0.6	1.7
Rajasthan	12.4	13.7	22.2	0.7	0.3	0.4
U.P.	8.5	9.9	15.6	0.7	0.5	1.1
Average for 14 States	16.9	20.9	28.3	1.7	1.4	2.0

Source: Rao, M.G. and Sen. T.K., *Government Expenditure in India: Level, Growth and Composition,* National Institute of Public Finance and Policy, New Delhi, Aug. 1993, p.119.

sustained agricultural productivity. This situation has been further complicated by decreasing level of public investment in agriculture during the Eight Plan. Private capital has not so far offset the decrease as contemplated by the proponents of India's economic reforms[9]. It is also observed that expenditures on the agriculture sector significantly varied. The high performing region had higher allocation of expenditure (both revenue and capital) and was closely followed

[9] Jha, S.C., *India's Economic Reforms and its Impact on Rural Poverty,* Paper presented at ESCAP Export Group Meeting, Bangkok, December 1995.

by the medium performing region. In contrast, again, the low performing region had the lowest allocation (both revenue and capital) to this sector.

Thus, the low performing region's poor performance can be very well related to inadequate capital formation in the public sector, aggravated by skewed agricultural credit distribution against this region[10]. The implications of all these are that the region having higher level of capital formation achieved better level of production base, leading to sustained agricultural productivity growth. Following the historical trend all over the world, and particularly the recent East and Southeast Asian experience, the agricultural sector provided impetus for the growth of the industrial economy in the high performing region. The low performing region, in absence of a dynamic agriculture, trailed far behind on the overall economic growth path. This has also added to the dimension of widening regional disparity over the period. Between 1990-91 and 1992, the standard deviation in per capita net State domestic product increased from 756.8 to 834.5 (see Table 1). As a result of economic reforms, there could be further widening in regional disparity. This is due to accelerated flow of domestic credit and foreign investment towards the better performing regions. The poor performing region is going to further suffer unless a drastic change is introduced in the development strategies and policy as well as institutional framework.

III. FUTURE SCENARIOS

The facts available in the preceding paragraphs clearly indicate that the low performing region, accounting for about 50 per cent of the nation's total population, has lagged behind in almost all aspects of socio economic development and hence, the cycle of stagnation and poverty has continued. There has emerged a vast pool of unemployed labour force. Their health is poor, life expectancy is low and illiteracy is high. The rate of population growth is also quite high. Housing conditions, drinking water, sanitation and household electric supply are also consistently low. All these have contributed to the low rate of economic growth and high incidence of poverty over the decades.

The low performing region need to accelerate their economic growth rate to catch up with the better performing regions. Ironically,

[10] Rath, N., "Agricultural Growth and Investment in India," *Journal of the Indian School of Political Economy,* 1989, Vol. 1. No. 1.

their planned investments have fallen sharply in the last five years, which has further jeopardized their prospects for economic growth and improvements in infrastructure and human capital development. In the years 1991-92 through 1993-94, the shortfall in achieving annual plan outlays has been increasing from year to year[11]. For instance, Bihar's shortfall in annual plan outlays increased from 30 per cent in 1990-91 to 67 per cent in 1993-94; UP's from 5 per cent to 31 per cent; and MP's from 11 per cent to 16 per cent in the corresponding periods.

As a result of economic reforms, the flow of both domestic and foreign investment is directed more towards the better performing region. The low performing region received only 20 per cent of commercial bank credit and 24 per cent of credit from all India financial institutions. All these indicate the likelihood of growing inter-regional disparities in the future if the present trend continues. The result of low growth in the vast low performing region could ultimately halt the future growth prospects of the better performing regions, due to limitations of the market. At present, the low performing region accounts for the major market for products emanating from the better performing regions. India's sustainable economic growth would very much depend not only on export demand but also on domestic demand, which would be largely influenced by the low performing region. Above all, there would be growing socio economic conflict, political turmoil and constraint to the overall economic growth prospects of the nation[12].

IV. NEED FOR MODIFIED DEVELOPMENT STRATEGY

In light of recent Asian experience, which has provided new models for sustained economic growth including the aspects of equity, India will have to find ways and means for attaining higher rate of economic growth (i.e. annual GDP growth rate of 7-8 per cent). Only higher level of growth could help achieve the goal of balanced regional development. Once the growth patterns picks up momentum, there could be gradual convergence, primarily through stronger market linkages and changes in total factor productivity.

[11] Indian Council for Research on International Economic Relations, *ibid.*

[12] The indications of political turmoil are already visible in the Hindi region, which has been marked by frequent changes in government. This trend is likely to continue if economic growth remains stagnant.

In order to accelerate the economic growth process in the high and medium performing regions (Northwest and South), let the market forces take care of resource allocation with the active participation of private sector initiatives. Macroeconomic environment should be favourable, in terms of tariff structure and taxation policies, for increased involvement of private sector, including investment in further infrastructure development in the region. The public sector should focus more on technological development and higher level of skill development to facilitate the scope of further industrialization. No attempt should be made to constrain the development process in the better performing regions in order to seek the goal of balanced regional development. Even if foreign investment has the preference in favor of better performing regions, this should not be discouraged.

For the low performing region, the development strategy would need drastic modification. The major thrust of strategy has to be fast human capital development (i.e. education, health and nutrition), agricultural modernization and rural industrialization. In order to introduce and expand growth centers in rural areas, infrastructure on transport and communication should occupy the highest priority. For agricultural modernization, there is a need to enhance both public and private sector investment, particularly in irrigation. Available statistics reveal that those States which have continuously increased investment in irrigation, agricultural productivity has increased[13]. As a result, the level of employment has gone up and incidence of poverty has declined. The reverse is the case with the low performing region which has reduced the level of investment in the agriculture sector. Ironically, even the expenditure under plan outlays (Eighth Plan) has significantly declined in recent years, which has further constrained the growth prospects.

As narrated in earlier paragraphs, India's overall growth was hampered due to wrong strategy of heavy industrialization in the initial stages of development. This experience suggests that the strategy for rural industrialization in the low performing region should focus on small scale industries supported by local resource endowment and available human skills. This would help improve the allocation efficiency of available resources (in terms of capital

[13] Rao, C.H.H., "Agriculture: Policy and Performance," in Bimal Jalan (Ed.), *Indian Economy: Problems and Prospects,* New Delhi, Viking Press, 1992.

output ratios) and add value to the products. If improved technology is required, this could be borrowed from outside the region. All these combined would give comparative advantages to the products of the region. As a result of this, the region can have better market access both domestically as well as externally (in terms of export and the provisions of GATT). Once the initial success adds to the stable GDP growth, it would then be possible to allocate more resources for further infrastructure, human skill and technology development in the low performing region. The rural sector would then provide the engine for sustained economic growth and thus would provide the low performing region the opportunity to gradually catch up with the better performing regions. The widening gap in regional disparity would tend to decrease.

The strategy proposed here has already been tested in the case of China and success has been achieved.[14] Indeed, the average 10-12 per cent of annual GDP growth in China can be attributed to this type of strategy.

In the low performing region, the market is not expected to play a major positive role in accelerating the process of growth. Therefore, the role of state intervention would be crucial in providing resources for basic infrastructure and human capital development. Only in the light of this development, and with a bit of increased micro-efficiency, would the market start playing its role. Therefore, all attempts should be made to determine the type of state intervention which could guide the play of market forces in the right direction. Once market forces become active, private sector participation would tend to grow. This did not happen in the past primarily due to wrong intervention of state and bureaucratic interference in each aspect of development. Even after the onset of economic reforms (1991), this has not substantially changed and hence, the flow of resources, both domestic and foreign, has not been that dynamic so far.

Another major constraint to the low performing region has been the weak organization of economic institutions. One of the major tasks for the state would be to bring significant improvements and strengthening in the organization of such

---

[14] Jha, S.C., "Economic Reforms in the People' s Republic of China and the Role of the Asian Development Bank," *China Economic Review*, 4(2), 1993, pp.235-42.

institutions at various levels. This should be done most urgently in order to encourage the initiative and participation of the private sector. This would also tend to facilitate the role of the market forces. So far, even the poor project performance, either domestically or externally financed, in all its aspects in the low performing region is generally attributed to the deficiencies in the institutions. The public sector projects (either road, irrigation or any other) on average, have been delayed by 3-4 years and costs have risen by about 30-40 per cent. The benefits to the State have been substantially reduced.[15]

One of the factors for enterprise development and increased level of productivity growth in the high performing region is the introduction of decentralized planning.[16] This particularly applied in the states of Gujarat, Maharashtra and Karnataka. This not only helped in promoting more and more use of local development and entrepreneurial skill but also in accelerating the pace of development. This has been lacking in the poor performing region. Therefore, future strategy would require the promotion of decentralized planning at the local level and detailed assessment of local resources, their level of utilization and constraints, and required types of technology. Local entrepreneurs can be provided with training and orientation to effectively participate in local raw material based enterprise development and expansion. The basic pre-requisite again would be infrastructure and institutional development, for which the initial initiative would have to come from the state.

In the persistent cycle of stagnation in the low performing region, with low resource base, low investment and low productivity growth, the States have lacked development vision, innovativeness and priorities. There is a prevailing sense of hopelessness. This would have to change. The state leadership would have to bring vision and innovativeness even at a low growth path, while setting priorities for quicker development in certain sectors and locations having reliable resource endowment.

Investment in infrastructure development could be selective in support of this high growth potential sector and location. It is in the overall interest of the states in the poor performing region to realize the urgency of faster economic growth. The time is running

---

[15] World Bank, *Post Evaluation Reports*, 1992.

[16] Mishra, G.P. (Ed.), *op cit.*, p.120.

fast against the possible serious socio-political turmoil. Once this happens, the prospects for growth would be jeopardized. Therefore, there is a need for vision in the leadership of the poor performing region.

V. CONCLUSIONS

India's Five Year Plans had no effective strategy of balanced regional development. Measures adopted were rather ad hoc and were very much influenced by political pressure groups. The ultimate result was a massive wastage of resources. Even after the implementation of the eight five year plans the concern for regional development remains serious. The recent measures of liberalization and economic reforms do not seem to have brought any impact on this aspect. As a matter of fact, the gap in regional development has been widening.

The main cause of regional imbalance can be attributed to faulty strategy of economic development by means of heavy industries. The gestation period of industrialization was too long and the cost very high. This did not bring the expected benefits either from the point of view of productivity or employment. The government's debt burden continuously remained heavy, and average economic growth remained at 3.5 per cent over a long period of time (1950-1980) against the national population growth rate of 2.2 per cent. With major part of the resource confined to industrialization, opportunity for large scale infrastructure development, improvements in human skill and indigenous techno-logies and dispersal of development activities turned out to be very limited throughout the country. The spill-over effect did not catch much ground and as a result, there was no trickle down effect of economic growth either on the regions and the sector performed in isolation, without much influence on the overall growth pattern.

However, the states which realized the pre-requisite of agricultural development as the major sector of the economy, and concentrated their efforts on this sector, emerged ahead in the growth path. Second, they allocated more resources to infrastructure and human capital development to support this. As a result of these two fundamentals, the growth pattern varied, with two regions (Northwest and South) improving in performance. The North east became low-performing. *Their* priority for the agriculture sector remained weak and investment in infrastructure and human skill development was very low. This region failed to take advantage of industrialization. With this variation in growth, even the flow of domestic resources, both private as well as institutional, slowed down. This added a further dimension to the widening of regional disparity. The per capita net domestic product during 1991-92 is estimated to be in the range of Rs. 3,288 (Bihar) to Rs. 5,056 (Assam) in the low performing region. For the high performing region, this ranged between Rs. 7,586 (Gujarat) and Rs. 11,106 (Punjab). The same pattern followed for per capita income. The low performing region's per capita income ranged between Rs. 2,539 (Bihar) and Rs. 3,983 (Rajasthan). But for the high performing region, this was in the range of Rs. 6,060 (Gujarat) and Rs. 8,281 (Punjab). The situation with regard to the level of unemployment and incidence of poverty was not any better for the low performing region.

The low performing region, accounting for about 50 per cent of the nation's total population, has lagged behind in almost all aspects of socio-economic development. This trend is expected to continue if no innovative strategy is adopted by the state governments in the low performing region. There is a need for drastic change in their development strategy. The central focus in this strategy has to be on human capital development, agricultural modernization and rural industrialization. The rural industrialization should be based on local resource endowment and available human skills. State governments will have to play the key interventionist role in infrastructure and institutional development. Market forces would not be able to make a positive contribution at this stage. It is the state that would have to guide the role of the market. In the past, state intervention was more bureaucratic and hindered the growth process in all its aspects. Second, the leadership of the state must have a development vision and must set out its priorities for investment and resource allocation in areas where the potential for growth is higher.

For the better performing region, state intervention has to be very selective in order for market forces and the private sector to accelerate their participation. The macroeconomic policies (particularly in terms of tariff structure and taxation) must be favourable for expanded role of the private sector. No attempt is needed to limit their development process in order to seek the goal of regional balanced development. As soon as the low performing region attains development momentum, there would gradually be convergence as a result of market linkages and changes in factor productivity. The low performing region would provide an opportunity to the investors for a high rate of return. However, the key for this scenario is the degree of infrastructure and human capital development, which must come on a priority basis by the state government, with reasonable support from the central government. If convergence does not take place, regional disparity would tend to widen and the opportunity for further growth in the high performing region would be rather limited. India's overall economic growth performance would remain low and the dream for entering the modern 21st century as a modern nation would be shattered. With a weak India and strong China, Asia's leadership would ultimately fall into the hands of China. This would have far reaching implications for the global socio-economic and political equilibrium.

REFERENCES

1. Barro, R.J., "Government Spending in a Simple Model of Endogenous Growth," *Journal of Political Economy*, (1990), 103-125.
2. Campano, F. and D. Salvatore, "Economic Development, Income Distribution and the Kuznets Hypothesis," *Journal of Policy Modelling*, 10 (1988), 265-280.
3. De Long, J.B. and L.H. Summers, "How Strongly Do Developing Countries Benefit From Equipment Investment," *Journal of Monetar Economics*, 32(1993), 395-415.
4. Jha, S.K., "The Kuznets Curve: A Reassessment," World Development, forthcoming April 1996.
5. Jha, S.K., "Fiscal Policy, Income Distribution and Endogenous Growth," mimeo, 1995, (University of Washington, Seattle, WA).
6. Kuznets, S., "Economic Growth and Income Inequality," *American Economic Review*, 45 (1955), 1-28.
7. Lucas, R.E., "On the Mechanics of Economic Development," *Journal of Monetary Economics*, 22 (1988), 3-42.
8. Perotti, R., "Political Equilibrium, Income Distribution and Growth," *Review of Economic Studies*, 60 (1993), 755-776.
9. Ram, R., "Economic Development and Income Inequality: Further Evidence on the U Curve Hypothesis," *World Development*, 16 (1988), 137 1-1375.
10. Romer, P.M., "Increasing Returns and Long Run Growth," *Journal of Political Economy*, 94 (1986), 1002- 1037.
11. Watson, M., "A Note on Estimating Deterministic Trends in the Presence of Serially Correlated Errors," mimeo, 1992, (Northwestern University, Evanston, IL).

3

Economic Reforms and Regional Disparities

Neeraj Kaushal

Regional disparities in India are human made. The potentially wealthiest state in the country has the highest proportion of the poor. Situated at the heart of the Gangetic belt, the most fertile part of the country, owning a third of its iron ore and coal, and almost all of the copper reservoirs, Bihar has the lowest per capita income in India. Orissa, the second lowest in terms of per capita income and the second highest in terms of poverty, has an equally impressive endowment of natural resources. In almost all the socio-economic parameters, whether it is per capita consumption, literacy or infant mortality, the two states are almost at the bottom of the ladder. In contrast, in Gujarat and Maharashtra, with relatively poor water resources, minerals and ores, most of these parameters are significantly better.

To some extent the backwardness of the eastern region is a hangover of the colonial past. The system of permanent settlement introduced by the British in eastern India led to absentee-landlordism, which created a parasitic culture in this region and stole away the entrepreneurship of its populace. The "land reforms" of the fifties and the sixties which had the potentiality of creating a class of kulaks worked in Punjab and Haryana, where the reforms were implemented, but not in Bihar where they were not. Even Nehru's 'temples of modern India' - steel plants, heavy engineering units and large river valley projects in the public sector- set up in this region could not improve the state of its economy. Non-implementation of land reforms, plus lack of industrial growth - indeed a significant flight of the capital to the growth centres - made the eastern region a captive of the vicious circle of low income, low consumption and low productivity.

All the states, including the backward ones like Bihar, Rajasthan, Orissa and Madhya Pradesh experienced growth, but the relatively developed states grew much faster than the less developed ones. A number of policies have been announced and implemented to develop backward regions. Disparities, however, have only widened. In 1971, the real per capita income in Punjab was 2.64 times that of Bihar (1). Twenty years later, the gap between the two widened with Punjab's per capita income rising to 3.35 times that of Bihar.

A study by N. Krishnaji (2) in 1993 showed that interstate disparities narrowed during the sixties but widened during the seventies. A more recent study by S.R.Hashim (3) which covered up to 1990-91 showed that disparities have been growing since 1970-71. The coefficient of variation in the per capita net domestic product between states, as calculated by Hashim was 31.49 per cent in 1970-71. It rose to 37.15 per cent in 1980-81 and further to 39.17 per cent in 1990-91. Inequalities, therefore, grew much faster during the seventies than during the eighties. Hashim's study goes a step further to show that in almost all the economic and social parameters, except crude death rate and literacy, both male and female, inter-state disparities widened during the eighties as well.

During the eighties, the states that lost significantly in terms of ranking were : Himachal Pradesh, Jammu and Kashmir, Kerala and West Bengal. Jammu and Kashmir was 11th in terms of per capita state domestic product in 1980-81. It fell to the 22nd position 10 years later, partly due the social and political turmoil which paralysed its economy since the mid-eighties. Himachal Pradesh fell from the 9th to the 13th position. Kerala, with its silver lining of achieving complete literacy, nonetheless fell from the 15th to the 20th position. And West Bengal, which saw a substantial increase in agriculture production, fell in its ranking from the 10th to the 14th position, because of almost wholesale industrial decline, for which its strong trade union movement proved to be one of the factors. Gujarat, on the other hand, while invited considerable amount of investment, also lost by two ranks from the eighth to the 10th position. Among the large states that improved their position considerably during this period were : Tamil Nadu, Sikkim, Assam and Rajasthan. (See Table 2)

Most of the other large states more or less maintained their ranking. That is, they grew almost as fast as the entire country. However, even within these states, the backward regions grew far more slowly than the developed regions, which resulted in political tensions between the slow growing and fast growing areas.

All this is despite the fact that both the state governments and the central government have implemented several schemes for the development of backward areas.

WHY DISPARITIES?

Why are the disparities widening? To some extent, disparities are inevitable. Capital, specially private, flows to regions endowed with high productivity, large buying power and good infrastructure. States which are deficient in these basic necessities have failed to attract investment.

These can be seen as obvious factors. However, inter-state disparities in India have widened due to multitude of complex factors. Among them are quality and standard of governance, resource endowments, proximity to raw materials, absence of genuine land reforms, quality of human capital and infrastructure.

Until recently several states actually followed policies which shied private investors away from these states. The parasitic culture of permanent settlement joined together with political patronage for negative trade union activism explains the relative economic backwardness of West Bengal. Kerala, which was not a victim of permanent settlement, lost in productivity and private sector investment on account of high official patronage to trade unions. Governments in these states basically believed in growth through public sector investment, which created industrial sickness in these states. The recent changes in the industrial policy of the West Bengal government has created a new investment climate. West Bengal has had the second largest number of foreign investment approvals, after Maharashtra since 1991, when the foreign investment policy was liberalised. Of course, approvals do not mean actual inflows. And to a certain extent actual inflows will depend on the future industrial policy in the state. But it is an indicator that industrialists no longer shy away from the state as they did merely a few years ago. Political parties in Kerala are still committed to protecting trade unions which discourage private investment, domestic or foreign. With fetters of control obstructing industrial growth, Keralite entrepreneurs like to set up industries outside the state.

Another factor which appears to have worsened income inequalities is the quality of governance. Maharastra, until recently and Gujarat are the two best governed states in the country (4). Bihar's decline in the quality of governance particularly since the sixties discourage industrialists to invest there. On the other hand, Karnataka, backward in terms of infrastructure and per capita income, has been able to entice investment merely because of better governance.

POLITICAL CONSEQUENCES OF DISPARITIES

Whatever be the reasons, disparities are not a unique feature of the Indian economy. Almost all countries in the world suffer from disparities. There, are disparities in the UK with the northern part of the country considerably backward as compared to its southern regions. The United States, the world's most industrialised country also labours disparities in growth and development among its 50 states. Industrial prosperity in this country has moved from the north-east to the mid-west and now to the west : Silicon valley rather than New York is now known for industrial leadership in America. Disparity within a state, is then, no matter of great concern if the state has one common language and a more or less unifying culture.

In an industrialising country like India with its diversity of languages and cultures, the assimilation of migrant population with the local population is far more difficult; it may take several decades. Nonetheless there is large scale migration of agriculture workers and semi-skilled or unskilled workers, who in fact travel from Bihar to Punjab-Haryana-Delhi or from the Karnataka and Andhra Pradesh to the Maharashtra-Gujarat region in search of agriculture, industrial or construction jobs.

Economists, in fact, argue that growth has a habit of creating disparities. But mobility of labour from slow growing regions to fast growing regions results in the benefits of high growth flowing to the people of slow regions. For instance, Bihari workers travel as far as Punjab for employment which gets them higher wages than what they could get in their own state. Outflow of workers from backward states reduces the supply of workers in these states, in turn raising the wages of those who stay back. So in the long run, the economic consequences of regional disparities may not be very serious.

However, disparities create serious political consequences. Disparities cause large scale political upheavals. Of late, inter-state disparities have been a source of growing political disturbance in several states. There are several illustrations of politically loaded inter-state disparities. For instance in Bihar, the populace of the less developed Jharkhand want a separate state for themselves. The entire tribal belt in Bihar of which Jharkhand is a part is rich in minerals, but it has seen little development. The people of Jharkhand have the grievance that their development has been sacrificed and all the funds of development have been poured into northern Bihar.

Similarly, in UP the less developed Uttrakhand wants the status of a separate state. The people of Uttrakhand too think that the state government and the centre have neglected them while western UP has been developed. In Maharashtra, there is Vidhrabha - from Nagpur to Chindwara, which is poorly developed; and its residents want a separate state. Saurashtra, the northern part of Gujarat is less developed. Earlier there have been demands for a separate state from the residents of Saurashtra. The entire tribal belt in Orissa is poorly developed. In Madhya Pradesh, the entire Chatesgarh area is poorly developed and is a hot bed for political tension. So even if, theoretically, the normal process of economic growth can take care of disparities, the political tensions they create in the meanwhile, make inter-regional disparities a very serious problem. As can be seen from the above examples, intra-state disparities are not such a serious issue as are two inter-state disparities. For instance, Rajasthan surrounded by two prosperous states, Punjab from one side and Gujarat from the other, does not suffer from any major political tension due to its poor growth. On the other hand, within

Gujarat there is a significant tension between the Saurashtra region and the rest of Gujarat.

DISPARITIES AND GOVERNMENT INTERVENTION

In the past four and a half decades, the government has initiated several schemes to reduce inter-and intra-state disparities. Regional equality has been a proclaimed basic objective of India's development strategy. There have been several backward area development programmes. Many taxes and other type of concessions have been offered to industrialists willing to invest in backward areas. But the heavy load of under-development has not become lighter. Industrialists it appears, price proper infrastructure, banking and financial services, much more than tax concessions. For all these reasons, the so-called growth centres, identified and sponsored by the Union government have failed to take off.

Besides announcing specific policies to encourage investment in backward areas, the central government has also been disbursing higher funds to states in the form of centrally sponsored schemes for backward regions. The centre also allocates more funds to backward states through Finance Commissions for non-plan purposes, and through the Gadgil formula for the plan. However, even all these together have made no perceptible difference to disparities either within or between states. On the other hand, as already noted, the inter-state disparities have sharpened. In fact, pouring more money into weaker and poorer states is not really a solution to the problem of backwardness in these states. Annual plans in several less developed states have become a complete farce. For instance, for several years Bihar has not been using its plan allocations fully; the government conveniently shifts most of the plan funds for non-plan expenditure. Nevertheless, it insists on raising the size of the plan every year. What is worse, the Planning Commission approves it, despite knowing that the Bihar government will divert a considerable proportion of the funds for paying salaries. In 1993-94, the government sanctioned a plan of Rs. 2300 crore, but the actual expenditure on the plan was Rs. 750 crore. The rest was used for paying salaries or for other unproductive purposes. In 1994-

95, the plan size was raised to Rs. 2500 crore. This shows higher plan outlays do not ensure that more funds would be devoted to development. In other words, growth in backward regions cannot be attained by pouring more funds. What is required is both fiscal and policy reforms, along with evenly administered rational regulations changing with the demands of time and growth of the economy.

DISPARITIES AND LIBERALISATION

Reforms, or the half-measures that have taken so far in the name of reforms, have not reached the state level. Their domain has mainly remained limited to the Centre. Several economists and experts, both in the government and outside, have expressed fears that liberalisation will increase disparities. Hashim is apprehensive that economic reforms will increase inter-state disparities. The mid-term appraisal of the Eighth Plan prepared by the Planning Commission echoes these fears too. International experience also shows that opening up of the economy to more competition leads to increased disparities. For instance, inter-regional disparities sharpened in the first few years of liberalisation in China and the laggards are still in the process of catching up with the fast growing regions. (5)

Will India go the Chinese way? There are no clear signals for that. Liberalisation paves way for a growing role for the market. Often market directs the flow of resources to states with higher purchasing power and better infrastructure and administration. This along with the decline in government role in production, both central and state, may increase inter-state disparities. The proponents of sharpening-disparities theory offer three more reasons in support of their argument (6). One, the ever growing size of the fiscal deficit which has reduced the central government's ability to repair inter-state disparities in any significant manner.

Two, transfer of resources from the Centre to the states takes place with tacit agreement between them. In the changing political scenario where most states are run by different political parties, and the party in power in the Centre rules over fewer states than at any time before, it is unlikely that such agreement would be reached easily. For instance, it may not be acceptable to the Maharashtra government that Bihar should get more money because it is poor and backward. Therefore, it is possible that the extra money flowing to weaker states through the Gadgil formula for plan funds (and through the Finance Commission formula for non-plan funds) may fall.

It can of course be argued that weaker states will continue to get additional funds through centrally aided schemes, even if the flow of funds through the Gadgil formula falls. But, richer states will also continue to get funds through externally aided schemes. On the other hand, weaker states, due to their poor fiscal position, may not be able to provide rupee resources to utilise externally aided projects.

The third factor given in favour of growing-disparities hypothesis is the growing demands for autonomy at the local level. Autonomy, it is argued, will sooner or later be extended to the financial sphere. This factor, too, will reduce the flow of funds from the Centre to the states and further to the local bodies in the form of Centre-states grants.

However, there is a possibility that cut in Centre-state transfers will force the state governments and the local bodies to exploit, more rigorously and ruthlessly, the resources at their disposal. So, in the years, factors, both for and against inter-state equality will be in force.

On balance, whether disparities will grow in future is an area of speculation. Liberalisation, which itself is a hesitant half-way house has not reached the state level. Looking with reasonable optimism to future, one can offer a number of reasons which may reduce inter-and intra-state disparities.

One, pressure on the existing infrastructure, as a result of large scale movement of people and capital, in a relatively industrialised state, may act as a hurdle to further investment there. If that happens, some industrialists may plough funds in less crowded and less industrialised states, specially those with better governance.

Two, more enterprising industrialists, who like to take risk, may also like to invest in states with poor infrastructure and bad administration. Some of the less developed states, particularly Bihar and Madhya Pradesh with their rich potential may be taken up by entrepreneurs for rapid development. The Ambanis have already put a welcome step forward. Their expectation is that they will get all encouragement and support from the state and the immense natural resources of Bihar will be for them to develop and exploit.

With this kind of capitalist adventure the relatively backward areas may not remain backward for a long time.

Three, since the locomotion of development in future will be trade, those areas will draw investment and enterprise which are within reasonable distance from ports. Port development, itself will have to be given a higher priority. A highly developed trade infrastructure will possibly work to the advantage of all areas reasonably close to ports or linked to ports by new railroads. Coastal India which has a number of backward state - Orissa, Karnataka, West Bengal and Andhra Pradesh will get faster development opportunities.

Four, in the next few years, industrialists would like to invest in states which are likely to stay surplus in power. A forecast made by the Central Electricity Authority shows that the eastern region would be power surplus , whereas the western and northern region would be highly deficient in power. Therefore, on this account the eastern region may attract more investment.

Five, the recent political trend of states or regional parties coming to power along with the acute diminishing of a hegemonic party system will almost certainly work for reduction of regional disparities, both within and between states. The less developed areas will have new political clout because of sheer numbers and the party in power at the state level will have to pay more attention to the development of the relatively deprived regions in order to get the support of the people of these regions at election time.

Six, liberalisation has scrapped policies like freight equalisation which discriminated against eastern states. This will have an overall effect of reducing disparities.

NOTES

1. See Table
2. Krishnaji N., Widening Distances: State Domestic Product Variations, 1961-81' in *'Development and Change Essays in Honour of K.N.Raj'*, edited by Pranab Bardhan, Mrinal Datta Chaudhuri and T.N. Krishnan, Oxford University Press, Bombay 1993.
3. Hashim S. R., 'Regional Disparities in India', *Planning Commission,* 1995. The study also calculates Gini coefficient to measure inequality in income

distribution, which shows that inequalities have increased over the years. The coefficient was 0.157 in 1970-71, 0.197 in 1980-81 and 0.207 in 1990-91

4. Desai, Ashok, The Next Gujarat ?, *Business Standard,* November 28, 1995.

5. Bhalla, A.S. *Uneven Development in the Third World: A Study of China and India,* Macmillan 1992. Tsai, Wen- Hui. In 'Making China Modernized: Comparative Modernisation between Mainland China and Taiwan' (Baltimore School of Law, University of Maryland, Occasional Papers 1993).

6. See note (3) and Mid-term appraisal of the Eighth Plan prepared by the Planning Commission, 1995.

Table 1
Per Capita net state domestic product * (at 1980-81 prices)

	1970-71	*1980-81*	*1990-91*
Andhra Pradesh	1216	1428	1803
Arunachal Pradesh	N. A.	1612	2726
Assam	1271	1312	1821
Bihar	817	904	1131
Goa	N. A.	2933	4490
Gujarat	1728	2021	2516
Haryana	1951	2357	3392
Himachal Pradesh	1574	1761	2123
Jammu and Kashmir	1487	1639	1673
Karnataka	1409	1630	2128
Kerala	1441	1529	1782
Madhya Pradesh	1281	1253	1615
Maharashtra	1986	2561	3386
Manipur	1135	1397	1871
Meghalaya	N. A.	1370	1760
Nagaland	N. A.	1513	1924
Orissa	1170	1103	1491
Punjab	2161	2889	3792
Rajasthan	1302	1284	1797
Sikkim	N. A.	1591	3243
Tamil Nadu	1472	1507	2212
Tripura	1071	1333	1651
Uttar Pradesh	1449	1142	1587
West Bengal	1465	1716	1961
A & N Island	N. A.	2608	2550
Delhi	3099	3563	4873
Pondicherry	N. A.	3017	3412

* Triennium average around the year mentioned
Source: Hashim S.R., 'Regional Disparities in India', *Planning Commission,* 1995.

Table 2
Ranking of states in terms of per capita net domestic product *
(at 1980-81 prices)

	1970-71	*1980-81*	*1990-91*
Andhra Pradesh	16	18	18
Arunachal Pradesh	N.A.	13	8
Assam	15	22	17
Bihar	20	27	27
Goa	N.A.	3	2
Gujarat	5	8	10
Haryana	4	7	5
Himachal Pradesh	6	9	13
Jammu and Kashmir	7	11	22
Karnataka	12	12	12
Kerala	11	15	20
Madhya Pradesh	14	24	24
Maharashtra	3	6	6
Manipur	18	19	16
Meghalaya	N.A.	20	21
Nagaland	N.A.	16	15
Orissa	17	26	26
Punjab	2	4	3
Rajasthan	13	23	19
Sikkim	N.A.	14	7
Tamil Nadu	8	17	11
Tripura	19	21	23
Uttar Pradesh	10	25	25
West Bengal	9	10	14
A & N Island	N.A.	5	9
Delhi	1	1	1
Pondicherry	N.A.	2	4

* Triennium average around the year mentioned
Source: Hashim S.R., 'Regional Disparities in India', *Planning Commission,* 1995.

4

Regional Disparity in the Industrial Development of India: An Inter-temporal Study

Srinath Baruah

1. INTRODUCTION

One of the basic objectives incorporated in the various five year plans at the national level is the removal disparity in regional economic development. The disparity in the regional economic development can be mainly attributed to widening regional imbalance in the level of industrial development. This paper, therefore, makes an attempt to examine the pattern of regional imbalance in industrial development over time with the help of econometric tools and to see how effective economic reforms are likely to be in narrowing down the regional imbalance in the level of industrial development.

2. PATTERN OF REGIONAL IMBALANCE

In our study, we consider the administrative jurisdiction of a state as an economic region although ideally economic region should be stratified on the basis of resource-base and economic homogeneity. There exists notable variation in the level of economic development of the various states over time in terms of per capita state income as well as the rate of growth of state income. The magnitude of the problem could be understood from

Table I showing the relative index of per capita State Net Domestic Product (SNDP) in the last two decades since 1970-71. However,. it must be stated that per capita SNDP figure alone may not always be a conclusive indicator of development as it is affected by the size of population. It is evident from Table 1 that there is distinct regional variation in the level of economic development. In 1970-71, we had states like Bihar having only Rs. 838 as per capita income and also the states like Delhi with per capita income of Rs. 3123 which was 3.73 times higher than that of Bihar. In fact, Delhi ranked first and Bihar touched the bottom of the rank in terms of per capita income in 1970-71. The same is true for 1981-81, the per capita income of Delhi was 4.09 times higher and in 1990-91 it was 4.17 times higher than that of Bihar reflecting the distinct increase in inter-state disparity. Another distinctive feature of regional disparity in the per capita income (or in the level of development) is that there are few states, namely, Delhi, Punjab, Maharastra, Haryana, Gujarat, Goa and Pondicherry whose per capita income was always higher than the national average while per capita income of Andhra Pradesh, Assam, Bihar, Karnataka, Madhya Pradesh, Kerala, Orissa, Uttar Pradesh, West Bengal, Tripura, Nagaland, Meghalaya and Manipur was consis-tently lower than the national average from 1970-71 to 1990-91. Another notable feature is that the relative index of per capita income in case of relatively richer states like Delhi, Punjab, Maharastra and Haryana has increased while that of states like Bihar, J & K, Kerala, Madhya Pradesh, Rajasthan, Uttar Pradesh, and West Bengal has decreased indicating that the disparity is widening the major states. In fact, the rank correlation coefficient of per capita SNDP between 1970-71 and 1980-81, and between 1980-81 and 1990-91 is very high being 0.97 in both cases, indicating thereby that the disparity has not narrowed down over the years.

In the field of industrial development also, the level of disparity among the states persists over the years. Although the village and small scale industries like handicrafts and handlooms are almost uniformly spread over the country, but the manufacturing sector is unevenly distributed among the states for there has been no noticeable disparity in the value added by the manufacturing factory sector over the years. The large scale industries are concentrated in the relatively rich states having strong base of infra-structural facilities and the backward states like those of north eastern region have recorded the lowest status in the industrial map of the country. The disparity in the per capita value added by manufacturing factory sector indicates the relative status of industrial development among the states although it is reiterated once again that the per capita concept may not be a conclusive indicator. The index of per capita value added of the manufacturing factory sector in the various states along with their rank (taking all India = 100) is furnished in Table-2.

Over the years 1970-71 to 1990-91, there is practically no remarkable change in the per capita value added by manufacturing factory sector. States like Goa, Gujarat, Haryana, Maharastra, Punjab, Tamil Nadu, Delhi and Pondicherry have much higher per capita value added by manufacturing factory sector compared to all-India average consistently from 1970-7o to 1990-91. Moreover, all the states mentioned above have high percentage contribution of industry and mining to State Net Domestic Product (SNDP) and except for Goa, they all have high percentage share of manufacturing output to all-India. On the other hand, Table 2 displays that states like Assam, Bihar, Orissa, Rajasthan, Uttar Pradesh and other north eastern states have per capita value added by manufacturing factory sector much lower than the all-India average over time, besides having lower percentage contribution by manufacturing sector to SNDP. We have already stated earlier that per capita concept alone cannot be a conclusive indicator of economic development or industrial development. That is why, we have computed a composite index of industrial development of the states for 1970-71, 1980-81 and 1990-91 on the basis of seven indicators of industrial development. This is done to analyse the spatio-temporal variation in the industrial development of the country from 1970-71 to 1990-91.

3. METHODOLOGY IN COMPUTATION OF INDUSTRIAL DEVELOPMENT INDEX

The principal component method first developed by Hotelling (1933) has been adoptea for computation of indices of industrial development of states for three time points 1970-71, 1980-81 and 1989-90. The aim of the method of principal components is the construction out of a set of variables, X_j s (j=1, 2.......k) of new variables P called "principal components' which are linear combination of X's such that

$$P_1 = a_{11}X_1 + a_{12}X_2 + \ldots\ldots\ldots\ldots\ldots\ldots a_{1k}X_k$$

.

.

.

$$P_k = a_{k1}X_1 + a_{k2}X_2 + \ldots\ldots\ldots\ldots\ldots\ldots a_{kk}X_k$$

The a_{ij}'s called loadings, are chosen so that the constructed principal components satisfy two conditions : (a) the principal components are uncorrelated and (b) the first principal component P_1 absorbs and accounts for the maximum possible proportion of the variation in the set of all X's, the second principal component absorbs the maximum of the remaining variation and so on.

The derivation of the loading factor $a_{ij,}$ j = 1, 2, ... k of the first principal component is made adopting the following steps as devised by C. Burt.

Step 1 : The variables (or indicators) X_j are first standardised using the simple formula

$$Z_j = (X_j - X)/SD_x$$

where SD_x is the standard deviation of X_j

Step 2 : The correlation coefficient between variables (or indicators) are obtained and they are arranged in a symmetric matrix form known as correlation matrix such that

$$r_{xi.xj} = r_{xj.xi}$$

and the principal diagonal elements being unity.

Step 3 : The square root of total sum of all elements of the correlation matrix is computed which is equal to

$$\sum_{i=1}^{k} \sum_{i=j}^{k} r_{xi.xj}$$

Step 4 : The column sum (or row sum) of the correlation matrix is obtained.

Step 5 : The loading factor (a_{ij}'s) of first principal component is derived by dividing each column (or row) sum of correlation coefficient such that

$$a_{ij} = \left(\sum_{j=1}^{k}\right)_{xi.xj}$$

where i refers to the ith variable.

Step 6 : The latent root of the first principal component has been found out to estimate the variation accounted by the first principal component. The latent root is defined as the sum of' the square the loading factors such that

$L_1 = {}^{k}a_{1j}$

Similarly latent root of mth principal component is given by

$$\left(\sum_{j=1}^{k} {}^{r}_{xi.xj}\right) / \surd \sum_{i-1}^{k} \sum_{j=1}^{k} r_{xi.xj}$$

The value of latent root of any p_i gives an idea of the importance of the amount of the total variation that the particular P_i has extracted from the set is X's. A convenient way of presenting the latent roots is to express them as a percentage of total variation in the set of X's. Thus, the percentage variance accounted by P_1 is given by

$$(L_1/k) \times 100$$

If the percentage variance of first principal component is more than 50%, normally it is not necessary to go for second and subsequent principal component.

Step 7 : Finally the first principal component is given by

$$P_{1i} = a_{i1}Z_1 + a_{i2}Z_2 + \ldots\ldots\ldots\ldots\ldots\ldots + a_{ik}Z_k \ldots\ldots (1)$$

The index of industrial development has been estimated from equation (1) above where Z_i is the standardised value of the X_i.

4. DATA SOURCE, RESULTS AND DISCUSSION

For finding out the level of industrial development of each of the state economy, we have taken the following seven indicators

X_1 = Percentage share of value of manufacturing outputs to all-India (ASI part)

X_2 = Percentage share of registered factories to all-India (ASI part)

X_3 = Per capita net value added by manufacturing factory sector at current prices

X_4 = Percentage contribution of industry and mining to NSDP at current prices

X_5 = Per capita value of output by manufacturing sector (ASI part) at current prices

X_6 = Index of selective development of infrastructure (all-India = 100) (relative weights for construction of infrastructure are given in Appendix –V)

X_7 = Percentage share of registered small scale units to all-India

For the computation of industrial development index all the seven indicators mentioned above are taken for 1980-81 and 1989-90, but the indicator X_4 could not be taken for 1970-71 as the reliable data were not available. The basic data on all the indicators are provided by the Centre for Monitoring Indian Economy's Report on "Basic Statistics relating to States of India", September 1994. The data on the seven indicators of industrial development for 1970-71, 1980-81 and 1989-90 are reproduced in Appendix I, II and III.

The first principal component for 1970-71, 1980-81 and 1989-90 is given by equations (2), (3) and (4) respectively.

Thus for 1970-71,

$$P_{1i} = 0.8712\ Z_1 + 0.9147\ Z_2 + 0.8654\ Z_3 + 0.8576\ Z_5 + 0.7034\ Z_6 + 0.8231\ Z_7 \ \ldots\ldots\ldots\ldots\ldots \ (2)$$

(variance of P_1 = 71 %)

For 1980-81,

$$P_{1i} = 0.7986\,Z_1 + 0.7658\,Z_2 + 0.8001\,Z_3 + 0.7425\,Z_4 + 0.8739\,Z_5 + 0.7096\,Z_6 + 0.5917\,Z_7 \ldots (3)$$

Finally for 1989-90,

$$P_{1i} = 0.7645\,Z_1 + 0.7230\,Z_2 + 0.8575\,Z_3 + 0.6689\,Z_4 + 0.8421\,Z_5 + 0.7440\,Z_6 + 0.5431\,Z_7 \ldots (3)$$

(variance of P_1 = 55 %)

The computed composite indices of industrial development of the states and their ranking for 1970-71, 1980-81 and 1989-9() are furnished in Table 3. It appears that the states like Maharashtra, Gujarat, Punjab, Tamil Nadu, West Bengal, Haryana and Andhra Pradesh rank among the first ten states at all the three points of time under our study while the states like Madhya Pradesh, Orissa, Himachal Pradesh, J & K and all the states of North Eastern region had consistently very low ranking during the period. More interestingly, all the states of north-eastern region under study rank the bottom in the composite index of industrial development at all the points of time. The rank correlation coefficient of the composite index of industrial development between 1970-71 and 1980-81 is 0.97 and it is 0.98 between 1980-81 and 1989-90 indicating that the pattern of ranking has not changed. In fact the imbalance has widened over time. This can be ascertained from the fact that the standard deviation of' the observations of either the per capita net value added by manufacturing factory sector (variable X_3) or the per capita net value of output by manufacturing factory sector (X_5) has increased. The standard deviation has increased from 41.09 in 1970-71 to 144.80 in 1980-81 and to 384.69 in 1989-90 in case of per capita value added by manufacturing sector and from 182.28 in 1970-71 to 727.74 in 1980-81 and to 2275.30 in 1989-90 in case of per capita manufacturing output. The arguments based on the above statistical analysis amply substantiate the view that the regional disparity in the level of industrial development has widened over time.

6. NEW ECONOMIC POLICY AND REGIONAL DISPARITY

We now turn to investigate whether the regional disparity which, existed in the pre-reforms period has really been narrowed down. The new economic reforms geared up through new industrial and trade policies in 1991 were expected to boost up the rate of industrial development both at national and regional levels. But the success of these polices to bring about industrial development depends on, *inter alia,* strong base of the infrastructural facilities. We have again used the principal component method to obtain the index of industrial development for 1992-93. However, we have taken only five indicators excluding the variables X_2 and X_4 for which state-wise data are not available. The data for the remaining five variables are obtained from the CMIE report on Industrial Statistics of India (January, 1996) and reproduced in Appendix IV. The ranking of the states on the basis of composite index of industrial development is furnished in Table 4. The rank correlation between the index of industrial development 1989-90 and 1992-93 is 0.9956 which indicates that the regional industrial imbalance is not narrowing down at all after the economic reforms; rather it has widened as evident from the fact that the standard deviation of the state level per capita value added by manufacturing factory sector has increased very significantly from 384.69 in 1989-90 to 610.28 in 1992-93 and the same is true in case of per capita output of manufacturing factory sector.

To be more specific, the percentage increase in per capita value added of manufacturing factory sector between 1989-90 and 1992-93 is much more in case of the richer states like Maharashtra, Punjab, Gujarat, Delhi, Haryana, Tamil Nadu, Karnataka, etc. compared to the industrially weaker states like Bihar, Orissa, J & K, Assam and all other states of north eastern region. In the post-reforms period (say in 1992-93), the condition of the states of north eastern region has not improved at all and their position remained at the bottom of the ranking of composite index of industrial development indicating that the economic reforms have not impacted favourably the north eastern region till date.

7. CONCLUDING REMARKS

From the statistical evidence as well as the logical views expressed in the previous sections, we can come to a definite conclusion that the inter-temporal regional disparity in the level of industrial development has not been narrowed down in spite of our solemn objective of removal of regional disparity. Rather, the disparity has widened. The same is true in the post reforms period also. More particularly, the industrial disparity appears to be more serious when we take into account all the states of the north eastern region. All of them are placed at the bottom of the ranking in the composite index of industrial development in spite of the fact that they are relatively rich in their natural resources. The economic reforms are welcome and can help in initiating higher rate of development only when the basic infrastructural facilities such as power, transport and communication, banking services, marketing services etc. are adequately provided as pre-condition. The whole of north eastern region lags far behind in these infrastructural facilities. So, the respective state governments and the Centre cannot wash off their hands and they, particularly the Centre, should came forward in a big way in providing of infrastructural facilities in order to enable the north eastern states to reap the benefits of economic reforms in future. The same is also true in case of other infrastructurally poor states like Himachal Pradesh, Jammu and Kashmir, Orissa, Rajasthan, Madhya Pradesh, Bihar etc. Otherwise, the removal of regional disparity in the level of economic development will remain a far cry.

REFERENCE

1. Centre for Monitoring Indian Economy (1994), "*Basic Statistics Relating to States of India*" September 1994.
2. Centre for Monitoring Indian Economy (1996), "*Industrial Statistics of India*" January 1996.
3. Government of Assam (1978), "*Statistical Abstract of Assam*" 1978.
4. Government of India (1986), "*Statistical Abstract of India*".
5. Hotelling, H. (1993), "Analysis of a Complex of Statistical Variables into Principal Components". *Journal of Educational Psychology.*
6. Johnston, J. (1984), *Economic Methods.*
7. Pal, M.N. (1975), "Disparities in the Levels of Development in India". *Indian Journal of Regional Science,* Vol. VIII, No. 1.

Table 1
Index of per capita Net State Domestic Product at Factor Cost at 1980-81 prices (all-India = 100)

Sl. No.	*Name of State*	*Index of net State Domestic Product*					
		1970-71	*Rank*	*1980-81*	*Rank*	*1990-90*	*Rank*
1	Andhra Pradesh	84.50	20	84.92	18	81.42	17
2	Arunachal Pradesh	75.29	20	96.06	12	109.51	9
3	Assam	77.93	18	73.85	25	80.35	18
4	Bihar	56.74	23	56.55	26	53.10	26
5	Goa	130.94	5	193.54	2	182.31	2
6	Gujarat	119.77	7	119.88	7	116.70	8
7	Haryana	145.70	2	145.85	6	154.04	5
8	Himachal Pradesh	105.62	9	104.86	9	96.07	10
9	Jammu & Kashmir	110.02	8	109.29	8	74.54	22
10	Karnataka	94.65	14	94.03	13	91.78	11
11	Kerala	98.71	13	92.92	14	77.53	19
12	Madhya Pradesh	84.36	16	82.03	20	77.22	20
13	Maharashtra	132.70	4	149.35	5	161.81	4
14	Manipur	74.54	21	87.94	17	82.63	16
15	Meghalaya	N.A.	N.A.	83.75	19	75.79	21
16	Nagaland	N.A.	N.A.	89.11	16	84.73	15
17	Orissa	75.29	19	75.75	23	72.13	25
18	Punjab	140.01	3	164.55	4	167.22	3
19	Rajasthan	100.61	11	75.20	24	84.77	14
20	Sikkim	N.A.	N.A.	96.68	11	150.47	6
21	Tamil Nadu	100.88	10	92.18	15	90.35	12
22	Tripura	72.17	21	81.42	21	73.07	23
23	Uttar Pradesh	81.04	17	78.65	22	72.71	24
24	Delhi	211.44	1	231.32	1	221.62	1
25	West Bengal	98.85	12	99.14	10	89.50	13
26	Pondicherry	128.23	6	186.95	3	148.01	7
	Richer States	133.45		150.34		155.83	
	Poorer States	77.12		72.31		69.81	

Source : Computed from CMIE Report on *'Basic Statistics Relating to States of India'*, September, 1994

Table 2
Index of State-wise per capita value added by Manufacturing Factory Sector at current price (all-India = 100)

Sl. No.	*Name of State*	*Index of per capita value added of manufacturing factory sector (all-India = 100)*					
		1970-71	*Rank*	*1980-81*	*Rank*	*1990-90*	*Rank*
1	Andhra Pradesh	50.88	14	62.29	14	64.01	16
2	Assam	82.63	13	36.57	20	65.37	15
3	Bihar	54.39	12	41.14	18	59.34	17
4	Goa	21.05		320.57	1	276.85	1
5	Gujarat	189.47	3	190.86	4	174.90	4
6	Haryana	122.81	7	153.14	6	140.27	7
7	Himachal Pradesh	66.67	11	82.86	12	97.86	9
8	Jammu & Kashmir	10.53	19	17.14	21	13.04	20
9	Karnataka	108.77	8	92.57	10	94.75	11
10	Kerala	73.68	10	88.00	11	95.72	20
11	Madhya Pradesh	47.37	16	65.71	13	70.04	13
12	Maharashtra	292.98	1	272.00	2	246.30	2
13	Manipur	N.A.		4.00	23	0.58	23
14	Meghalaya	N.A.		60.00	15	10.70	21
15	Orissa	47.37	15	42.86	17	70.04	12
16	Punjab	91.23	9	131.43	9	207.00	3
17	Rajasthan	45.61	17	55.43	16	51.75	19
18	Tamil Nadu	131.58	6	145.14	7	164.98	6
19	Tripura	0.00		8.57	22	5.84	22
20	Uttar Pradesh	42.11	18	38.86	19	58.75	18
21	Delhi	224.56	2	174.29	5	128.60	8
22	West Bengal	170.18	4	144.00	8	66.15	14
23	Pondicherry	149.12	5	208.00	3	165.18	5
	Richer States	233.33		229.71		224.32	
	Poorer States	45.61		43.29		61.09	

Source: Computed from CMIE Report on *'Basic Statistics Relating to States of India'*, September, 1994

Table 3
Index of Industrial Development of States 1970-71 to 1989-90

Sl. No.	*Name of State*	*1970-71 Index*	*1970-71 Rank*	*1980-81 Index*	*1980-81 Rank*	*1989-90 Index*	*1989-90 Rank*
1	Andhra Pradesh	0.976439	8	- 1.37184	10	0.999451	10
2	Assam	- 2.75993	16	- 4.83930	18	- 2.57367	17
3	Bihar	- 0.66519	12	- 2.90991	14	- 1.14314	15
4	Goa	- 3.45737	19	1.444030	7	3.922370	5
5	Gujarat	5.563905	3	4.022148	2	5.340469	4
6	Haryana	0.541838	9	- 0.15281	9	1.781527	7
7	Himachal Pradesh	- 3.14917	18	- 4.92933	19	- 2.63219	18
8	Jammu & Kashmir	- 4.15702	20	- 5.58756	21	4.94535	21
9	Karnataka	0.431898	10	- 1.56244	12	0.210418	12
10	Kerala	- 0.08915	11	- 1.48127	11	- 0.04988	13
11	Madhya Pradesh	- 1.30860	14	- 3.23033	15	- 0.21947	14
12	Maharashtra	12.32951	1	7.890392	1	8.427266	1
13	Manipur	- 4.74975	23	- 6.56217	23	- 5.41146	23
14	Meghalaya	- 4.53918	22	- 5.56944	20	- 5.15018	22
15	Nagaland	- 4.42700	21	- 6.21570	22	- 4.66095	20
16	Orissa	- 3.00914	17	- 4.52619	17	- 2.68929	19
17	Punjab	4.524526	5	1.496026	6	5.756496	2
18	Rajasthan	- 2.59322	15	- 3.74270	16	- 2.05420	16
19	Tamil Nadu	5.841144	2	3.298992	3	5.342646	3
20	Tripura	- 4.91725	24	- 6.95462	24	- 6.06761	24
21	Uttar Pradesh	1.828278	7	- 2.36531	13	1.449536	9
22	Delhi	3.699992	6	1.36558	8	0.849828	11
23	West Bengal	5.124160	4	1.769312	4	1.762369	8
24	Pondicherry	- 1.03962	13	1.580381	5	2.183715	6

Table 4
Index of Industrial Development of States – 1992-93

Sl. No.	*Name of State*	*Index*	*Rank*
1	Andhra Pradesh	0.127144	12
2	Assam	- 2.43653	19
3	Bihar	- 1.37711	15
4	Goa	3.687676	3
5	Gujarat	3.448966	4
6	Haryana	1.863851	8
7	Himachal Pradesh	- 1.77979	17
8	Jammu & Kashmir	- 3.5332	23
9	Karnataka	0.023095	13
10	Kerala	0.147632	11
11	Madhya Pradesh	- 0.01711	14
12	Maharashtra	5.167128	1
13	Manipur	- 3.72509	20
14	Meghalaya	- 3.85105	22
15	Nagaland	- 3.85072	21
16	Orissa	- 2.09162	18
17	Punjab	4.453781	2
18	Rajasthan	- 1.59286	16
19	Tamil Nadu	3.343362	5
20	Tripura	- 4.00498	24
21	Uttar Pradesh	1.213184	9
22	Delhi	0.226773	10
23	West Bengal	1.919780	7
24	Pondicherry	2.637750	6

The first Principal Component for 1992-93 being
$P_{1i} = 0.6451\ Z_1 + 0.8841\ Z_3 + 0.7994\ Z_6 + 0.5407\ Z_7$
(Variance of P_1 = 55 %)

APPENDIX I
Indicators of Industrial Development of States – 1970-71

Sl. No.	*Name of State*	*X1*	*X2*	*X3*	*X4*	*X5*	*X6*
1	Andhra Pradesh	5.0	8.4	29	158	93	7.8
2	Assam	1.4	2.3	30	135	73	0.3
3	Bihar	5.5	2.3	31	133	98	3.6
4	Goa	0.1	0.2	12	100	100	0.3
5	Gujarat	9.7	10.9	108	501	111	6.6
6	Haryana	2.3	1.7	70	318	129	3.2
7	Himachal Pradesh	0.2	0.2	38	92	72	1.7
8	Jammu & Kashmir	0.1	0.3	6	30	83	0.5
9	Karnataka	4.1	5.4	62	193	90	4.8
10	Kerala	2.7	3.6	42	175	135	6.3
11	Madhya Pradesh	4.2	4.1	27	138	53	5.6
12	Maharashtra	24.6	18.2	167	671	117	10.7
13	Manipur	neg	neg	10	8	63	neg
14	Meghalaya	neg	neg	20	80	63	neg
15	Nagaland	neg	neg	10	54	81	neg
16	Orissa	1.7	1.8	27	108	69	0.7
17	Punjab	3.2	6.3	52	326	201	12.9
18	Rajasthan	1.9	2.0	26	103	59	4.2
19	Tamil Nadu	10.3	10.6	75	342	171	9.6
20	Tripura	neg	0.1	10	13	48	0.1
21	Uttar Pradesh	7.3	7.0	24	114	107	11.9
22	Delhi	1.9	2.6	128	637	140	3.8
23	West Bengal	13.5	9.9	97	419	152	8.1
24	Pondicherry	0.2	0.1	85	445	140	0.2

Source: CMIE Report on *'Basic Statistics Relating to States of India'*, September, 1994

APPENDIX II
Indicators of Industrial Development of States – 1980-81

Sl. No.	*Name of State*	*X1*	*X2*	*X3*	*X4*	*X5*	*X6*	*X7*
1	Andhra Pradesh	5.2	11.6	109	17.6	595	98	4.8
2	Assam	1.1	1.6	64	11.6	538	93	0.8
3	Bihar	5.1	4.4	72	19.5	444	97	4.8
4	Goa	0.4	0.2	561	35.1	2123	100	0.3
5	Gujarat	11.7	11.6	334	29.4	2100	215	6.1
6	Haryana	3.1	2.6	268	19.4	1448	154	4.5
7	Himachal Pradesh	0.2	0.2	145	13.5	334	79	1.2
8	Jammu & Kashmir	0.2	0.3	30	17.1	182	73	1.6
9	Karnataka	4.2	5.6	162	25.4	698	101	3.8
10	Kerala	3.4	3.2	154	22.9	182	137	3.7
11	Madhya Pradesh	4.0	3.6	115	24.5	461	62	7.9
12	Maharashtra	23.6	16.1	476	35.3	2295	118	5.8
13	Manipur	neg	neg	7	9.3	10	73	0.7
14	Meghalaya	neg	neg	105	16.2	202	60	0.0
15	Nagaland	neg	neg	25	10.5	90	77	0.1
16	Orissa	1.7	1.6	75	16.2	388	82	1.8
17	Punjab	4.1	5.9	230	17.5	1484	215	7.8
18	Rajasthan	2.6	2.8	97	19.8	470	77	5.8
19	Tamil Nadu	10.9	10.7	254	34.0	1371	153	6.9
20	Tripura	neg	0.2	15	6.7	63	55	0.2
21	Uttar Pradesh	6.2	7.4	68	16.2	341	107	7.4
22	Delhi	2.2	3.3	305	30.8	2166	138	3.1
23	West Bengal	9.8	6.6	252	32.2	1098	132	20.4
24	Pondicherry	0.1	0.2	364	54.9	1424	138	0.2

Source: CMIE Report on *'Basic Statistics Relating to States of India'*, September, 1994

APPENDIX III
Indicators of Industrial Development of States – 1989-90

Sl. No.	Name of State	X1	X2	X3	X4	X5	X6	X7
1	Andhra Pradesh	5.9	14.8	329	17.7	2053	101	5.8
2	Assam	1.3	1.5	336	22.4	1330	95	0.8
3	Bihar	4.9	3.2	305	23.8	1313	96	4.7
4	Goa	0.4	0.2	1423	38.3	3359	128	0.4
5	Gujarat	10.4	10.1	899	34.3	5829	125	5.7
6	Haryana	3.5	2.9	721	19.5	4873	149	5.2
7	Himachal Pradesh	0.4	0.3	503	22.0	1700	85	0.9
8	Jammu & Kashmir	0.2	0.2	67	13.1	500	71	1.6
9	Karnataka	4.2	5.3	487	27.6	2246	99	5.0
10	Kerala	2.6	3.2	492	20.8	2030	140	3.5
11	Madhya Pradesh	5.3	2.2	360	26.4	1844	72	11.0
12	Maharashtra	21.6	14.3	1266	35.6	6311	112	4.8
13	Manipur	neg	neg	3	12.4	60	78	0.3
14	Meghalaya	neg	neg	555	16.2	163	71	0.1
15	Nagaland	neg	neg	40	24.6	231	67	neg
16	Orissa	2.1	1.3	360	20.3	1504	82	1.6
17	Punjab	5.3	5.7	1064	20.2	6004	214	8.2
18	Rajasthan	3.6	2.9	266	18.0	1635	82	5.5
19	Tamil Nadu	10.4	12.8	848	30.9	4308	139	7.02
20	Tripura	neg	0.3	30	4.8	174	66	0.2
21	Uttar Pradesh	9.6	9.1	302	20.4	1590	108	10.4
22	Delhi	1.8	2.9	661	28.2	4492	122	2.3
23	West Bengal	6.1	12.8	340	27.8	2066	166	14.2
24	Pondicherry	0.2	0.3	849	51.0	186	122	0.2

Source: CMIE Report on *'Basic Statistics Relating to States of India'*, September, 1994

APPENDIX IV
Indicators of Industrial Development of States – 1989-90

Sl. No.	*Name of State*	*X1*	*X3*	*X5*	*X6*	*X7*
1	Andhra Pradesh	6.8	626	3660	103	6.3
2	Assam	1.0	354	1594	93	0.9
3	Bihar	4.3	381	1437	96	5.0
4	Goa	0.4	1919	11952	171	0.3
5	Gujarat	11.2	1891	5786	125	5.9
6	Haryana	3.4	944	7445	152	4.8
7	Himachal Pradesh	0.4	829	2861	84	0.7
8	Jammu & Kashmir	0.2	114	812	69	1.4
9	Karnataka	4.8	887	1775	97	5.5
10	Kerala	2.5	606	3215	140	5.6
11	Madhya Pradesh	5.8	569	3122	75	12.4
12	Maharashtra	21.2	1995	9610	111	3.8
13	Manipur	neg	17	141	81	0.3
14	Meghalaya	neg	156	350	65	0.1
15	Nagaland	neg	68	378	71	0.0
16	Orissa	2.1	431	2343	89	1.0
17	Punjab	4.7	1411	8309	205	7.5
18	Rajasthan	3.3	503	2627	80	3.8
19	Tamil Nadu	10.3	1275	6634	138	9.1
20	Tripura	neg	78	244	53	0.4
21	Uttar Pradesh	9.2	448	2341	109	15.1
22	Delhi	5.6	694	2926	113	8.1
23	West Bengal	2.0	1187	10133	140	1.6
24	Pondicherry	0.2	1728	11782	140	0.2

Source: CMIE Reports on *"Basic Statistics Relating to States of India"*, September, 1994 and *"Industrial Statistics of India"*, January, 1996

APPENDIX V
Weight used in the Computation of Infrastructure Index by Centre for Monitoring Indian Economy

Item	*Weight*
Power	**20**
1. Per capita consumption of electricity (kwh)	10
2. Per capita industrial consumption of electricity (kwh)	5
3. Percentage of villages electrified to total	5
Irrigation	**20**
4. Percentage of net/gross area irrigated to total net/gross area cropped	20
Roads	**15**
5. Road length per 1000 sq. km.	5
6. Motor vehicle per lakh population	5
7. National Highway per 1000 sq. km.	5
Railways	**20**
8. Railway route in km. Per '000 sq. km. of area	20
Post Office	**5**
9. Number of Post Office per lakh population	2.5
10.Number of letter boxes per lakh population	2.5
Education	**10**
11.Literacy percentage	10
Health	**4**
12.Number of beds per hospital	4
Banking	**6**
13.Per capita deposits (Rs.)	2
14.Per capita bank credit (Rs.)	2
15.Number of bank offices per lakh population	2

Source: CMIE Report on *"Basic Statistics Relating to States of India"*, September, 1994

5

New Economic Policy and Regional Disparities

Jayanta Madhab

Forty years of economic planning and nine finance commissions' awards have not really reduced regional economic disparities. States like Bihar, Orissa, Uttar Pradesh and Rajasthan still remain at the bottom of the list in terms of per capita net state domestic product. In fact, in certain cases, the gap has been widened with those of the leading states like Punjab, Maharashtra and Haryana. The question is whether the new economic policies (NEP) now being implemented since 1991 will help to bridge the gap or further widen the disparities; and what sort of interventions are to be adopted to prevent further widening of disparities.

I

Far reaching changes were initiated by the Government of India (GOI) since 1991 in the industrial, financial, trade, transport and infrastructure sectors. Most important of these reforms were in the industrial sector. Only six out of seventeen industries are now in the reserved list. For all purposes, industrial licensing was abolished. Industry houses can now expand without reference to government. Foreign participation is allowed up to 51 per cent and in some cases up to 100 per cent. Restriction on foreign technology is eased; liberal royalty payment allowed. Controller of capital issue office is abolished.

As far as public sector undertakings are concerned, greater management authority has been given. Disinvestment of part of the holdings by government is also introduced. Competition is encouraged. Budgetary supports are to be phased out. And, a national renewal fund is set up for protecting the interest of the workers who might be retrenched.

A national minerals policy was announced in 1993. This policy permits private and foreign investors in the mining sector including coal in specific cases.

The government opened the power sector to private investment with foreign participation allowed up to 100 per cent of equity. In the transport sector, private airlines have been allowed to compete in the domestic sector.

In the financial sector, several important changes have been made. First, the government has allowed new private sector banks to be established; second, reduction of SLR and CRR limitation has been effected enabling banks to make available more funds for the private sector; third, opening up the financial market to the private mutual funds and entry of foreign institutional investors are likely to attract more foreign capital to India. Permission to approach international markets through GDR or Euro issues is also granted. Fourthly, interest rate above Rs. 2 lac advances was regulated in October 1994. And lastly, income tax, corporate tax, custom and excise duty rates are lowered.

On the trade sector, rupee is made fully convertible under current account and initially devalued by 21 per cent to make exports more competitive. Since then further depreciation of the rupee has taken place.

The liberalisation process, a part of NEP, has a long way to go. In fact in several important sectors the reform process has not started; or is coming slowly. No reforms have yet been initiated in the agricultural sector. No progress has been made, even after five years, on labour market reform and particularly 'exit policy'. Similarly, state taxation is another area where reforms have yet to start.

2

Prior to a discussion on the impact of NEP on regional disparities, some observations on NEP itself are helpful to put the discussions in the proper perspective.

It has to be recognised that in 1991, two sets of policy measures were introduced by Government of India. One, short-term austerity measure for immediately correcting the balance of payments position, the other, long term liberalisation measures, aimed at improving India's competitiveness in the world market. The former can be called 'structural programme' (SP), and the second 'structural adjustment programme' (SAP). While SP elements were, by and large, one time measures; SAP started in 1991 and continued, though with a much slower pace. Both the programmes overlapped; and, in many cases, policy instruments were the same.

Secondly, SAP essentially aimed at industry, medium and large; it was urban in character. Therefore agriculture and the vast majority of rural populace were left unaffected except indirectly. Those states which were predominantly agricultural were not affected as much as the others.

Thirdly, the success of SAP depended heavily on the initiative of the private sector. It was about harnessing the private sector. States which did not have a sizeable and vibrant private sector could not take full advantage of SAP. At least not immediately.

Fourthly, private sector flourished in those states which provided a congenial environment with infrastructure and policies to encourage private sector investment.

Fifthly, the liberalisation measures started by the Central Government have not really reached many State Governments. Very few State Governments have followed up with their programme for and support of liberalisation. State politicians and bureaucrats are still averse to give up the 'license raj' benefits. Those State Governments which had followed a more 'market friendly' approach garnered the bulk of domestic and foreign investments.

Lastly, while the adverse impact of SP and SAP was felt most immediately, the benefits are expected to accrue over a period of time. Therefore, it is premature to measure the benefits of liberalisation process. Furthermore, there are hardly any statistics available; while there are some data available on all-India basis, state level statistics are difficult to come by.

Having, however, said this, an attempt will be made to assess the impact of NEP on two regions, one economically advanced, the other economically backward. The advanced states comprise Goa, Gujarat and Maharashtra (western states) and the backward states are the north eastern states of Arunachal Pradesh, Assam, Manipur, Meghalaya, Mizoram, Nagaland and Tripura.

3

The characteristics of these two regions could not have been more different. Having had access to the sea, the western states of Goa, Gujarat and Maharashtra have been trading with the rest of the world for centuries. As these states had come under the colonial rule long before many other states, they had access to western technologies and had an early start in industrialisation. In fact both Gujarat and Maharashtra have now become the home of India's biggest industry houses. Homogeneity of the population is another strong point.

On the other hand, the eastern states are landlocked, geographically isolated form the main centres of industry and trade. These states came under the British rule in the nineteenth century. The British rule earlier, the Government of India later, left the tribal to themselves. No attempt was made to bring them into the Indian mainstream till the mid sixties. The region is predominantly agricultural and largely tribal. Indeed there are as many as 200 tribes with their own dialect and culture. They live on subsistence economy producing very little surplus. The region has produced very few entrepreneurs. The Brahmaputra and the Barak valleys, which are densely populated, have some resemblances with the rest of India.

Table I highlights the disparities between the two regions. Except Arunachal, in the rest of the NE states' per capita income is only about half of that of western states. Again, save for Nagaland and Arunachal, NE region's average size of operational holding is less than half of its counterpart. That NE states are largely agricultural and western states are industrial can be seen from the composition of state net domestic product. While the contribution of agriculture sector ranges from 25 per cent in Nagaland to 53 per cent in Arunachal, Goa's share is a mere 18 per cent and Maharashtra's 23 per cent. Industry sector contributes between 33 per cent and 36 per cent in the western states, NE states' figures range between 6 per cent (Tripura) and 26 per cent (Assam). The contribution of manufacturing sector is even less. Except Assam the rest of the NE states do not have a manufacturing sector worth the name.

Except Mizoram which has a high literacy rate, the rest of NE states trail behind the western states. In terms of per capita consumption of electricity, the western states are way above the NE states. Same is true for consumption of petroleum products and saleable steel. Fertilizer consumption also shows a dismal picture; Assam showing a use of 7 kg./ha. as against 73 kg./ha. by Gujarat. Per capita net value added by the manufacturing sector figures show a very discouraging picture. The figure for Assam is Rs. 336 (Manipur has only as low as Rs. 3 and Meghalaya Rs. 55), Goa's comparable figure is Rs. 1423, Gujarat's Rs. 899 and Maharashtra's Rs. 1266. This shows the productivity as well as age and state of technology of the machinery.

But the most important difference is in the CMIE's relative development infrastructure index. All-India being 100, western states are well ahead of NE region, none of which is even close to all-India level. Arunachal has a figure of 44 as against Goa's 171. The growth rate of state domestic product, however does not show any great divergence between these two regions.

The question is whether NEP has caused any changes in the existing disparities. Due to non-availability of post reform state level data, no meaningful analysis can be done. Nonetheless, an analysis of investment data will give an indication of future trend.

Government investment is determined by the five year plans. The current plan was prepared prior to reform. No shift in investment pattern is noticeable to prevent further deterioration of regional disparities. However, Government of India has increased its allocation to programmes affecting the weaker section of the community to shield them from the adverse effects of liberalisation.

Tables II, III and IV illustrate the investment bias in favour of the three western states. Needless to say the NE region fared the worst. Of the 17,064 industrial entrepreneurial memorandum entered between August 1991 and December 1994 (Table II) involving an investment of Rs. 344,929 crore, only 47 involving Rs. 2167 crore were for the NE states. Industries however entered into 5958 memoranda for location in Goa, Gujarat and Maharashtra, with project cost of Rs. 129,836 crore (nearly 38 per cent of total approvals).

Similarly, Foreign Direct Investment shows (Table III) same bias in favour of the three western states. While Goa, Gujarat and Maharashtra received 640 approvals with an investment figure of Rs. 9718 crore up to June 1995, the NE states obtained 7 approvals, out of total of 3322, with Rs. 14 crore as investments.

Assistance sanctioned by the all India fiinancing institutions (Table IV) to the enterprises by the states in the post reform era also demonstrates that both Maharashtra and Gujarat lead the rest of the states. In 1994-95, enterprises in Maharashtra and Gujarat obtained sanctions worth Rs. 13,727 crore and Rs. 10,125 crore respectively. Same year, enterprises in Assam obtained only Rs. 136 crore, Arunachal Rs. 4 crore, Meghalaya Rs. 6 crore, and Rs. 2 crore each for Nagaland and Tripura. Per capita total assistance up to March 1995 shows extreme position. Tripura received only Rs. 139 as against Goa's Rs. 12,627, a state half of Tripura's size.

Because of better infrastructure and market friendly environment in the western states more and more investments are flowing there. This has caused a 'virtuous circle of prosperity'. Higher the investment, higher is the output, higher employment and wages, higher taxes, higher expenditure on education, health and infrastructure leading to further investments. The circle is completed.

The reverse is true in the NE states. Because of lack of infrastruc-ture and local entrepreneurs, despite having a reasonably good resource base, investments are low. Lower the investments, lower is the output, lower employment, lower taxes and lower spending on education, health and infrastructure leading to a vicious cycle of poverty. Added to this is the fact that all the NE states are weary of "outsiders coming to exploit"; and in most states there is an active insurgency which further prevents external capital to come in.

From the investment data, it is quite clear that the new economic policies will further widen the regional disparities, unless counter measures are initiated immediately.

4

In a federal structure with wide regional disparities amongst its consti-tuent states, the central government has the responsibility of ensuring a reasonable level of inter-regional equity. NEP encourages the private sector to be the engine of growth. Private sector however makes investment decisions based on market conditions. Left to itself, most of the investments will concentrate, as in the past in the market friendly-states having adequate infrastructure. Under these circum-stances, the central government's role becomes much more important. It becomes a regulator, facilitator and provider, together with the state governments of infrastructure.

Most state governments' finances are in doldrums; this is particularly so in the North Eastern states. There is growing imbalance between the state governments responsibilities and resources. The successive finance commissions have given marginal increases to the states. A bold new approach is required to solve the dual problem of giving reasonably adequate resources to the states to discharge the development responsibilities on one hand, and to make the states responsible and accountable on the other. The Tenth Finance Commission itself made a suggestion. Since then several suggestions have come to light, the most recent being that of the Andhra Pradesh Government. These are worthy of consideration.

State governments' finances are characterised as inefficient, mismanaged, full of leakage and debt ridden. There is hardly any accountability. The Government of Assam receives 70 per cent of its revenues from the Government of India in terms of shared taxes and grants. Other NE states receive even higher percentages. All the NE states are "special category states" meaning that resources other than constitutional, coming from the central government are given on the basis of 90 per cent grant, 10 per cent loan. The Government of Assam spends 40 per cent of its total resource in interest payment and repayment of loans; another 40 per cent on salaries, wages, pensions and establishment. Only 20 per cent, the residual, is spent on maintenance of capital assets and development work. Unless this pattern of spending is changed in favour of development works and maintenance of capital assets, infrastructure development etc., private sector investment is unlikely to grow.

Besides infrastructure (particularly power, roads, railways and telecom), private sector wants transparent laws, less political and bureaucratic intervention and of course less corruption. Various tax concessions are not of great importance.

Apart from investments in infrastructure and human resources development the state governments of the North East have to change the strategy of development. They must invest or promote investment on a priority basis, on a sector which is less susceptible to security condition, but will generate enough surplus for further investment. Indeed surplus generation is the critical variable for development of the region. This can be achieved only through the development of agriculture, horticulture, livestock and fish culture. These are known trades; training requirement is marginal. Most of these states produce only one crop, rice. If three or more crops can be made to grow, consider the amount of surplus that will be generated, with it the effect on absorption of unemployment or under unemployment. This surplus will generate further activities in different spheres including the government, and will have a snow balling effect.

Unless timely action is taken to prevent further widening of regional disparities, the federal structure will come under a great stress. Because of a feeling, based on certain amounts of facts, that the north eastern states have been left out of the development process, although a small elite minority has benefited immensely, insurgency groups have survived and indeed in some states prospered.

Coordinated actions between the central and state governments to prevent further deterioration of the situation are urgently required.

Table 1
Economic Characteristics of Two Regions

States	Pop. Mn.	Literacy %	Per Capita Income Rs.	Contribution to SDP Agri.	Contribution to SDP Indust.	Av. Size of Op. land holding /Ha	Per Capita Consumption Elect. Kwh	Per Capita Consumption Petrol Prod. Kg.	Fertilizer use Ha/kg.	Per Capita value added per worker Rs.	Relative Dev. Infra. Index
Goa	11	76	11,658	18	33	1.02	663	545	45	1423	171
Gujarat	41.3	61	76,000	26	35	3.15	622	140	73	899	125
Maharashtra	78.9	65	10,984	23	36	2.65	524	123	52	1266	111
Arunachal	0.9	42	8,172	53	10	4.82	128	93	—	—	44
Assam	22.4	53	5,916	41	26	1.31	91	38	7	336	93
Manipur	1.8	60	5,362	42	13	1.21	140	35	49	3	81
Meghalaya	1.8	49	5,519	33	20	1.76	159	63	12	55	65
Mizoram	0.7	82	—	41	16	1.57	126	54	16	—	63
Nagaland	1.2	62	5,397	29	29	7.15	100	39	4	—	71
Tripura	0.9	60	3,781	50	6	1.03	84	23	21	30	63
All India	846	39	6,929	30	31	1.68	331	(-)	67	514	100

Figures are 1991-92
Source: CMIE : *Basic Statistics Relating to the States*, September, 1994
Government of India : *Handbook of Industrial Policy and Statistics*, 1995

Table 2
State-wise Distribution of Industrial Entrepreneurial Memorandum August 1991 – December 1994

	Number	*Investment Rs. Crore*
Goa	103	2,170
Gujarat	2446	59,708
Maharashtra	3409	67,958
Arunachal	—	—
Assam	39	1,038
Manipur	—	—
Meghalaya	3	38
Mizoram	—	—
Nagaland	2	53
Tripura	3	1,038
All India	17064	344,929

Source: Government of India : *Handbook of Industrial Policy and Statistics*, 1995

Table 3
Foreign Direct Investment Cases Approved August 1991 – December 1995

	Number	*Investment Rs. Crore*
Goa	22	90
Gujarat	143	2,414
Maharashtra	475	7,214
Arunachal	—	—
Assam	2	11
Manipur	4	2
Meghalaya	—	—
Mizoram	—	—
Nagaland	—	—
Tripura	1	1
All India	3322	35,087

Source: *Monthly Newsletter* : All India Investment Centre, November 1995

Table 4
Assistance Sanctioned by All India Financing Institutions
Rs. Crore

	1991-92	*1992-93*	*1993-94*	*1994-95*
Goa	138	110	298	270
Gujarat	2,247	3,988	6,863	10,125
Maharashtra	3,409	67,958		
Arunachal	1	1	1	4
Assam	118	94	85	136
Manipur	3	2	1	—
Meghalaya	8	2	3	6
Mizoram	2	1	—	—
Nagaland	6	1	—	2
Tripura	3	1	1	2
All India	**20,906**	**31,069**	**39,101**	**57,792**

Source: Government of India : *Handbook of Industrial Policy and Statistics*, 1995

6

Impact of Growth on Access to, and Change in Possession of Land, Education, Employment and Consumption and Disparities Between SC, ST and Others

G.Parthasarathy
Jayashree Anand
C.V.R. Sankar

OBLIGATIONS IMPOSED ON THE STATE UNDER INDIAN CONSTITUTION

It is obligatory on the state, under the Indian Constitution, to initiate measures to improve the lot of Scheduled Castes and Scheduled Tribes, who comprise the unprivileged and the discriminated groups of the society.

Special provisions are enshrined in the Constitution for the uplift of SCs and STs which include abolition of untouchability, reservation of seats in educational institutions and Government services, prohibition on transfer of land of tribals to non-tribals; reservation of seats in Lok Sabha, etc.

The Constitution also spells out setting up of administrative machinery to monitor the effective implementation of these safeguards. The Commissioner of Scheduled Caste and Scheduled Tribes appointed under Article 338 of the Constitution is required to investigate all matters relating to the safeguards provided for the uplift of these communities and submit to the President a report which is placed before the two houses of Parliament for discussion.

NEED FOR PERIODIC MONITORING

SCs and STs face manifold problems. There is no doubt that they have progressed to some extent but the fact remains that they have not come on par with the other sections of the society. In spite of the various administrative and legislative measures undertaken to help them, the fact remains that this segment of society has not progressed economically to the desired extent.

REVIEW OF LITERATURE AND GAPS IN KNOWLEDGE

There are only a few studies which throw light on access to and dispari-ties among ethnic groups. Saradamoni (1981) presented a micro-level study based on a village near Thiruvananthapuram in Kerala on 'Landlessness, Employment and Education'. She concludes that the existing policies for the SCs and STs have not helped them.

Vijay Nayak and Prasad (1984), analysed the ungrouped NSSO data of the 28th and 32nd Rounds to examine the level of living of the SC/ST vis-a-vis the non SC/ST in Karnataka and inequality in their lifestyles during 1973-74 and 1977-78. They conclude that SC/ST had a lower standard of living than the non SC/ST. There was a fall in the standard of living in real terms for SC/ST and non SC/ST over the period 1973-74 to 1977-78. The decrease was greater for the SC/ST, leading to a widening of the disparity.

Mridul and Pan (1994) analysed NSSO data on consumption for four eastern states of India. Their major findings are (1) The eastern region as a whole suffered from economic backwardness as was reflected in low MPCE which was below the all-India level. This was particularly true for SCs and STs; (2) the rural-urban divide existed in eastern India, with a lower MPCE and higher poverty incidence in rural areas as compared to urban areas; (3) the study showed that

SC and ST households had lower consumption standards than non SC/ST households and suffered from high incidence of poverty.

In a study (Parthasarathy, 1995) of employment and unemployment in Andhra Pradesh, it is seen that the percentage of female headed households is 16.07 among SCs whereas the corresponding figures for the others is 13.2 per cent. Rural agricultural labour households among SCs form a higher percentage (69.3). The incidence of poverty as in 1987-88 in rural Andhra Pradesh among SCs was 22.5 per cent and among STs 44.9 per cent as against 19.7 per cent for others. In Andhra Pradesh the highest rate of unemployment is among SC females.

The rate of unemployment among SCs is more than double the rate recorded for others. Rural SC males have similar rates of unemployment as others. SC females are the worst affected among all female groups. In brief, there is no clear evidence that public intervention programmes have reduced the disparity among SCs, STs, and others.

FACTORS BASIC TO IMPROVEMENT

Three factors are basic to the uplift of SCs and STs. Since the bulk of them are in the rural areas and are dependent on agriculture, access to land is critical. Land is essential to improve their employment opportunities. In the rural society land is not only a source of income, it is also a source of credit. The household which is landless is dependent on others for employment, credit and other basic requirements. In that context, possession of land becomes very critical to human dignity. Similarly, education is needed for intergenerational mobility. An educated person has better opportunities for mobility into other sectors. Education is not only a means of development but it is also essential for its own sake. SCs and STs are known to be illiterate and this illiteracy has been persisting for generations. So, any improvement in literacy and education should be considered a progressive step. Employment is not only a fundamental right, but also a means of supporting oneself. In the context of widespread landlessness among these groups, improvement in employment opportunities in agriculture and non-agriculture sectors is considered a progressive step, while deterioration in the employment situation is retrogression.

In the light of the above, the proposed study monitors changes in access to, and disparities between the SCs and STs on the one hand and 'others' on the other on an all-India and state levels. We pay special attention to the impact of growth on these groups. There is not adequate literature available on growth and access and disparities despite the importance of the subject, though literature exists for growth and poverty.

OBJECTIVES

The specific objectives of the study are to examine :

i Access of SCs and STs to land, education, employment etc., and changes thereof

ii Disparities between SCs, STs and others

iii Impact of growth on 'access' and 'disparities.

DATA BASE

The data base for access and disparity are the special survey of NSSO on SC and ST – 38th round, i.e. 1983 and 43rd round for 1987-88. For the study on impact of growth, we used Central Statistical Organisation data on per capita Net State Domestic Product for the years 1983-84 and 1987-88 at constant prices.

Change and disparity measure applied : Change and disparity between SCs and STs and others, over a time period selected for analysis is measured by the difference in absolute per cent between 'others' on one hand and SCs and STs on the other.

The analysis of access and disparities is preceded by an examination of changes in the distribution of SC and ST population in the states between 1981 and 1991.

DISTRIBUTION SC AND ST POPULATION IN STATES (1981)

SC Population

The total SC population as in 1981 is 105 million, 88 million in rural area and 17 million in urban areas on an all-India level. As against urban population of 23 per cent of the total at all-India level, SC

Table 1
State-wise Distribution of Total SC and ST Population by Rural and Urban

State	Total				SC				ST			
	Rural		Urban		Rural		Urban		Rural		Urban	
	1981	1991	1981	1991	1981	1991	1981	1991	1981	1991	1981	1991
India	525.46	628.69	159.79	217.61	87.99	112.34	16.76	25.88	48.43	62.75	3.20	5.01
Andhra Pradesh	41.06	48.62	12.49	17.88	6.75	8.76	1.21	1.83	2.98	3.88	0.197	0.319
Bihar	61.20	75.02	8.72	11.35	9.26	11.44	0.860	1.13	5.45	6.15	0.362	0.463
Gujarat	23.48	27.06	10.60	14.25	1.64	1.90	0.797	1.16	4.49	5.66	0.354	0.499
Haryana	10.095	12.41	2.82	4.05	2.09	2.68	0.371	0.5757	—	—	—	—
Himachal Pradesh	3.95	4.72	0.325	0.449	0.997	1.23	0.0565	0.08298	0.194	0.2129	0.000314	0.00541
Jammu & Kashmir	4.73	5.88	1.26	1.84	—	—	—	—	—	—	—	—
Karnataka	26.41	31.67	10.73	13.91	4.37	5.65	1.23	1.72	1.59	1.63	0.235	0.286
Kerala	20.68	21.42	4.77	7.68	2.24	2.35	0.309	0.534	0.256	0.310	0.00499	0.0112
Madhya Pradesh	41.59	50.84	10.59	15.34	6.04	7.52	1.32	2.10	11.55	14.65	0.434	0.746
Maharashtra	40.79	48.40	21.99	30.54	3.07	5.55	1.41	3.21	5.17	6.41	0.601	0.913
Manipur	1.05	1.33	0.375	0.506	0.01479	1.0177	0.0030	0.0194	0.343	0.579	0.0452	0.053

(Contd.)

Meghalaya	1.09	1.44	0.241	0.33	0.00295	0.00497	0.0025	0.0041	0.943	1.312	0.134	0.206
Nagaland	0.654	1.001	0.120	0.208	—	—	—	—	0.587	0.933	0.0636	0.128
Orissa	23.26	27.42	3.11	4.23	3.50	4.58	0.363	0.00551	5.64	6.670	0.273	0.362
Punjab	12.14	14.29	4.65	5.99	3.67	4.56	0.845	1.18	—	—	—	—
Rajasthan	27.05	33.94	7.21	10.07	4.79	6.10	1.048	1.51	4.03	5.22	0.156	0.254
Sikkim	0.265	0.369	0.051	0.037	0.01437	0.0213	0.0039	0.00275	0.062	0.08349	0.011	0.00742
Tamil Nadu	32.46	36.79	15.95	19.08	7.09	8.43	1.79	2.28	0.470	0.5052	0.0504	0.0690
Tripura	1.83	2.34	0.226	0.422	0.291	0.380	0.01955	0.071	0.576	0.8393	0.00769	0.0141
Uttar Pradesh	90.96	111.51	19.90	27.61	21.00	25.82	2.45	3.45	0.222	0.2710	0.01098	0.0169
West Bengal	40.13	49.37	14.45	18.71	10.51	13.61	1.49	2.48	2.96	3.612	0.1155	0.196
A & N Islands	0.139	0.206	0.0496	0.1749	—	—	—	—	0.022	0.026268	0.000271	0.000512
Arunachal Pradesh	0.590	0.754	0.0414	0.111	0.00194	0.002858	0.000979	0.00119	0.431	0.518	0.01006	0.03213
Chandigarh	0.0288	0.0662	0.423	0.576	0.006813	0.01414	0.0568	0.091	—	—	—	—
D & N Haveli	0.09676	0.127	0.0069	0.0117	0.00182	0.00224	0.000223	0.000487	0.0789	0.106	0.00279	0.003516
Delhi	0.452	9.42	5.77	8.47	0.104	0.2077	1.0176	1.59	—	—	—	—
Goa, Daman & Diu	0.735	0.744	0.352	0.527	0.0141	0.01514	0.00936	0.01311	0.0082	0.00928	0.00249	0.002819
Lakshadweep	0.0216	0.0226	0.0186	0.0291	—	—	—	—	0.0209	0.02148	0.0169	0.02669
Mizoram	0.372	0.3718	0.1218	0.318	0.000097	0.000456	0.000038	0.000235	0.353	0.3581	0.109	0.2955
Pondicherry	0.228	0.291	0.316	0.517	0.0625	0.0777	0.03411	0.0536	—	—	—	—
Assam	17.85	19.93	2.05	2.49	—	1.430	—	0.229	—	2.78	—	0.09713

urban population formed only 16 per cent in 1981. In the states, the concentration of SC population is in Bihar, Andhra Pradesh, Uttar Pradesh, West Bengal and Tami Nadu. These five states account for two thirds of SC population in the country in 1981 in rural areas. When urban areas are considered SC population is concentrated in Andhra Pradesh, Karnataka, Madhya Pradesh, Maharashtra, Rajasthan, Tamil Nadu, Uttar Pradesh and West Bengal. The eight states together accounted for nearly 80 per cent of urban SC population (Table 1).

ST Population

The ST population as in 1981 at all-India level was around half of the total SC population. ST population is more concentrated in certain states. Rural ST population is concentrated in Bihar, Andhra Pradesh, Gujarat, Madhya Pradesh, Maharashtra, Orissa and Rajasthan. These states accounted for four fifths of the total ST population in rural areas.

Urban ST population is much less than the comparable percentage for SC. At the national level urban ST population accounted for only 6.20 per cent of the total population as against 16 per cent for SC. ST urban population is concentrated in Andhra Pradesh, Bihar, Gujarat, Karnataka, Madhya Pradesh, Maharashtra and Orissa. These seven states together accounted for 76 per cent of the total ST urban population. Among north-eastern states, Arunachal Pradesh and Mizoram have significant urban ST population.

INTER-STATE VARIATIONS IN RATES OF GROWTH OF POPULATION FOR SC, ST BETWEEN 1981 AND 1991

The total population at the all-India level increased from 685 million in 1981 to 846 million in 1991 with a growth rate of 2.11 per cent per annum. Rural population has increased from 525 million in 1981 to 629 million in 1991 at an annual growth rate of 1.79 per cent whereas urban population has increased from 150 million in 1981 to 218 million in 1991 with an annual growth rate of 3.09 per cent. This reflects rural-urban migration. The percentage of SC population was 15.29 in 1981. It has grown up to 16.34 per cent in 1991 with an annual growth rate of 2.77 per cent. 84 per cent of the SC population lived in rural areas; and 16 per cent in urban areas in 1981; the percentage of urban population in total was 23 in 1991; the SC percentage in urban areas was 18.78 whereas the percentage of urban population was 25.7 (Table 2).

Table 2
State-wise Growth Rates of Total SC and ST during 1981-1991

State / UT	*Total*		*SC*		*ST*	
	Rural	*Urban*	*Rural*	*Urban*	*Rural*	*Urban*
India	1.79	3.09	2.43	4.35	2.59	4.48
Andhra Pradesh	1.69	3.59	2.61	4.14	2.64	4.82
Bihar	2.04	2.64	2.09	2.73	1.21	2.46
Gujarat	1.42	2.96	1.47	3.75	2.32	3.43
Haryana	2.07	3.62	2.49	4.39	—	—
Himachal Pradesh	1.78	3.23	2.10	3.84	0.93	5.55
Jammu & Kashmir	2.18	3.79	—	—	—	—
Karnataka	1.62	2.60	2.57	3.35	0.25	1.96
Kerala	0.26	4.76	0.48	5.47	1.91	8.08
Madhya Pradesh	2.01	3.71	2.19	4.64	2.38	5.42
Maharashtra	1.71	3.28	5.92	8.23	2.15	4.18
Manipur	2.36	3.60	1.80	18.67	5.74	1.64
Meghalaya	2.78	3.19	5.22	4.95	3.32	4.30
Nagaland	4.26	5.50	—	—	4.55	12.60
Orissa	1.65	3.08	2.69	4.17	1.68	2.82
Punjab	1.63	2.53	2.17	3.34	—	—
Rajasthan	2.27	3.34	2.42	3.65	2.59	4.87
Sikkim	3.31	3.21	3.94	3.49	2.98	- 3.96
Tamil Nadu	1.25	1.79	1.73	2.42	0.72	3.14
Tripura	2.46	6.25	2.67	12.90	3.76	6.06
Uttar Pradesh	2.04	3.28	2.07	3.42	1.99	4.31
West Bengal	2.07	2.58	2.58	5.09	1.99	5.29
A & N Islands	3.93	4.12	—	—	1.78	6.17
Arunachal Pradesh	2.45	9.86	3.87	1.95	1.84	11.61
Chandigarh	8.29	3.09	7.30	4.71	—	—
D & N Haveli	1.72	5.28	2.19	7.81	2.95	2.27
Delhi	7.34	3.84	6.92	4.46	—	—
Goa, Daman & Diu	0.12	4.04	0.71	3.37	1.26	1.24
Lakshadweep	0.45	4.44	—	—	0.28	4.57
Mizoram	- 0.005	9.60	15.48	18.22	0.14	9.97
Pondicherry	2.44	4.92	2.18	4.43	—	—
Assam	1.10	1.94	—	—	—	—

Much lower percentage of ST population as compared to SC lived in urban areas in 1981. During 1981-91, the rate of growth of ST urban population exceeds both the rate for SC and all. As a result urban ST population increased from 6 per cent in 1981 to 7.4 per cent in 1991.

As in the case of all-India, the rate of growth of SC population in all states is higher than that of others. The exceptions are Bihar and Gujarat.

In most states, the rate of growth of SC population is around the all-India average; the exceptions are Gujarat, Kerala, Manipur and Tamil Nadu. In these four states, the rate of growth of SC population is much less than the all-India average. Kerala recorded the least growth of SC population followed by Gujarat. In Maharashtra and Meghalaya, the rate of growth of SC population is abnormally high exceeding 5 per cent per annum.

As regards ST people, they show the highest rate of growth among all ethnic groups. There are large inter-state variations. The north-eastern states, Manipur, Nagaland, Tripura, Meghalaya show a higher growth rate than all-India level. Bihar, Himachal Pradesh, Karnataka, Kerala, Orissa, Tamil Nadu show much lower rate of growth than the all-India average. In comparison with others, ST rates of growth are generally higher than rate of growth of others, the only exceptions being Bihar, Himachal Pradesh, Karnataka and Tamil Nadu.

Urban rate of growth for all ethnic groups is higher than the rural. This reflects rural urban migration. In case of SC urban rate of growth (annual), it varies from 2.42 per cent in Tamil Nadu to 8.19 per cent in Manipur. Considering state-wise, Bihar, Gujarat, Haryana, Karnataka, Orissa, Punjab, Rajasthan, Tripura, Tamil Nadu, Uttar Pradesh and Himachal Pradesh show less than the average growth rate than the all-India average. Kerala, Maharashtra, Madhya Pradesh, Manipur, Meghalaya, West Bengal and Tripura record a higher growth rate when compared to the all-India level.

With regard to SC urban growth rate in comparison with the growth of total, except in Sikkim in all other states, the urban growth rate is uniformly higher than that of others.

As regards ST urban growth rate, this is higher than the urban growth rate of all-India average in Andhra Pradesh, Himachal Pradesh, Kerala, Madhya Pradesh, Meghalaya, Mizoram, Nagaland, Rajasthan, Tripura, West Bengal, Tamil Nadu and Gujarat. In the states of Bihar, Maharashtra, Manipur, Orissa, and Sikkim, ST growth rate is lower than the all-India average. ST growth rate is higher in almost all states except Orissa, Karnataka, Manipur, Tripura and Bihar.

It seems from earlier analysis that growth rates for SCs and STs are higher than that of the total population growth rate in urban areas. This reflects distress migration of this class of people to urban areas.

ACCESS TO LAND SCS, STS AND OTHERS AND DISPARITIES BETWEEN SC, ST GROUPS AND OTHERS

A major programme for the alleviation of poverty among the SC and ST population groups relates to improvement in access to land. It therefore, becomes necessary to monitor the extent to which the programme has achieved its objectives. The data available for such monitoring are limited to a few years. NSSO has published data for SC, ST and others separately in their 38th and 43rd rounds with a gap of a five-year-period.

The all-India and states/UT data for various social groups for 1983-84 and 1987-88 are presented in Table 3.

The first two size classes of land may be said to represent absolute landlessness (ABLL) without/with homestead. The change in access for the two time periods selected indicates that for all social groups percentage of households in ABLL without homestead has been increasing over the period, though the change is more significant among SCs, followed by others and STs. The percentage of households (0.00 ha) with own homestead has been decreasing for all social groups during the two time periods and the decrease is more for STs and SCs than others.

Thus, for the two size classes representing ABLL, SC households are at a disadvantage compared to 'others' over the two time periods. The disparity is widening between 'others' and SCs for ABLL without homestead and there is only a marginal narrowing down of disparity for ABLL with own homestead.

For the STs, the disparity with others has increased over time with respect to ABLL with own homestead, and decreased over time with ABLL without own homestead.

Table 3
Percentage Distribution of Households by Possession of Land by Size Class and by Social Groups 1983-84 and 1987-88 (All-India)

	Without own homestead 0.00 ha	*With own homestead 0.00 ha*	*0.00 to 0.40 ha*
SC			
1983	2.48	5.28	68.74
1987-88	15.50	4.90	75.26
Change in access	13.02	- 0.38	6.52
ST			
1983	3.90	4.27	37.82
1987-77	10:30	2.30	46.35
Change in access	6.40	- 1.97	8.53
Others			
1983	2.50	2.86	44.66
1987-88	9.80	2.70	43.00
Change in access	7.30	- 0.16	- 1.66
Disparity			
Others and SC			
1983	0.02	- 2.42	- 24.08 *
1987-88	- 5.70	- 2.20	- 32.26
Others and ST			
1983	- 1.40	- 1.41	6.84
1987-88	- 0.50	0.40	- 3.35

* deviation shown from 'Others' households

ACCESS TO LAND AND DISPARITIES BETWEEN 1983-84 AND 1987-88

The total landless households have increased as a percentage of total households over time both in the case of SCs and STs. But the percentage has declined only in the case of others. As a consequence, the disparities between others and SCs, and others and STs have increased over time.

It appears that the redistribution policies of the Government did not have any effect in reducing the total landless among SC and ST households. Instead, they have succeeded in reducing the landless among the others, though marginally.

IMPACT OF GROWTH ON ACCESS TO LAND FOR SCs, STs AND OTHERS

For studying the impact of growth on access to land of various social groups, cross sectional data on per capita NSDP for all states and union territories, are used (Table 4). In 1982-83, the range of per capita NSDP varied between Rs. 2875 in Punjab and Rs. 536 in Madhya Pradesh among the major states. The other states at the bottom one third included Tripura, Assam, Meghalaya, Uttar Pradesh, Rajasthan, Orissa, Bihar and Kerala. Others among the top states and union territories are Delhi, Goa, Pondicherry, Haryana, Maharashtra, Andaman and Nicobar Islands, Gujarat and Sikkim.

For some of the states such as Gujarat 1987-88 proved to be a bad agricultural year. As a result there was a sharp fall in NSDP. In Andhra Pradesh, Kerala, Jammu and Kashmir and Rajasthan also it was a very bad agricultural year. At all-India level, per capita NSDP increased only by 13.91 per cent in a period of five years. The growth rate is generally low, except in a few states/union territories. Such exceptions are Assam, Goa, Madhya Pradesh, Nagaland, Sikkim, Tamil Nadu and Delhi. These include states with low as well as high levels of income. No pattern is observable on the relationship between growth rate and initial level of per capita income.

CROSS SECTIONAL ANALYSIS OF GROWTH AND ACCESS TO LAND FOR SC, ST AND OTHERS

States are ranked on their levels of per capita Net State Domestic Product (NSDP) for 1982-83. Similarly they are ranked on the basis of near landlessness (0.00 to 0.40 ha) (Table 4). Punjab and Haryana with highest income show highest landlessness. The rank correlation between near landlessness and per capita NSDP without own homestead gives a positive value, suggesting positive relationship between growth and landlessness without own homestead for SC. Positive relationship is also seen between growth and landlessness without own homestead and others. Negative value is recorded only in the case of ST but it is not statistically significant.

Table 4
Per Capita NSDP State-wise at 1980-81 Prices for 1983-84 and 1987-88

State	*1982-83 (in Rs.)*	*1987-88 (in Rs.)*	*% Change*
Andhra Pradesh	1545 (16)	1530 (18)	- 0.97
Arunachal Pradesh	1744 (10)	2184 (9)	25.23
Assam	1367 (21)	1521 (20)	11.27
Bihar	873 (26)	979 (26)	12.14
Goa	3152 (2)	3493 (2)	10.18
Gujarat	2025 (8)	1842 (11)	- 9.038
Haryana	2475 (5)	2588 (8)	4.57
Himachal Pradesh	1673 (11)	1818 (15)	8.67
Jammu and Kashmir	1671 (12)	1575 (17)	- 5.74
Karnataka	1665 (13)	1809 (12)	8.65
Kerala	1462 (19)	1413 (23)	- 3.35
Madhya Pradesh	536 (27)	849 (27)	58.39
Maharashtra	2473 (6)	2813 (5)	13.75
Manipur	1485 (18)	1693 (16)	14.01
Meghalaya	1361 (22)	1485 (21)	9.11
Nagaland	1616 (14)	2016 (10)	24.75
Orissa	1133 (25)	1320 (24)	16.51
Punjab	2875 (4)	3310 (3)	15.13
Rajasthan	1278 (24)	1241 (25)	- 2.89
Sikkim	1746 (9)	2678 (7)	53.38
Tamil Nadu	1527 (17)	1821 (14)	19.25
Tripura	1443 (20)	1470 (19)	1.87
Uttar Pradesh	1360 (23)	1455 (22)	6.99
West Bengal	1571 (15)	1828 (13)	16.36
A & N Islands	2414 (7)	2695 (6)	11.64
Delhi	4018 (1)	4601 (1)	14.51
Pondicherry	3088 (3)	3309 (4)	7.16
All India	1697	1933	13.91

Source: CSO, *Estimates of State Domestic Product and Gross Fixed Capital Formation*, pp. 12-13
(a) Figures in brackets are ranks.

For 1987-88, there is a slight improvement in the position of SC because the relationship between growth and near landlessness without own homestead turns out to be negative. However, the value is not statistically significant.

Rank correlations are also computed for SC, ST and 'others' in the case of landless households with own homestead. For SC, the relationship between growth and landless households with own homestead is positive, suggesting that growth did not help them to acquire own homestead. There is a negative relationship between growth and landless households with own homestead for ST. The rank correlation between growth on the one hand and SC and ST near landless on the other is negative, only for 'others' it is positive. The situation has not improved for SC and ST in 1987-88 though ST shows a slight favourable turn in 1987-88. As regards disparities there has been a shift from a negative to positive sign in the case of SC between 1983-84 and 1987-88, suggesting widening of disparities in the case of near landless. Similarly, in the case of landless with own homestead also there has been a shift for the worse, if the shift from negative to positive sign is considered. In 1987-88 however the relationship between growth and landlessness without and with own homestead turned out to be negative for both SC and ST and positive for 'others'. But none of these is statistically significant.

IMPACT OF GROWTH ON DISPARITIES

Disparities are measured by the difference between 'others' and SCs on access to land. The rank correlation coefficient between growth and disparities between SCs and STs 'others' and SCs on the one hand and 'others' and STs on the other, for 1983-84 and 1987-88, for near landlessness, landlessness with and without own homestead are presented in Table 5. The rank correlation between growth and disparities between 'others' and SCs is negative in 1983-84 and positive in 1987-88 in respect of near landlessness, suggesting an unfavourable change. But both the values are not statistically significant. Disparities in 'others' and STs show a negative rank correlation coefficient in both the periods which are significant at 5 per cent level suggesting a favourable situation for STs during both the periods as regards near landlessness.

Growth and landless households without own homestead : The rank correlation coefficient between 'others' and SCs are negative whereas for STs and 'others' it is positive in 1983-84. In 1987-88 also, the correlation coefficient of disparities between 'others' and SCs shows negative sign while for 'others' and STs there is a positive sign. But none of the values is statistically significant suggesting that growth has no impact in improving access to land for SCs and STs and in disparities also growth has no effect in reducing disparities (Table 6).

Table 5
Rank Correlation Between Growth and Access to Land

	1983-84			*1987-88*		
	SC	*ST*	*Others*	*SC*	*ST*	*Others*
Without own homestead (0.00 ha)	0.0027	- 0.1236	0.2466	- 0.0928	- 0.0788	0.2650
With own homestead (0.00 ha)	- 0.1163	- 0.1306	0.0299	- 0.2442	- 0.2277	0.0717
0.00 to 0.40	- 0.1841	- 0.0656	0.1905	- 0.0641	0.0604	0.0470

Table 6
Rank Correlation Between Growth and Disparity in Land

	1983-84		1987-88	
	Others & SC	Others & ST	Others & SC	Others & ST
Near landlessness	- 0.0760	- 0.4112	0.0165	- 0.4145
Without own homestead 0.00 ha	- 0.1221	0.0095	- 0.0403	0.0211
With own homestead 0.00 ha	- 0.0290	- 0.2320	0.2234	- 0.1716

The data on percentage distribution of person-days of usually employed (Age 5+) in the principal status by broad person-days of usually employed (PDUE) activity status for 1983-84, are drawn from Sarvekshana (NSSO) 38th round for rural and urban areas. (Data presented in Table 7a and 7b).

The change in access could not be analysed as the data are available for only one year by this classification. Thus, the analysis is restricted to disparity between 'others' and SC & ST, and also of the differences in access between rural and urban areas.

Table 7a
Percentage Distribution of Person-days of Usually Employed (Age 5 and Above) in the Principal Status by Broad Current Daily Activity Status 1983-84

States UT All India		*Urban Male*			*Rural Male*	
	SC	*ST*	*Others*	*SC*	*ST*	*Others*
Punjab	92.33	0	94.76	84.02	91.36	94.55
Haryana	93.93	0	97.09	87.15	0	0
Maharashtra	90.78	87.63	94.83	81.57	85.34	89.87
Gujarat	94.35	93.06	94.46	85.92	91.00	92.41
Himachal Pradesh	95.72	0	98.13	95.52	97.60	97.91
Jammu & Kashmir	99.33	0	97.62	96.49	83.94	89.78
Karnataka	88.47	86.56	92.58	79.59	0	89.52
West Bengal	91.62	96.62	94.25	81.35	82.60	86.69
Andhra Pradesh	83.45	92.75	93.27	80.57	85.40	88.65
Tamil Nadu	79.98	88.50	89.03	70.84	80.69	82.00
Kerala	63.70	0	81.76	65.18	72.9	78.78
Uttar Pradesh	92.37	94.65	95.22	89.70	94.64	95.35
Rajasthan	89.21	94.76	96.62	90.56	95.76	95.37
Orissa	97.10	82.73	96.07	87.62	88.60	91.03
Bihar	94.67	92.94	97.84	84.68	95.23	93.37
Madhya Pradesh	91.46	95.74	95.11	90.85	93.74	94.08
Sikkim	0	96.69	94.57	0	99.22	97.28
Arunachal Pradesh	0	0	0	0	0	0
Nagaland	0	100.00	99.95	0	0	0
Manipur	0	88.32	98.45	0	89.67	99.32
Tripura	98.94	0	98.27	96.30	92.31	96.38
Assam	95.50	0	97.52	96.24	98.35	95.81
Meghalaya	0	98.2	99.05	0	95.54	94.03
Delhi	96.33	0	98.96	82.60	0	95.04
Goa	0	0	90.81	91.00	0	91.83
Pondicherry	0	0	91.33	49.53	0	79.41
A & N Islands	0	0	96.52	95.40	9.58	98.14
All India	90.36	91.71	94.07	84.22	90.96	91.16

Source: *Sarvekshana* (NSSO) 38th Round (Jan-Dec. 1983) Vol. XIII, No. 1, Issue No. 40 (July-Sept. 1989) pp. 26-29

Table 7b
Percentage Distribution of Person-days of Usually Employed (Age 5 and Above) in the Principal Status by Broad Current Daily Activity Status 1983-84

States UT All India	*SC*	*Urban Female ST*	*Others*	*SC*	*Rural Female ST*	*Others*
Punjab	84.26	74.74	81.77	76.32	100.00	71.56
Haryana	98.76	0	97.00	80.23	0	63.93
Maharashtra	74.61	70.77	78.78	61.71	67.31	68.06
Gujarat	83.31	55.31	78.00	70.08	72.58	70.64
Himachal Pradesh	95.15	0	78.61	67.10	78.13	73.54
Jammu & Kashmir	100.00	0	94.76	78.08	0	73.44
Karnataka	77.78	82.75	86.76	67.20	73.47	77.36
West Bengal	90.47	97.97	92.71	68.13	64.61	78.76
Andhra Pradesh	65.73	77.97	76.72	62.52	66.49	72.23
Tamil Nadu	70.81	68.00	84.15	55.86	72.43	67.41
Kerala	70.28	0	78.89	56.44	45.66	65.88
Uttar Pradesh	89.93	100.00	86.08	74.10	80.49	81.08
Rajasthan	88.18	95.65	84.17	82.54	90.11	87.86
Orissa	84.26	74.44	81.77	70.82	67.91	68.56
Bihar	84.16	80.60	93.62	65.97	84.33	77.43
Madhya Pradesh	87.55	72.45	83.73	74.82	79.29	73.91
Sikkim	0	97.21	95.58	0	97.17	98.59
Arunachal Pradesh	0	0	0	0	0	73.91
Nagaland	0	100.00	100.00	0	0	0
Manipur	0	86.40	99.62	0	82.38	93.10
Tripura	100.00	0	100.00	74.12	78.26	93.17
Assam	96.20	0	97.61	80.81	90.52	90.21
Meghalaya	0	98.86	98.86	0	90.50	82.55
Delhi	95.45	0	97.56	73.96	0	97.41
Goa	0	0	85.72	0	72.01	85.84
Pondicherry	0	0	94.01	40.78	0	68.17
A & N Islands	0	0	0	80.23	94.17	94.71
All India	81.61	75.76	84.00	- 67.66	75.94	73.75

Source: *Sarvekshana* (NSSO) 38th Round (Jan-Dec. 1983) Vol. XIII, No. 1, Issue No. 40 (July-Sept. 1989) pp. 26-29

We observe that for SCs, the percentage distribution of PDUE is uniformly lower than for STs and 'others' for rural and urban areas for males and females. The PDUE for females is lower than for males for all social groups for rural and urban areas. Except for rural females, even for STs the PDUE is lower compared to 'others'.

Thus, the access to PDUE for SCs is lower compared to STs and 'others'.

Table 8
Percentage Distribution of Person-days of Usually Employed (Age 5 +) in the Principal Status by Broad Current Daily Activity Status (1983-84)

	Rural		*Urban*	
	M	*F*	*M*	*F*
All India				
SC	84.22	67.66	90.36	81.61
ST	90.96	75.94	91.71	75.76
Others	91.16	73.75	94.07	84.00
Disparity				
Others and SC	6.94	6.09	3.71	2.39
Others and ST	0.29	- 2.19	2.36	8.24

The disparity between 'others' and SCs is wider in rural areas, when compared to urban areas. The disparity between 'others' and STs in both rural and urban areas is lower compared to disparity between 'others' and SCs. Thus, the overall PDUE for SCs is lowest for rural and urban, and males and females among the social groups considered.

Rank correlation coefficients between growth and disparities in respect of 'others' on the one hand and SCs and STs on the other, show a positive sign and the values are also significant. Only in urban areas they are negative but the values are significant statistically (Table 9).

Table 9
Rank Correlation Between Growth and Disparities in Employment SC, ST and Others

	Others and SC		*Others and ST*	
	M	*F*	*M*	*F*
Rural	0.5350	0.4365	0.4766	0.6261
Urban	0.0270	- 0.0114	- 0.3457	- 0.3596

In brief, 1983-84 data suggest that the growth is positively related to disparities in employment between 'others' and SCs and 'others' and STs in rural areas reflecting the disadvantageous situation for SCs and STs in relation to employment.

ACCESS TO AND DISPARITIES IN EDUCATION

Access to education is measured by the number of children enrolled in schools (Table 10). The rank correlation coefficient indicates a positive relationship in growth and access to education for SCs in 1983-84, and negative relationship in 1987-88 suggesting a deterioration in position in rural areas for both sexes. For urban areas also, the negative relationship exists for SC males in both the time points. Only in case of SC females, there is a shift from positive to negative. In ST position also, the general picture is one of deterioration. For 'others' alone, there is a favourable change in the case of both males and females and the changes are statistically significant too.

Rank correlation suggest a widening of disparities between SCs and 'others' and 'others' and STs also, both in urban and rural areas. In rural areas, the gap is evident much more and is statistically significant too.

SUMMARY AND CONCLUSION

This paper sought to judge the access of SCs and STs to three important determinants of development viz., access to land, access to employment and access to education and disparities between 'others' on one hand and SCs and STs on the other. Landlessness has grown both among SCs and STs. Disparities between 'others' and SCs and STs also show general increase. Growth has no effect in reducing either landlessness of SCs and STs or reducing disparities.

Table 10
Percentage of Children (5-14 yrs) Currently Attending Educational Institutions For Each Household Group for Different States/UT/All-India

Urban *Scheduled Castes*

States / UT	*1983-84*		*1987-88*	
/All-India	Male	Female	Male	Female
Punjab	62.6	57.0	64.2	57.3
Haryana	58.7	18.2	73.2	46.2
Maharashtra	75.4	65.5	81.2	64.3
Gujarat	67.9	57.9	67.4	60.0
Himachal Pradesh	74.2	15.9	—	—
Jammu & Kashmir	64.7	27.2	72.3	62.2
Karnataka	69.3	57.7	71.3	50.5
West Bengal	66.3	55.8	69.3	55.6
Andhra Pradesh	79.5	62.2	73.2	66.4
Tamil Nadu	71.0	68.0	80.1	69.9
Kerala	90.4	95.6	100.00	92.8
Uttar Pradesh	50.4	41.2	54.2	37.5
Rajasthan	60.9	34.7	71.5	31.9
Orissa	71.4	46.9	58.6	33.0
Bihar	42.9	24.7	41.6	28.8
Madhya Pradesh	72.8	50.5	69.8	54.7
Sikkim	—	—	81.9	100.0
Arunachal Pradesh	—	—	—	—
Nagaland	—	—	—	—
Manipur	—	—	—	—
Tripura	70.6	60.8	71.2	89.5
Assam	57.6	64.8	82.3	72.1
Meghalaya	—	—	65.1	50.6
Delhi	75.8	62.5	65.1	56.2
Goa	—	—	—	—
Pondicherry	—	—	92.3	97.2
A & N Islands	—	—	—	—
All India	66.7	52.3	68.2	53.8

Source: *Sarvekshana* (1983), NSSO, 38th Round Jan-L[illegible]. 83, Issue No. 40 (July-Sept. 1989) pp. 14
Sarvekshana (1987 - 88), NSSO, 43rd Round (July 87 - June 88), Vol. XII No.2, Issue No. 49 (Oct-Dec. 1991) pp. 55

Table 11
Rank Correlation Coefficients for Growth and the Percentage Number of Children (5-14) Currently Attending Educational Institutions and PCNSDP

Year	*SC*		*ST*		*Others*	
	M	*F*	*M*	*F*	*M*	*F*
Rural						
1983-84	0.2369	0.2067	- 0.0027	0.0791	0.3663*	0.4466*
1987-88	- 0.1587	- 0.1706	0.1056	0.0635	0.0635*	0.5078*
Urban						
1983-84	- 0.1181	- 0.1517	- 0.3172	- 0.3455*	0.5404*	0.4267*
1987-88	- 0.0754	0.0140	- 0.2002	0.0598	0.4396*	0.4860*

* indicates significant at 5 per cent.

Table 12
Rank Correlation Coefficient for Disparities Between Others and SC and Others and ST

Year	*Rural*				*Urban*			
	Others & SC		*Others & ST*		*Others & SC*		*Others & ST*	
	M	*F*	*M*	*F*	*M*	*F*	*M*	*F*
1983-84	0.5350	0.4365	0.4766	0.6261	0.0270-	0.0114-	0.3457-	0.3596
1987-88	0.2289	0.1332	0.4177	0.4899	0.1809	0.2332	0.4177	0.4899

7

Investment Gaps in Primary Education : A State-wise Study

V.K. Ramachandran
Vikas Rawal and
Madhura Swaminathan[1]

1. INTRODUCTION

Investment is needed on a very large scale in order to provide for universal primary education, and this paper is an attempt to provide state-wise estimates of the magnitude of resources that need to be mobilised to achieve this goal.[2]

India is a country characterised by very low levels of development. It is a country where the majority of the people earn low incomes, a country where illiteracy is widespread, and where large numbers suffer from ill-health, undernourishment, inadequate shelter and different forms of exploitation. The tasks of development are immense and require large-scale and commited public intervention. Specifically, the international

---

1. We have revised our initial estimates of expenditure following suggestions from Abhijit Sen and we are grateful to him for his comments.

2. The most recent previous paper on resource requirements, and the only one of which we are aware with respect to the contemporary period, by Tilak and Kar (1994) has serious methodological flaws (see Annexure).

historical experience shows that mass literacy is a precondition for the elimination of the worst forms of poverty and deprivation.[3]

We believe that "universal education and mass literacy cannot be achieved without the establishment of universal formal schooling" (Ramachandran, 1995b). Although valuable, systems of non-formal schooling, which in some cases are combined with child labour, and campaigns for mass literacy cannot achieve mass education. Universal schooling "requires that school education be made *compulsory*" (*ibid.*). Compulsory school education, in turn, requires systematic programmes of public action; a commitment to mobilise the necessary financial resources; and the will to make the necessary socio-political changes. Establishing universal schooling is likely to entail basic land reforms and public action against gender and caste discrimination.

2. FAILURES ON THE EDUCATION FRONT IN INDIA

Although the benefits of education to individuals and to society are widely known,[4] India is a country with very low levels of achievement in education. In 1991, India had around 321 million illiterate people (125 million males and 196 million females above the age of 7), the largest collection of illiterates in the world. The number of illiterate people today is greater than the population at the time of independence (in 1951, the number of persons above the age of four was 314 million). Between 1981 and 1991 (excluding Jammu and Kashmir), 19 million persons were added to the population of illiterate persons in the country. The situation is one of low overall literacy combined with large variations across states, rural-urban regions, communities and sex. The lowest female literacy rate in the country was 20 per cent in Rajasthan in 1991 (in rural areas, the rate was only 11.6 per cent), and the lowest male literacy rate was 52 per cent in Bihar. Illiteracy is acute among deprived communities. The male and female literacy rates among scheduled castes were 46 and

3. In a review of a book on the comparative economic development of small resource-rich countries of Scandinavia in the mid-19th century and a similar group of countries in Latin America in the 20th century, Thorp points out that two points emerge strongly in respect of the strategy of successful development: "the role of early agrarian reform...and the role of education" (Thorp, 1993, p 1324). As Thorp notes, this is, of course, also the lesson from East Asia.

4. An excellent account of the contribution of education to development can be found in Dreze and Sen (1995).

19 per cent respectively and the corresponding figures for scheduled tribes were 41 and 18 per cent. And among some of the most deprived sections of the population such as the tribal women of Rajasthan, the rate of literacy was as low as 4.4 per cent in 1991.[5]

Today, every child in India does not have easy access to a primary school. Notwithstanding official data, school attendance and enrolment ratios are low. The data from the 43rd round of the National Sample Survey (NSS) for 1987-88 on school attendance have been tabulated state-wise for 18 major states in Tables 1, 2 and 3.[6] We shall first discuss the data on children in the 5 to 14 year age group, which have been computed from information in the NSS reports (Table 3). The general picture is one of low school attendance (with the exception of Kerala). Again, with the one exception of urban Kerala, attendance rates for girls were lower than for boys in all states, and in general, attendance rates were lower in rural than in urban areas. Attendance rates were extremely low in the rural areas of Bihar, Madhya Pradesh, Rajasthan and Uttar Pradesh, (commonly referred to as the BIMARU states) as well as in Haryana, Orissa and Jammu and Kashmir. Less than 25 per cent of girls aged 5 to 14 years were attending school in rural Bihar, Rajasthan, Madhya Pradesh, Uttar Pradesh and Orissa. At the all-India level, about 40 per cent of rural children and 74 per cent of urban children were attending school. The figures in Table 1, for children aged 5 to 9 years are even more appalling. In eight states, attendance rates for rural girls in this age group were less than 5 per cent![7]

In this paper, we have used the attendance data for 5 to 14 year old pupils for further analysis. However, even the attendance rates cal-culated for 5-14 year old pupils may be an over-estimate in some cases. Data from village studies in Uttar Pradesh, for example, suggest that actual attendance is much lower. In 1993 in Palanpur, Dreze and Saran (1995) found that reported female enrolment was 20 per cent whereas observed or actual female school attendance was only 4 per cent.

---

5. On the lack of educational achievements among tribal women and girls, see National Commission for Women (1994)

6. Unfortunately, we could not get these data for the north eastern states.

7. These data are partially misleading because many children, particularly in rural areas, do not enter school till they are 7 or 8.

To get an idea of the scale of the problem, we have estimated the number of children not attending school in 1995 in different states using the 1987-88 attendance rates for 5-14 year old pupils and population projections for the 6-11 age cohort in 1995 (Table 4). The figures are staggering. A total of around 35 million boys and 41 million girls are estimated to be out of school in 1995 in the 18 states listed. In Uttar Pradesh alone, 8.7 million boys and 9.2 million girls are out of school. Over a million girls are not attending school in the rural areas of Andhra Pradesh, Bihar, Gujarat, Karnataka, Madhya Pradesh, Maharashtra, Orissa, Rajasthan, Tamil Nadu and West Bengal.

The quality of available schooling facilities is also deplorable. The Education Survey of 1986 found that 28 per cent of primary schools in the country were single-teacher schools and another 32 per cent had two teachers each. In some states like Rajasthan, 50 per cent of schools were reported to be single-teacher schools. According to a report prepared by the Ministry of Education in 1985 "many schools remain without any teacher for varying periods of time" (cited in Weiner, 1991, p 92). The same report notes that 40 per cent of primary schools did not have a pucca building and 9 per cent had no building at all. Further, 40 per cent of schools had no blackboards, 70 per cent had no library facilities, 60 per cent had no drinking water and 89 per cent lacked toilet facilities (*ibid.*).[8]

India also has a record number of child labourers. The estimates of the number of working children range from 13 million (Census of India 1981), to 44 million (Operations Research Group, 1983), to a 100 million according to voluntary organisations.[9]

This is the context in which we must consider the long-run trends and the more recent, structural adjustment-induced changes in expen-diture on education in India.

3. STRUCTURAL ADJUSTMENT PROGRAMMES AND EDUCATION

There is now a large volume of literature that documents the consequences of stabilisation and structural adjustment programmes

---

8. See also Dreze and Saran (1993) on the vandalisation of school buildings in Palanpur, Uttar Pradesh

9. The last figure is given by Swami Agnivesh, who has been leading a struggle for the abolition of child labour.

on the economies and peoples of developing countries in all parts of the world, and shows unambiguously that the poor suffer in the process of structural adjustment.[10] Expenditure reduction which is a part of an orthodox stabilisation package usually results in reduced spending on education, health, social welfare and programmes that directly benefit low-income groups in the economy.

In the 1980s, UNICEF commissioned a study of the impact of structural adjustment programmes on children. The study, published in two volumes under the title *Adjustment with a Human Face* was edited by Giovanni Cornia, Richard Jolly and Frances Stewart. This was a landmark study and the first to attempt an analytical framework to measure the direct and indirect consequences of structural adjustment programmes on children. The study makes one point emphatically : in the 1980s, structural adjustment programmes and the prolonged recession that followed them did great harm to the welfare of children. The study concludes that "there is widespread and growing evidence that in the early 1980s these economic changes.....triggered a sharp reversal in the trend towards improvement in health, nutrition and education standards of children". The study also notes that "nutrition and education seem to be the areas where deterioration is most evident and pronounced, an alarming sign in view of the permanent damage caused by malnutrition at an early age, and in view of the negative long-term implications of declining literacy" (*ibid.*).

To take one example from their case studies, here is some evidence on the effects of the adjustment policies on child welfare in the state of Sao Paulo (the most populous of the 23 states of Brazil, and one that accounts for the major share of Brazil's industrial output).[11] The economy went into a big recession in the eighties : GDP declined at an annual rate of 2.2 per cent (1981-84), unemployment grew from 5.8 per cent in 1982 to 7.1 per cent in 1984 and wages declined at almost 6 per cent per annum. While consumer prices grew annually at 25 per cent, the rise in food prices was much faster (31 per cent). Income distribution worsened. Social expenditures declined sharply, by 8 per cent annually between 1981 and 1984. There were absolute declines in expenditures on health

---

10. See, for example, Chomsky (1993), Chossudovsky (1992), Commonwealth Secretariat (1989), Cornia et. al. (1987), Ramachandran and Swaminathan (1993) and Taylor (1988).

11. This section is based on Roberto Macedo's study in Cornia *et. al.*, 1988

and education. While the share of health expenditures in total expenditures was maintained at around 3.5 per cent, there was a decline in the share of education, from 17.1 per cent in 1980 to 15.3 per cent in 1984. School attendance worsened. There was a sharp increase in drop-out rates (that is, in drop-outs as a proportion of children enrolled in schools). For children in the first grade, the drop-out rate increased from 4.6 per cent in 1979 to 13.4 per cent in 1983. Further, in the mid-eighties, only 22 per cent of those who enrolled in grade one reached the final grade of primary school. Among eighth graders, the drop-out rate increased from 7.5 to 12.3 per cent over the same period. There was also evidence of an increase in the number of children abandoned by their families between 1979 and 1985.

There are two recent papers that document the effects of structural adjustment on education. A World Bank review of the literature on education and adjustment states that "evidence of reductions in public expenditures during adjustment is pervasive" (Noss, 1991). Adjustment is associated with declines in all education indicators : in public education financing, in gross primary enrolment rates in student-teacher ratios and in the growth of teachers (Kakwani *et. al.*, 1990, cited in Noss, 1991). Pauline Rose looks at the experience of 86 countries (including countries that did not receive any adjustment lending) and finds that "there has been a slowdown in the increase in female enrolment rates at the combined first-and second-level in countries that have agreed to World Bank adjustment operations" (Rose, 1995). For a subset of 59 countries, time series analysis showed that while female enrolment increased in the 1970s with one exception (Guyana), in the 1980s, female enrolment declined in 16 countries, of which 15 were "adjusting" countries (*ibid.*).

Expenditure on education in India: long run trends and changes in the nineties

The following features of education expenditure in India need to be noted prior to an analysis of trends. First, since education is on the concurrent list, both central and state governments are responsible for education. However, the centre accounts for only a small proportion of total expenditure; in 1992-93, for example, the centre accounted for 11 per cent of total expenditure on education. Secondly, education expenditure is predominantly on the revenue account, that is, the main component is recurrent expenditure; in 1992-93, only 1 per cent of expenditure was from the capital account (for states and centre combined). Thirdly, the bulk of education expenditure is on the non-plan account. Taking expenditure on elementary education, in 1991-92, around 12 per cent of total expenditure was plan expenditure.

Table 5 shows the share of development expenditure allocated to education in the different Five Year Plans. Education's share of expenditure declined sharply during the Fifth and Sixth Five Year Plans. The trend was reversed during the Seventh Five Year Plan but allocations (as a percentage of total expenditures) remained lower than in the First Plan.

Public expenditure on education has grown at a positive rate over the last 40 years : between 1950-51 and 1989-90, expenditure per pupil grew at 1.9 per cent per annum in real terms (Tilak, 1995).[12] However, expenditure on education remains grossly inadequate and is also very low (both in absolute terms and as a proportion of GDP) as compared to other developed and developing countries.[13] In 1990-91, public expenditure on elementary education was only 1.8 per cent of GDP *(ibid.)*.

Turning to the more recent period, real expenditure on education by the central government declined sharply between 1990 and 1992 (see Table 6). Outlays increased in real terms in 1993-94.[14] Per capita expenditure declined from Rs. 7 in 1989-90 to Rs. 6.32 in 1992-93 (Jalan and Subbarao, 1995).

Since a large part of the expenditure on education comes from state budgets, a complete picture of changes in spending on the social sectors requires that state-level expenditures also be taken into account.[15] In absolute terms, between 1974-77 and 1989-92, real per capita expenditure by states on social sectors increased, on average, from Rs. 281 to Rs. 578 (at 1982-83 prices) for 17 major states (Prabhu and Chatterjee, 1993). The rate of increase, however, decelerated

---

12. We assume that these estimates are based on official data on enrolment. They do not, of course, take into account the children who are not enrolled.

13. See Dreze and Sen *(1995)* and Tilak (1994).

14. Unlike in other developing countries, cutbacks in social sector spending have to some extent been reversed under popular pressure.

15. However, a focus on central government expenditures is inevitable if we are to monitor the impact of fiscal adjustment on social sector spending (Nayyar, 1993).

from 1985-86 to 1991-92 *(ibid.)*. Further, a very small share (around 10 per cent in 1991-92) of state-level expenditures on the social sectors was on capital expenditures.[16]

Gupta and Sarkar (1994) examine expenditures under the broad head of "human resource development" for all states combined. They show that the share of this expenditure going to "education, sports, art and culture" has declined on both capital and revenue accounts in the early 1990s (Table 7). Further, per capita expenditure on education for all states combined declined from Rs. 84.52 in 1989-90 to Rs. 80.05 in 1992-93 (Jalan and Subbarao, 1995).

Table 8 documents the changes in expenditure on elementary education in the last few years at the state level. A quick glance at the data shows that the overall trend was one of stagnation. In real terms, expenditures declined in 7 states between 1991 and 1992 and in 10 sates between 1992 and 1993. If in this period population grew at 2.15 per cent per annum (growth rate between 1981 and 1991), growth rates of expenditure per capita would be much lower than the figures given in Table 8.

The effects of the recent decline in expenditure can be observed by the "*decline* in the *absolute number* of teachers in primary and upper-primary schools between 1991-92 and 1992-93" (Dreze and Sen, 1995, p 123, emphasis in original). The brunt of the job losses was borne by women; there was almost no change in the number of male teachers. As Dreze and Sen rightly argue, "there could hardly be a more inappropriate response to the current failures of basic education in India" *(ibid.)*.

4. EXISTING INTER-STATE INEQUALITIES IN ENROLMENTS AND INVESTMENT REQUIREMENTS

The history of education policy in India is one of seemingly good intentions; without the necessary financial and socio-political backing,

---

16. In another paper, Seeta Prabhu (1994) shows that, first, the share of total expenditure allocated to development purposes by all states combined declined between 1990-91 and 1993-94 (Prabhu, 1994). Secondly, over the last three years, there was a reduction in the share of social services in the total development expenditure of states. Thirdly, the financial position of many states is precarious and with a decline in the transfer of resources from centre to states in 1994-95, only a further decline in state-level development expenditures (including expenditures on social sectors) is possible.

however, the policy has become a collection of pious statements. The National Policy on Education (NPE) 1986 gives "an unqualified priority to universalisation of elementary education......universal enrol-ment.....and universal retention of children up to 14 years of age" (Ministry of Human Resource Development, 1989). The Report goes on to argue that "neither normal linear expansion nor the existing pace and nature of improvement can meet the needs of the situation". The NPE called for an investment of 6 per cent of national income or GDP in education during the Eighth Five Year Plan.

India has also ratified the UN Convention on the Rights of the Child which clearly states that "State parties recognise the right of the child to education, and with a view to achieving this right progressively and on the basis of equal opportunity, they shall, in particular, make primary education compulsory and free to all" (Article 28).[17]

In this paper, we take the goal of universal primary schooling for the 6 to 11 year age group and estimate the costs of schooling the children in this age group who are currently out of school. We refer to these estimates as investment requirements.

METHODOLOGY

Colclough and Lewin (1993) have proposed a methodology for calculating investment requirements to finance universal education. Colclough - Lewin's method involves a three-step estimation - first, the calculation of flows of students through each grade, second, the, calculation of the unit cost of schooling, and, third, by combining the two, the calculation of investment requirements. To use the Colclough - Lewin methodology for calculation of number of children in each grade, we require data on parameters like population of children of school-going age, proportion of children who enter first year of primary school at the age of six, rates of repetition, promotion and drop out for each grade, number of students per class and student-teacher ratios. To calculate the unit cost of schooling, we require, data on factors contributing to costs like building, salaries and operating expenses.

---

[17] Cited in UNICEF (1994).

Detailed and reliable data on all the parameters required for calculation of flow of children in each grade are not available in India. In the absence of the required data, Ramachandran (1995b) modified the Colclough - Lewin method to calculate investment requirements for universal education in West Bengal. This alternative method used attendance rates to estimate the number of children in the age-cohort 6-11 years who are attending school and who are not attending school. Norms for unit recurrent costs, unit capital costs for new schools and unit capital costs for improvement of existing schools were identified and used to calculate recurrent costs and capital requirements for universal primary education. Yearly investment requirements were then calculated assuming that the target of universalisation was to be achieved in the next five years. The norm for unit costs used by Ramachandran (1995b) are based on an interview and subsequent discussions with the Minister for School Education, Government of West Bengal, in which major heads of investment and school-operating expenses were identified. He prepared the following estimate of costs for establishing a school of 150 children.

Estimated capital and recurrent costs for a primary school for 150 children with five teachers, West Bengal, 1995, in rupees

Expenditure head	Cost (Rs.)
• Building	3,00,000
• Sanitary Provision and water	40,000
• Furniture and blackboards	35,000
• Mats, chalks, dusters	500
• Teaching aids, recreational materials, playing materials, library facilities, teacher reference books etc.	10,000
• Text books	10,000
• Teachers' salary (for 5 teachers)	1,54,740
• Cost of teacher' training	26,190
Total capital expenditure	3,75,000
Unit capital cost	2,500
• Maintenance (10% of capital expenditure)	37,500
Total Recurrent expenditure (including maintenance)	2,38,930
Unit recurrent expenditure	1,593

Source: Office of the Minister, Primary and Secondary Education, Government of West Bengal cited in Ramachandran *(1995b)*.

Note: The statement from the office of the minister mentions that the costs involved in establishing a school, other than the cost of building, are same in rural and urban areas. As far as the building is concerned, a relatively cheaper option for urban areas is to hire buildings rather than construct them. This, the statement mentions, is a general practice in West Bengal. The rent for a building or five classrooms in West Bengal is about Rs. 2,500 per month.

We have applied this methodology to calculate investment requirements for 17 states of India. As far as we are aware, this is the first exercise that calculates state-wise investment requirements for universal primary education in India using data on unit costs of schooling (that is, using norms as opposed to past expenditure) and data on attendance other than the official enrolment data.[18] The estimates presented of expenditure required are based on the unit capital costs of Rs. 2,500 for all children not attending school. For the children who are attending school, we assume that 50 per cent of the unit capital cost is needed to improve the existing school infrastructure. Unit recurrent costs (as shown in the Table above) are assumed to be the same for all children. NSS data on school attendance for 1987-88 are used along with population projections for 1995 to estimate the number of children in the 6-11 year age-group who are attending/not attending school.

It is to be noted that the estimates obtained by the present method can be improved. Owing to limitations of data, we have not been able to incorporate factors like current utilisation of resources, existing teacher-pupil gap, distribution of villages according to number of children out of school, etc. Use of these parameters would have improved the estimates. Further, using separate norms for each state will give different estimates. Again, owing to the lack of data (as for example, on building costs in different states), we have applied the norm for West Bengal to all the other states.[19]

Our results on investment requirements for 17 major states are presented in Table 9. The table gives state-wise estimates of expenditure needed for the first five years to all 6-11 year old. Columns 3 and 4 of the table show the total expenditure as a proportion of current expenditure on elementary education and State Domestic Product (SDP) respectively. Column 6 shows the additional expenditure as a proportion of SDP. These figures tell us by how

[18] There have been some earlier attempts to estimate the requirement of investment for primary education. These generally used past unit expenditure as a norm for cost and official data on enrolment. Problems associated with these estimates are discussed in the Annexure.

[19] We have used data on proportion of children attending school from the NSS quienquennial survey of employment and unemployment, 1987-88. The data on population of children between age-cohort 6-11 have been taken from the Census of India, 1981 and projected using 1981-91 growth rates for the respective states to 1995. For Assam 1971 data were used for projections. For both Jammu & Kashmir and Assam, population projections were calculated using all-India growth rates.

much current expenditure needs to be scaled up and the commitment to be made in terms of SDP.

The figures clearly show that very high levels of investment need to be made to achieve the target of universalisation of primary education. Andhra Pradesh, for example, needs to spend Rs. 2,324 crore yearly if all 6-11 year old children in the state are to be in primary school. For Delhi, a smaller state, and one where current attendance is high, the estimated yearly expenditure is Rs. 301 crore.

Turning from absolute figures to the commitment in terms of SDP (see column 6), the only state that seems to have come close to meeting the estimated expenditure requirement is Kerala, where the additional expenditure is only 0.6 per cent of SDP. In all other states the additional expenditure required is a high proportion of SDP. Bihar and Uttar Pradesh are worst off in this respect : in Bihar the additional expenditure amounts to 5.7 per cent of SDP.

In terms of the total investment on primary education as a percentage of SDP (column 4), the commitment required is less than 4 per cent of SDP in the states of Delhi, Punjab, Kerala, Maharashtra, Haryana , Tamil Nadu and Gujarat.[20] Next come states which need to commit between 4 and 5 per cent of SDP. These include Karnataka, Andhra Pradesh and West Bengal. Finally, there are the laggard states: Jammu and Kashmir, Orissa, Rajasthan, Uttar Pradesh, Madhya Pradesh and Bihar. These states have, not surprisingly, to make a huge investment effort (more than 5 per cent of SDP) to do justice to a policy of universal primary schooling. Bihar, in particular, needs to make an annual investment of the order of 8 per cent of SDP.

5. CONCLUDING REMARKS

The costs of getting every child in India into school in the next five years are large and vary across states, depending on current achievements. Resources alone cannot transform conditions without appropriate socio-political changes and commitment from

---

[20] Kerala falls in this category because of low SDP and not due to low attendance. The correct indices to look at for Kerala are investment requirement as a proportion of existing expenditure and additional investment requirement as a proportion of SDP. As column3 and 6 show, Kerala has a much easier road ahead.

governments, teachers and parents. At the same time, to make the policy of universal primary schooling meaningful, a financial commitment of the order of magnitude estimated in this paper is required.

Annexure
A Note On Alternative Estimates of Investment Requirements for Primary Education

In this annexure we shall comment mainly on two alternative estimates of expenditure requirements for primary education, namely, the Reports of the Finance Commissions and Tilak and Kar (1994). The State Plan of Action on Universalisation of Primary Education in West Bengal has also estimated investment requirements for the state of West Bengal [Government of West Bengal 1994]. These estimates have been discussed in Ramachandran (1995b).

Non-plan expenditure forms the bulk of expenditure on primary education. In 1991-92 the non-plan expenditure on elementary education was close to 92 per cent of the total expenditure on elementary education. The Finance Commissions recommend allocation of the non-plan expenditure of the central and the state governments into different services. Estimation of the non-plan expenditure for primary education by the Finance Commissions is, thus, of great importance. Up to the Eighth Finance Commission, the recommendations were based on projections from past trends of expenditure on education. The projected estimates of allocation of resources for different services would occasionally be adjusted to the other policy objectives like an emphasis on backward states, construction of additional schools, promotion of girls' education. None of the Commissions, including the Ninth and the Tenth Finance Commissions, estimated the expenditure required for universalisation of primary education. The Ninth Finance Commission attempted what they called a "normative" estimation of expenditure requirements for 14 major states. This was done with the objective of ensuring "inter-state equity in relation to central transfers". Their approach was based on estimating unit cost functions for a variety of ends including general services (administrative expenditures of various kinds), social services (education and health services) and economic services.

To identify the unit cost function for primary education, they estimated the following regression.

$$X = a + b_1E + b_2T + b_3S + b_4P$$

Where

X is the expenditure on primary education per enrolled child

E is the enrolment rate (ratio of number of children enrolled in primary schools to the population of children)

T is the student teacher ratio in primary schools in different states (ratio of number of enrolled students to number of teachers)'

S is the differences in the average salaries of primary school teachers across states

P is the price differentials across states

This regression equation was estimated using data for 14 major states. They used the data averaged over two periods, 1981-82 to 1983-84 and 1984-85 to 1986-87. These data (28 observations) were pooled to estimate the parameters. From the estimated cost function, expenditure requirements were calculated for each state for 1986-87 using actual values of enrolment and average values for the other explanatory variables. The estimates of expenditures for the states as a whole for 1986-87 were then projected to the future using all-states growth rates of expenditure on elementary education. Since the expenditures were estimated from an *average norm,* as estimated by the regression equation, estimates were higher than actual values for the low income states and lower than actual values for the high income states.

We feel this methodology is inadequate in many respects, as indicated below.

First, despite the introduction of a much more complicated methodology, the Ninth Finance Commission did not incorporate the most desired target in the education sector, namely the universalisation of enrolment in primary schools. The Tenth Finance Commission also estimated the expenditure for education by projecting the actual expenditure in the past as was done prior to the Ninth Finance Commission.

Secondly, the official data on enrolment are highly inflated. The unit expenditure in the past per enrolled child would thus be an underestimate of actual expenditure per child. In the regression equation shown above enrolment appears in three variables, viz., the expenditure per enrolled child, enrolment rates and the teacher-pupil ratio. This is bound to bias the estimates.

Thirdly, this approach uses unit cost functions based upon past expenditures on education. The Ninth Finance Commission report states that "the normative expenditures..... have to be estimated at the justifiable cost of providing the existing standards of services". In practice, however, the estimates aimed to provide the existing standards of services, known to be education is concerned. Thus, even without other data problems, using past expenditure as a proxy for cost cannot give anything more than estimates for existing standards of services.

Another estimate of state-wise expenditure requirements for universalisation of primary schooling has been made by Tilak and Kar. Tilak and Kar explicitly mention having followed the methodology of "normative estimation" developed by the Ninth Finance Commission. They have estimated the unit cost (expenditure) function separately for each state by using data for 12 years (1980-81 to 1991-92). They, however, have used only enrolment as the explanatory variable in the regression equation. The equation estimated by them is:

$$\ln (C) = a + bE^*,$$

where C and E* refer to unit expenditure and *total enrolments* respectively, and ln is the natural logarithm.

For primary education they have taken the target of universal enrolment to be achieved by the year 2000 and calculated enrolment figures for the intermediate years by interpolation. Using these enrolment estimates they have calculated the expenditure requirements for each state in each year.

Clearly, the Tilak and Kar method, contrary to their claim, is completely different from that of the Ninth Finance Commission. The *norm* as referred to by the Finance Commission was an average cost function introduced, as mentioned before, to ensure inter-state equity in central transfers. All it does is to calculate expenditure requirements for each state for providing the "average" quality of services instead of the actual quality of services. Tilak and Kar, on the other hand, estimate state-wise unit expenditure functions. They use the estimated functions, which are nothing more than an approximation of actual values, as the *norms* for the cost to be used with the projections for enrolment to calculate the expenditure requirements. Tilak and Kar have improved the methodology of the Ninth Finance Commission by introducing externally specified targets of enrolment (universalisation by the year 2000) to estimate the expenditure requirements. They, however, have not made a lot of other necessary changes in the methodology. This has led to various problems in their estimation.

First, they have also used official data on enrolment, which are known to be highly inflated. This leads to an under-estimation of the expenditure requirements. Also, enrolment and attendance are two different things. While enrolment in primary classes refers to children (of all ages) studying in primary schools, attendance refers to the percentage of children in a specified age-group attending school. It is therefore conceptually incorrect to talk of a gap between universal attendance and present enrolment. This would lead to further under-estimation of expenditure.

Secondly, Tilak and Kar also use expenditure as a proxy for unit cost. This, as we mentioned earlier, is seriously flawed.

Thirdly, the regression equation has not been correctly specified. If at all one is to calculate unit expenditure functions for the past, then factors like student-teacher ratio, density of population, salaries, etc. should be included as explanatory variables in the estimation of the expenditure function. The existing large teacher gap, for example, is an important variable in explaining low investments in the past.[21] Tilak and Kar have dropped all these variables from their equation. Also, they have used absolute figures on enrolment (E*) as against enrolment rates (E) used by the ninth Finance Commission[22].

---

[21] Relatively large increases in teacher salaries accounted for the increase in expenditure on education during eighties [Sen and Dreze 1995].

[22] Given the equation has been specified in the semi-log form, the estimated values of coefficients of enrolment are very small. The results, as reported by them, present the values of coefficients only up to four decimal places. Many of these coefficients, up to four decimal points, are zero. Seeing the published report, it is difficult to comment on the accuracy of the estimates.

Table 1
Proportion of Children Attending School, Aged 5-9 Years, 1987-88

State	*Rural*			*Urban*			*Rural +*
	Male	*Female*	*Total*	*Male*	*Female*	*Total*	*Urban*
Andhra Pradesh	63.30	45.20	54.23	79.70	72.80	76.31	61.98
Assam	48.60	47.80	48.23	72.60	66.10	69.70	51.90
Bihar	18.80	10.60	18.80	53.70	45.80	50.13	28.43
Delhi	36.00	0.00	18.58	84.40	81.10	82.84	76.11
Gujarat	63.10	52.40	57.89	72.00	74.90	73.35	63.88
Haryana	3.60	2.40	3.04	81.80	71.00	77.11	22.60
Himachal Pradesh	0.00	0.00	0.00	90.30	82.40	87.04	10.36
Jammu & Kashmir	0.90	1.10	1.00	73.50	67.00	70.27	17.67
Karnataka	57.00	50.60	53.82	70.20	69.50	69.84	59.91
Kerala	86.90	82.80	84.81	93.40	90.50	92.95	86.87
Madhya Pradesh	33.00	17.00	25.28	71.30	64.50	67.97	36.56
Maharashtra	64.00	54.40	59.42	79.70	76.60	78.18	67.53
Orissa	2.70	2.10	2.41	75.80	66.60	71.13	17.14
Punjab	4.00	3.40	3.72	83.30	80.70	82.04	33.51
Rajasthan	6.00	2.70	4.49	68.30	54.70	62.08	20.57
Tamil Nadu	39.70	34.30	37.03	90.40	86.00	88.26	60.90
Uttar Pradesh	5.70	3.50	4.70	58.90	49.40	54.37	17.83
West Bengal	34.30	33.10	33.73	64.40	61.60	63.03	41.81
All-India	27.60	23.50	25.65	72.60	67.70	70.24	38.85

Source: National Sample Survey Organisation, 1992

Table 2
Proportion of Children Attending School, Aged 10-14 Years, 1987-88

State	*Rural*			*Urban*			*Rural +*
	Male	*Female*	*Total*	*Male*	*Female*	*Total*	*Urban*
Andhra Pradesh	57.00	30.90	44.29	79.30	66.20	72.62	54.55
Assam	76.10	70.90	73.79	90.50	84.30	87.85	76.56
Bihar	54.60	28.70	54.60	75.00	64.00	70.06	59.57
Delhi	96.00	86.10	92.25	89.80	84.20	87.11	87.67
Gujarat	76.50	52.20	65.39	82.10	76.10	79.32	71.32
Haryana	81.80	51.60	68.28	85.10	78.70	82.38	71.96
Himachal Pradesh	92.50	73.00	83.07	93.30	95.10	94.08	84.68
Jammu & Kashmir	77.50	45.80	61.58	80.70	74.60	77.93	65.80
Karnataka	65.00	45.50	55.31	78.00	73.00	75.55	63.27
Kerala	93.30	91.20	92.31	93.40	94.30	93.83	92.69
Madhya Pradesh	31.60	29.90	30.85	88.30	76.80	83.10	46.07
Maharashtra	79.40	55.70	68.55	90.00	83.50	86.91	76.72
Orissa	61.20	38.90	49.94	81.80	71.20	77.07	56.26
Punjab	72.10	59.30	66.25	83.10	81.30	82.24	72.02
Rajasthan	69.60	19.20	47.01	83.20	55.20	70.00	53.71
Tamil Nadu	70.70	48.70	59.97	78.60	69.70	74.21	66.70
Uttar Pradesh	63.80	30.70	49.24	71.30	60.80	66.50	54.10
West Bengal	64.30	52.80	58.81	79.60	74.50	77.20	64.58
All-India	67.00	42.30	55.59	81.30	72.40	77.11	62.38

Source: National Sample Survey Organisation, 1992

Table 3
Proportion of Children Attending School, Aged 5-14 Years, 1987-88

State	*Rural*			*Urban*			*Rural +*
	Male	*Female*	*Total*	*Male*	*Female*	*Total*	*Urban*
Andhra Pradesh	60.36	38.73	49.66	79.51	69.63	74.57	58.54
Assam	62.38	58.97	60.84	82.36	75.69	79.45	64.27
Bihar	34.90	19.77	34.90	63.66	54.25	59.42	42.60
Delhi	69.70	39.14	56.57	87.12	82.69	85.01	81.99
Gujarat	69.63	52.31	61.44	77.21	75.51	76.42	67.53
Haryana	43.19	26.43	35.54	83.45	74.77	79.72	47.15
Himachal Pradesh	47.51	37.28	42.55	91.99	89.79	90.06	49.01
Jammu & Kashmir	37.93	22.84	30.38	77.30	70.69	74.16	41.28
Karnataka	60.92	48.10	54.55	74.22	71.23	72.72	61.58
Kerala	90.43	87.09	88.80	93.40	93.43	93.41	89.96
Madhya Pradesh	32.33	22.60	27.82	79.94	70.29	75.39	41.00
Maharashtra	71.65	55.02	63.87	84.92	80.00	82.54	72.06
Orissa	29.90	20.01	25.02	78.99	68.76	74.12	35.98
Punjab	38.35	31.25	35.08	83.20	80.99	82.14	52.52
Rajasthan	35.50	10.20	24.04	75.28	54.94	65.84	35.95
Tamil Nadu	55.27	41.43	48.47	84.48	77.71	81.16	63.81
Uttar Pradesh	32.92	15.87	25.30	65.02	54.80	60.24	34.81
West Bengal	48.12	42.15	45.27	72.22	68.01	70.20	52.59
All-India	46.47	32.25	39.80	76.96	70.00	73.64	50.14

Note: Attendance rates in the NSS survey results (for source see Tables 1 and 2) have been reported for age-groups 5-9 and 10-14. Attendance rates for age-group 5-14 are weighted averages of the attendance rates for age-groups 5-9 and 10-14.

Table 4
Number of Children, Aged 6-11, Not Attending School, 1995

State	*Rural*		*Urban*		*Total*
	Male	*Female*	*Male*	*Female*	
Andhra Pradesh	1,734,359	2,636,282	333,100	494,612	5,198,352
Assam	764,482	802,621	41,478	56,232	1,664,814
Bihar	5,033,684	5,297,293	397,705	457,400	11,186,083
Delhi	34,522	58,512	92,831	115,171	301,036
Gujarat	752,844	1,072,258	278,563	275,535	2,379,200
Haryana	721,782	798,670	60,092	85,104	1,665,649
Himachal Pradesh	218,051	252,733	2,651	3,323	476,759
Jammu & Kashmir	344,345	397,700	36,088	44,332	822,465
Karnataka	1,085,882	1,471,507	308,680	346,145	3,212,214
Kerala	143,621	191,309	40,015	39,378	414,322
Madhya Pradesh	3,278,272	3,549,820	281,731	404,268	7,514,091
Maharashtra	1,264,279	1,935,309	387,208	511,451	4,098,247
Orissa	1,713,962	1,947,212	79,980	116,994	3,858,149
Punjab	746,031	728,877	82,573	84,540	1,642,021
Rajasthan	2,239,368	2,793,818	238,677	408,194	5,680,057
Tamil Nadu	1,261,996	1,603,218	226,549	319,838	3,411,601
Uttar Pradesh	7,812,295	8,129,294	936,955	1,111,159	14,989,702
West Bengal	2,441,236	2,636,151	393,384	440,141	5,910,913
Total	31,591,011	36,302,584	4,218,260	5,313,817	77,425,675

Source: Census of India 1981 (1988), Part IV-A, Social and Cultural Tables, Tables C-1 to C-6, by P. Padmanabha, Registrar General and Census Commissioner, India

Notes: To estimate the population of children aged 6-11 in 1995, state-wise population growth rates (based on Census of India) for the period 1981-1991 have been used. For Jammu & Kashmir, all-India population growth rates have been used. For Assam, base year population was from 1971 and this was projected to 1995 using all-India population growth rates.

Attendance rates used are as in Table 3.

Table 5
Expenditure on Education in Different Five Year Plans By Government of India

Plan Period	*Expenditure on education as percentage of expenditure on all heads of development*
First (1951-56)	6.79
Second (1956-61)	4.50
Third (1961-66)	4.87
Fourth (1969-74)	5.21
Fifth (1974-79)	3.26
Sixth (1980-85)	2.59
Seventh (1985-90)	3.55
Eighth (1992-97)	4.91

Source: Seeta Prabhu (1994), Table 1.

Table 6
Central Government Plan Outlay on Education

	Actual	*Constant Prices (1980-81 prices)*	
	Rs. Million	*Rs. Million*	*Index*
1989-90	6485	3194	100.0
1990-91	6772	3010	94.2
1991-92	7454	2923	91.5
1992-93	8412	2983	93.4
1993-94	11069	3689.6	115.1
1994-95 (B.E)	13176	3875.3	121.3

Source: Government of India, Expenditure Budget, different years.
Note: Actual values are deflated with the GDP deflator.

Table 7
Percentage Share of Human Resource Development Expenditure Allocated to Education, Sports, Art and Culture, All States, 1989-90 to 1991-93

	Plan Expenditure		*Non-plan Expenditure*		*Total*
	Revenue account	*Capital account*	*Revenue account*	*Capital account*	
1989-90	14.0	2.2	24.6	0.10	1.6
1990-91	9.0	2.1	24.7	0.03	1.5
1991-92	10.0	1.9	22.9	0.08	1.4
1992-93	11.9	2.0	22.4	0.17	1.5

Source: Gupta and Sarkar (1994), Table 5.

Table 8
Changes in State-Wise Plan and Non-Plan Expenditure, Revenue Account, on Elementary Education, 1991-1993

State	*Expenditure on elementary education (at 1980-81 prices)*					
	1991-92		*1992-93*		*1993-94*	
	Rs mill.	*Index*	*Rs mill.*	*Index*	*Rs mill.*	*Index*
Andhra Pradesh	1960.5	100	2147.2	109	2173.6	110
Arunachal Pradesh	115.5	100	114.1	99	124.3	107
Assam	1212.6	100	1256.6	103	1339.5	110
Bihar	3102.3	100	3003.9	97	3163.9	101
Goa	76.9	100	81.0	105	79.6	103
Gujarat	2124.8	100	1992.4	94	2302.0	108
Haryana	617.2	100	685.7	111	674.0	109
Himachal Pradesh	397.2	100	435.8	109	548.9	138
Jammu & Kashmir	242.0	100	218.9	90	205.7	85
Karnataka	1836.6	100	2123.3	115	2512.3	118
Kerala	1606.7	100	1625.4	101	1786.6	111
Madhya Pradesh	2318.1	100	2537.4	109	2507.0	108
Maharashtra	3477.9	100	3598.0	103	3294.5	95
Manipur	136.3	100	145.6	107	135.6	99
Meghalaya	156.6	100	163.5	104	184.4	118
Mizoram	109.2	100	110.8	101	103.7	95
Nagaland	116.4	100	122.4	105	125.9	108
Orissa	1227.7	100	1482.4	121	1360.5	111
Punjab	660.8	100	744.9	113	792.6	120
Rajasthan	1776.8	100	1862.9	105	1961.6	110
Sikkim	59.8	100	61.9	103	58.7	98
Tamil Nadu	2883.6	100	2617.9	91	2949.1	102
Tripura	196.1	100	192.9	98	183.3	93
Uttar Pradesh	4180.0	100	4307.3	103	4445.2	106
West Bengal	1891.6	100	1787.4	94	1812.3	96

Source: Ministry of Human Resource Development (1995)
Note: Actual values were deflated with the GDP deflator, and then indexed to expenditure in 1991-92.

Table 9
Investment Requirements for Five Years for Universal Schooling of Children in Age-Cohort 6-11

State	*Yearly Investment required (I) (Rs.)*	*I/Existing expenditure(%)*	*I/SDP (%)*	*Existing expenditure/SDP 1994-95 (%)*	*Excess expenditure/SDP (%)*
[1]	*[2]*	*[3]*	*[4]*	*[5]*	*[6] = [4-5]*
Andhra Pradesh	23249131348	325	4.2	1.3	2.9
Assam	8611406470	189	5.2	2.8	2.4
Bihar	33017620233	310	8.4	2.7	5.7
Delhi	3011021198	301	1.7	0.6	1.1
Gujarat	13609031862	160	3.5	2.2	1.3
Haryana	6038894033	286	2.8	1.0	1.8
J & K	2744917500	445	6.7	1.5	5.2
Karnataka	15545239870	164	4.0	2.4	1.6
Kerala	7807205783	122	3.5	2.9	0.6
Madhya Pradesh	21313505768	294	5.4	1.8	3.5
Maharashtra	26571420093	269	2.5	0.9	1.5
Orissa	11328896713	274	6.1	2.2	3.9
Punjab	6308829725	234	2.1	0.9	1.2
Rajasthan	16972264140	258	5.9	2.3	3.6
Tamil Nadu	16402494378	155	3.3	2.1	1.2
Uttar Pradesh	53143981120	363	6.5	1.8	4.7
West Bengal	23651268239	403	4.6	1.1	3.5

Notes: Current expenditure on elementary education and SDP are for 1994-95. Current Expenditure for 1994-95 has been estimated by projecting the 1993-94 expenditure figures using growth rates between 1992-93 and 1993-94, and with a constraint that expenditure cannot decline. SDPs for 1994-95 have been estimated by projecting SDPs for 1993-94 using growth rate in GDP between 1993-94 and 1994-95.

REFERENCES

Chomsky, N., 1993, *Year 501: The Conquest Continues,* Boston: South End Press.

Chossudovsky, M., 1992, "Globalization of Poverty", *Frontline,* March I 3.

Colclough, C. with K. M. Lewin, 1993, *Educating All the Children,* Oxford: Clarendon Press.

Commonwealth Secretariat, 1989, *Engendering Adjustment for the 1990s,* Report of a Commonwealth Expert Group on Women and Structural Adjustment.

Cornia, G. A., Jolly, R. and Stewart, F. (eds.), 1987, *Adjustment With A Human Face,* Vol. 1, New York: Oxford University Press.

Cornia, G. A., Jolly, R. and Stewart, F. (eds.), 1988, *Adjustment With A Human Face,* Vol. 2, New York: Oxford University Press.

Dreze, J. and Amartya Sen, 1995, *India: Economic Development and Social Opportunity,* Oxford University Press.

Dreze, J. and M. Saran, 1993, Primary Education and Economic Development in China and India : Overview and Two Case Studies:, LSE-STICERD DEP No 47.

Gupta, S.P. and A.K. Sarkar, 1994, "Fiscal Correction and Human Resource Development : Expenditure at Central and State Levels", *Economic and Political Weekly,* March 26.

Jalan, J. and K. Subbarao, 1995, "Adjustment and Social Sectors in India" in R. Cassen and V. Joshi (eds.), *India: The Future of Economic Reform,* Delhi : Oxford University Press.

Ministry of Human Resource Development, 1989, *National Policy on Education —- 1986.* Ministry of Human Resource Development, Department of Education, Planning and Monitoring Unit,1995, *Analysis of Budgeted Expenditure on Education, 1991-92 to 1993-94.*

National Commission for Women, 1994, *Report on Development of Female Education Among Tribal Communities,* New Delhi.

National Sample Survey Organisation, 1992, *Sarvekshana,* Results of the 4th Quinquennial Survey of Employment and Unemployment, NSS 43rd round (July 1987-June 1988), Special Issues.

Nayyar, D., 1993, "Economic Reforms in India: A Critical Assessment", ILO-ARTEP Working Papers, New Delhi.

Noss, A., 1991, "Education and Adjustment: A Review of the Literature", World Bank, WPS 701.

Prabhu, K. S. and S. Chatterjee, 1993, Social Sector Expenditures and Human Development: A Study of Indian States, Reserve Bank of India, Development Research Group, Study 6, Bombay.

Prabhu, K. S., 1994, "The Budget and 'Structural Adjustment with a Human Face'", *Economic and Political Weekly,* April 16-23.

Ramachandran, V. K. and M. Swaminathan, 1993, "Structural Adjustment Programmes and Child Welfare", a paper presented at the seminar on New Economic Policies: Their Impact and Implications, Hyderabad, December 3-5.

Ramachandran, V.K., 1995a, Kerala's Development Achievement: A Review, Indira Gandhi Institute of Development Research, Preprint No 200, Bombay.

Ramachandran, V. K., 1995b, "Universalising School Education: A Case Study of West Bengal", draft paper, Indira Gandhi Institute of Development Research, Bombay.

Report of the Tenth Finance Commission (for 1995-2000), 1994.

Second Report of the Ninth Finance Commission (for 1990-1995), 1989.

Report of the Eighth Finance Commission, 1984.

Rose, P., 1995, "Female Education and Adjustment Programmes: A Cross-Country Statistical Analysis", *World Development,* 23, 11.

Shariff, A. and R. Sudarshan, 1996, "Education in India: Selected Gender Disaggregated Indicators", paper presented at a workshop on Gender, Health and Development Perspectives in India, January 12-14, New Delhi.

Taylor, L., 1988, *Varieties of Stabilization Experience,* Oxford: Clarendon Press.

Tilak, Jandhyala. B. G, 1994, *Education for Development in Asia,* Sage Publications.

Tilak, Jandhyala. B. G. and D. K. Kar, 1994, "Requirements of Resources for Education in India: Implications for the Tenth Finance Commission", New Delhi: NIEPA.

Tilak, Jandhyala. B. G, 1995, "Costs and Financing of Education in India", Studies on Human Development in India, Discussion Paper No 5.

Thorp, R., 1993, "Diverging Paths : Comparing a Century of Scandinavian and Latin American Economic Development edited by M. Blomstrom and P. Melier", *Economic Journal,* Vol. 103, No. 4, September.

UNICEF, 1994, "The Right to be a Child', India Background Paper.

UNICEF, 1995, *The Progress of Indian States.*

Weiner, M., 1991, *The Child and the State in India,* Princeton University Press.

8

Women and Regional Development

Gunilla Sterner

THE GENDER SYSTEM

Women and men do not live the same types of lives or share the same life conditions even if they share the same household and family. In the same way women and men in a certain region live their lives under different terms. In every society, at every given time, there exists an invisible contract between women and men of what is expected from each sex. This pattern is usually called the gender system by social scientists, and it regulates what kind of tasks, jobs, education are to be assigned to females or males. The gender system also regulates the distribution of power and influence between the sexes as well as the control of reproduction. If one, by accident or with a conscious mind, crosses that border and fulfils a task defined for the other sex, one will immediately become aware of it through the reactions from people around. That is what happened to the first pioneers, whether they were female doctors or priests, or the first men who took parental leave in Sweden.

The theory of gender system gives an explanation as to why our society is so divided between the sexes on labour market, education, power, income and wealth. Of course there is also a value dimension in it, male superiority and female subordination. (Just check with the insurance companies, they have implemented this system and completed it in every detail !)

The hopeful part of it is that the system is not eternal, it is changing over time. What is called a female task today could be that of a male tomorrow, and vice versa. Jobs such as milking cows, were once typically female in Sweden but today with the new technical systems milking is mostly done by men. Teaching, on the other hand, was a male job earlier which today is dominated by women.

REGIONAL DEVELOPMENT AND GENDER PERSPECTIVES

I work for the Country Administrative Board in Stockholm, which is involved in regional development. Every year the Board distributes a big amount of state grants to stimulate growth of enterprise and business, occupations and services in the region. Stockholm is the capital city and economically most advanced in the country with a diversified industry and commerce.

Education and infrastructure are some basic needs when you want to attract foreign companies to make investments in a region. A skilled labour-force, with low wages and salaries, a high level of know-how, existence of other companies with a similar production (the Silicon Valley-syndrome), good public services and peaceful environment are the other important pre-requisites. But it is also important to integrate a gender perspective in regional development policy and form the policy in the interest of women. Development is more a question of how every region could mobilize its own population and use its own resources. Investments in education, infrastructure and research have become more important than economic subsidies to enterprise. To stimulate the region's own inhabitants, male and female, to start and develop enterprises of different kinds, to refine goods, to increase growth and export is as important as to attract foreign investors.

The national goal in Sweden for regional development policy is to give people access to occupation, service and a good environment wherever they choose to live in the country. The policy should contribute to develop stable and vital regions in all parts of the country. All regions should receive equal opportunities for economic, social and cultural development.

The north of Sweden has a small population with high unemploy-ment, and a very limited labour market for women. The women and the young girls there move to the south to get higher education and jobs in the urban areas. The southern parts, specially the urban areas, are well developed with a variety of industries and services. The regions that are most rapidly growing are the ones around the university cities. It seems that today higher education and technical know-how are more important than roads and airports. The new electronic communication systems can bring new opportunities for remote and isolated regions.

HISTORICAL BACKGROUND

Sweden has gone through many phases of development during the last 100 years. A century back, Sweden was an agrarian country but could not feed its inhabitants. As a result, more than one million people (one fifth of the population) left the country and emigrated to America. At the end of the sixties the country was industrialized and urbanized. This was accompanied by the growth of the service sector. Today half of the labour force is occupied in the service sector. Only about 3 per cent of the labour force is now occupied in agriculture, 21 per cent in the manufacturing industry, 12 per cent in commerce, 7 per cent in com-munications, 17 per cent in private services and 33 per cent in public services. One million people or one fourth of the Swedish labour force are employed by the public sector and 70 per cent of them are women.

Between 1950s and the 1980s Sweden had a long period of governance by a social democratic government and it experienced fairly good economic growth during this period. During this time it built up the public sector with child care centres, schools, care of elderly and hospitals. This growth was the result of political reform, of decentralization of powers and responsibility to local governments. For the past 15 years, public sector expenditure has exceeded 60 per cent of Gross Domestic Product (GDP). Women got increased access to paid work in the enlarged public sector. About half of the women, the majority of the mothers, chose to work part-time, so that they could also manage the unpaid work at home.

In the 90s the situation has changed radically. State finances became weak. The same is true of the municipalities and the country councils. Although local governments (municipalities and country councils), since long ago have the constitutional right to levy taxes on their inhabitants, they now also have to borrow money to pay for their consumption. Almost half of the expenditure consists of labour costs. As a result the expenditure of local governments has decreased in recent years and lots of women have lost their jobs. In the 90s we had a severe recession combined with structural changes in many branches with increasing unemployment as a fallout. The unemployment rate is still high (around 10 per cent). The mounting unemployment has also worsened the financial position of the local governments, whch are legally responsible for disbursing social assistance to the growing number of unemployed persons.

The unemployment rate today is almost the same for men and women, but the new jobs are more technical and very few women have technical education.

Sweden also had a non-socialistic government between 1991 and 1994, at the central as well as most local levels. During this time the public sector became more market-oriented, business-minded, and commercialised. The organisation was decentralised and most units became be self-financed by fees instead of depending on grants. So during these years the fees for childcare and care of elderly have almost doubled. Further, the public-sector undertakings were exposed to competition.

The users of public services have now more options to choose between different providers of publicly financed services. Today it is possible for parents to start a cooperative childcare centre or a school with a special pedagogics and get state or municipal grants for the endeavour. An even greater influence of parents and pupils compared to what is currently available in the ordinary school is being contemplated by the government, where they are going to be the majority on the steering committee of the school.

Now we again have a social democratic government, but the new structure of organization and management remains, since all govern-ments today are interested in minimising expenses of the public sector.

For women in general the situation has worsened during the 90s. Their salaries have almost been standing still, while expenses like housing, food, childcare and medical care have risen. The salaries for women are around 80 - 90 per cent of that of their male counterparts but many women do not work full time. Today it is not easy to get full time jobs while the municipalities are cutting down on expenditure. A new tendency has been to offer more time limited jobs with less security. About one third of all the jobs in Stockholm city are time limited. The last two years experienced many cuts in the public transfer and welfare systems, like child allowances, sickness benefits and parental insurance, and lower unemployment insurance benefits. At the same time the fees for public services have gone up. All families, irrespective of their size, have felt the pinch of the general cut. Many households today have one or more of the grown-ups unemployed. The unemployment rate is specially high among refugees and immigrants, who number about one million of eight million population. The diversity of ethnic groups and culture also means that we have to seek new methods to achieve equality. The old methods were designed for the ancient society. New problems demand new solutions, while at the same time we must know our history.

EQUALITY POLICY AND EFFECTS

Since the 60s there has been an active effort for equality between women and men in Sweden. The overall goals, as expressed in the 1994 Parliamentary Bill, can be summarized as follows

- An equal distribution of power and influence between women and men
- Equal opportunities for women and men to achieve economic independence
- Equal terms and conditions for women and men as regards entrepreneurship, work, terms of employment, conditions in working life and opportunities for development at work
- Equal access for girls and boys, women and men, to education, including the same opportunities to develop personal ambitions, interests and talents
- Equal responsibilities for women and men for the work at home and with children
- Freedom from gender specific violence.

LABOUR MARKET

The aim has specially been to break down the segregated labour market and equalise access to education. So far the results have not been impressive. Women still work in a few occupations just as they did 15 years ago, occupations and sectors reflecting the traditional role of women, such as childcare, nursing, care of elderly, routine industrial jobs and office jobs. Sweden has, in spite of the internationally high female employment participation rate, the most gender segregated labour market in Europe. There have been some structural changes in female dominated branches, for example the level of education has been heightened in office works, the new computer techniques demand new skills and general service works with low demands in education are disappearing. The banks are cutting down their staff because of newer ways of communicating with the customers. The hospitals employ only highly educated nurses and cut down on assistant personnel. In the 70s the female dominated textile industry quietly passed out while the male dominated shipyards got all attention from the state and in the public debate. Today we have a parallel between the office women and the building workers. Both sectors are going down but the men are protesting more loudly.

Since 1980, we have the Equal Opportunities Act., which was amended in 1992 and 1994, to break down the segregated labour market. The Act consists of two parts, one that requires an employer to take active measures to promote equality at the workplace, and the other part that prohibits an employer from discriminating against a person because of her or his gender.

Today, the Act is more accepted by the employers and trade unions and now it can also be used for trying cases where work of equal values are compared. All employers with more than 10 employees have to draw up a plan to promote equality. The quality of the plans is slowly rising, under the supervision of the Equal Opportunities Ombudsman.

EDUCATION

At secondary school levels the proportion between the sexes has become better in the theoretical programmes, but in programmes directed to special occupations the imbalance continues. But more women today go in for higher studies. Around 60 per cent of all first year students at Swedish universities and colleges are women and nearly twice as many women as men graduated from higher education institutions in the 80s. And women in technical education rose from 9 to 22 per cent during the decade. This is partly due to changes in pedagogics. Earlier, the technical high schools were very much male dominated and so were the problems to solve. For example girls were asked to detonate a hand grenade. Instead when girls are allowed to formulate the problems themselves, they get more interested to use technique to solve their problems. Fields like multi-media, medical technology, and environmental protection attract women.

There has been a clear policy to spread out universities and high schools over the whole country, but many of them are still located in Stockholm.

It has been noticed that the new universities have exerted a good influence on the growth of industry and services in the surrounding areas. Today many remote regions are competing in the new technologies, and they have been successful to a large extent.

POWER AND INFLUENCE

The greatest success for the equality policy came during the elections in 1994. The social democratic party had voting lists with every other representative a woman. The women secured 40 per cent of the seats in the Parliament and 50 per cent of the ministers in the government were women. In the local governments the women got 41 per cent of the seats in the council and 48 per cent of the seats in the country councils. This had never happened before. But in case of chairmen of municipal committees the bias still exists. The same is true in the case of the steering committees. Female politicians are most interested in areas like social services, school systems, education/culture and health/medical services. Berit Aas, the well known Norwegian social scientist warned the female politicians to forget why they went into politics. She says that women must also change the politics, otherwise they will not be effective.

PARENTAL RESPONSIBILITY

Sweden has a higher fertility rate than most of the Western European countries (2.1 children per woman in 1992). Financial support to families and access to good living enabled parents to combine parenthood with gainful employment. From January 1995 parental benefit will apply for twelve months, six for the father and six for the mother. A parent may, however, declare in writing that he or she gives up the right to parental benefit to the other parent, except for a period of thirty days. During this period the parents get about 90 per cent of salary, but for the rest of the days, only 80 per cent.

But these reforms had a limited impact on the behaviour of parents. From 1974 the number of days taken by men on parental leave has increased from 0 to 10 per cent. But in the same period the number of days taken by men for taking care of sick children has declined from 40 to 33 per cent. (But if you count the sum of days it is an increase from 300 to almost 2000 days). Fathers in the rural parts of the country take more days off than men in the cities. Immigrant fathers are also using these benefits. And the attitudes of people have already changed; you can see lots of fathers every morning taking their kids to schools or nursery.

PAID AND UNPAID WORK

A study carried out in 1990 about time-use showed that the time women spend on work is about the same, 60-61 hours a week However, women spend more time on unpaid housework (33 hours a week) and less time on paid work (27 hours a week) while men spend 20 hours on unpaid and 41 hours on paid work. Men seem to have better chances of coming home to rest after a long day at work. For women, there is a great deal more unpaid work. In Sweden it is very rare to have domestic help, only a small segment of the population can afford it. And there is also discussion on the morality and ethics in having another woman serving in your own household. You are expected to manage both fields, if you are a woman, even if you are the vice prime minister.

WHAT METHODS HAVE BEEN MOST SUCCESSFUL?

The Equal Opportunity Act and the Ombudsman

The above Act along with the institution of the Ombudsman is one method used to slowly change the society. For example the number of female judges in general courts has risen from 12 to 17 per cent for the permanent judges, and from 40 to 54 per cent for non-permanent judges, during the last seven years. And today we have 13 per cent female chiefs in the police, which means that the proportion of women in leading positions within the police forces has more than doubled during the last seven years. But change in attitudes is to be accompanied by increase in resources and knowledge of women.

The Principle of Mainstreaming

The other method is the principle of mainstreaming, which should be followed in all areas. This means that the unequal power relationship between the sexes at an overall level in society must be revealed, recognized and taken into account in all major policy decisions. Equality work aims at changing the structures in society which contribute to maintaining gender segregation, female subordination and male domination.

At the regional level this means that the Equality Affairs Division requires that all government proposals include an analysis of proposed measures from a gender perspective. and that all budget proposals analyse what will be the expected effects on women and men. At the regional level, where I work, we have the same mission. We should see to it that plans and programmes of the Country Administrative Board do have a gender perspective, that the individual statistics is divided in female and male, that the effects on women and men is analysed, and that the resources are equally distributed between men and women. Here we have not yet finished our mission. The expert function that I uphold was enforced just one year ago, so my experiences are limited. A lot of work remains to be done. I have found out that only 20 per cent of the state grants for regional development goes to women, and even less when it comes to subsidies directed to enterprises (about 2%). Why is that so? Well, my colleagues tell me, it is so difficult to find out if it is a man or a woman that runs the company. And fewer female entrepreneurs apply for subsidies. But the fact is that none has cared to find out if there are different needs for female and male entrepreneurs.

So we have now started to support female entrepreneurs in a more explicit way. First of all we divide all statistics on gender basis even for companies (which is possible), and make some surveys among female and male entrepreneurs to find out more about what kind of support they need. Women have more difficulties with getting bank loans and they do not want to take loan as much as the men. They also have needs for child care and networks with other women. They also prefer to become a female business-adviser.

So we address more explicitly to the kind of support and subsidies for women; we have supported female business-advisers both in my region and in the rural areas of the country.

To take life and work in your own hands - resource centres for women

We are also building up special resource centres for women, where one can get support, advice, training, and knowledge about how to start a company and come into contact with different women networks. In these resource centres the regional boards for labour, education and the municipalities allocate their resources and cooperate with organisations The centre is built on the empowerment principle; it is built up by and for the local women, who also dominate on the steering committee.

Today we have these regional resource centres in half of the regions. In my region we have about five local centres. And at the national level we have the National Resource Centre that supports us. I think these centres have been very successful in mobilising the women, specially in the rural areas of the country. But I think the concept is equally applicable to the city areas.

SUMMARY

Sustainable development can only be attained when the needs and interests of both women and men are fully recognised in the planning and implementation of projects and programmes.

One important goal for regional development policies in all countries must be to contribute to women's independence so that women, regardless of which part of the country they live, can live a worthy life measured from a female perspective. That includes equal conditions for women and men regarding education, incomes and properties, health, and influence in society. That means that all resources of society should be equally distributed between sexes. And that all unpaid work of women should be fully recognised and valued. It also means a freedom from male guardianship, sexual harassment and gender violence.

And maybe some of the methods we use in Sweden could be useful in India also.

9

Regional Disparity and Resource Flows Across States

Atul Sarma

Balanced regional development has been one of the most cherished goals of Indian planning. Despite this, at the end of four and a half decades of planning, the distance between the advanced and backward states has widened rather than narrowing down in terms of income realization. Even between 1985 and 1990, the distance of the poorer five states from the all-India average per capita SDP increased as can be seen from the first two columns of Table-1. For example, taking all-India per capita SDP as 100, the per capita income index of Bihar declined to 53.9 in 1990 from 59.4 in 1985. On the other hand, the same index for Maharashtra and Punjab rose to 147.4 and 170.5 respectively from 135.3 and 163.6 during the corresponding period.

One of the critical factors contributing to this differential rates of income generation across states is the varying levels and qualities of administrative, social and economic infrastructures available in different states. Precisely for this reason, the development of infrastructures has constituted major components of the successive plans of both the Centre and states in the entire planning era.

It is to be noted that at the beginning of the planning era, the initial level of infrastructures was widely different in different states. But despite balanced regional development being one of the explicitly stated plan objectives, the interregional disparity in the availability of infrastructures, leaving aside their quality, has deteriorated over the years. Table 1 which presents two sets of infrastructure index - the one without and the other with civil administration - for high, middle and low income states and special category states clearly brings out this point. For example, for most of the low income and special category states, the infrastructure index is far below the all-India average index even in 1990. With all-India average as 100, the index for Bihar, M.P., Orissa and Rajasthan lies between 66 and 92 and that for special category states other than Nagaland between 49 and 84. On the other hand, this index is far above the all-India average for the high and middle income states : it ranges from 102 for Karnataka to 219 for Punjab. The situation would further worsen if quality variables which are not incorporated in this exercise are introduced in the construction of the infrastructure index.

By and large, similar pattern emerges from the examination of the indices separately for administrative, social and economic infrastructures as presented in Tables 2, 3 and 4.

The above analysis highlights the fact that infrastructure development is critically important for the pace of economic growth. But it should also be noted that while the infrastructure development largely depends on government investment, the final outcome in terms of income generation in a state is influenced by the total resource flows inclusive of private investment. It is, therefore important to examine interregional income disparity on the basis of total resource flows across states.

The income and employment generation (and the welfare level in an economy) depends to a large extent, on the level of investment. The level of investment, on the other hand, is dependent on the government's role in economic management and its capacity to invest directly or through its instrumentalities and to create environment to stimulate private investment. This holds true even in the case of a state economy in a federal system operating in a mixed economy framework like ours.

But a state in our federal system operates under a hard budget constraint, and therefore its capacity to invest on its own is rather limited; more so, for the relatively backward states, their economic bases being narrow and less diversified.

A state government has limited taxation and borrowing powers while it has no access to foreign resources nor has it any power to create money. Imbalance inherent in the allocation of functions and revenue sources for a sate government has been sought to be corrected through the distribution of shared and assigned taxes and grants-in-aid under the dispensation of the Finance Commission. In actual practice, however, two other forms of fiscal transfers viz. plan assistance and discretionary, have come to enhance the state's capacity to play their role in their respective economies. The former is provided under the formulae-based recommendation of the Planning Commission while the latter type of transfers is made by the individual ministries of the Central government without referring to the Finance and Planning Commissions. Apart from these direct fiscal transfers from the Centre, there are several other forms of resource flows to the states. These are:

(i) Allocation of market loans;

(ii) Negotiated loans from LIC, GIC, etc.;

(iii) Loans from term lending institutions e.g. IDBI, NABARD etc.;

(iv) Investment by Central Public undertakings;

(v) Commercial Bank Credit;

(vi) Private foreign investment;

(vii) Private Domestic Investment; and

(viii) Mobilization through Capital markets.

All these various resource flows on both public and private sector accounts together determine the level of investment and the resultant income and employment generation in a state economy. The data on all these various flows are not readily available. On the basis of the available data for some of the above variables for 1990-91, this paper highlights the nature of distribution of these flows across states at different income scale. Having done so, the paper argues for redefining the role of fiscal transfers in the context of current liberalized economic environment.

Examining the relative share of these resource flows against the income and population shares of the respective states as presented in Table 5, the following important observations can be highlighted.

The total fiscal transfers which include Finance Commission (F.C.) & Planning Commission (P.C.) transfers under centrally sponsored schemes, discretionary transfers and transfers for natural calamities are much higher for the ten special category states than their respective population and income shares. Special category states together claimed 18.3 per cent of the total fiscal transfers in 1990-91 as against their population share of 5.4 and income share of 4.8. Low income states also benefited from a larger flow of fiscal transfers from the Centre. Their share in fiscal transfer (41.3 per cent) was much higher than their income share (32.9 per cent) However, these were lower than their population shares (44.1 per cent).

Both high and middle income states received much lower share in fiscal transfers as compared to their income or population proportions. High income states received only 14.52 per cent of the total fiscal transfers as against their population and SDP share of 18.91 per cent and 29.86 per cent respectively. Similarity, five middle income states received 25.73 per cent of the total fiscal transfers against their population and income shares of 31.68 per cent and 32.56 per cent respectively.

On the whole, it appears, therefore, that fiscal transfers in totality were equity-oriented favouring special category and low income states.

Disaggregating the fiscal transfers by agencies, it can be observed that P.C. transfers rather than F. C. transfers were more in favour of special category states. In the case of low income states or even middle income states, F.C. transfers were more favourable than P.C. transfers. High income states received lower share both in F.C. and P.C. transfers as compared with their population and SDP shares, although their share in P.C. transfers was much higher – almost close to their population share. It is noteworthy that between middle and high income state, P.C. transfers favoured the middle income states. Discretionary transfers favoured special category and low income states.

In contrast to the above observations, the special category states received a share in small savings almost equal to their population share but high (30.54 per cent) and low income (35.15 per cent) category states received more than their income shares while the middle income states (28.57 per cent) received less than their population and income share. Thus, in terms of share in small savings, high and low income states were better off as compared to middle and special category states.

It is interesting to note that low income and middle income states benefited more from market borrowing, their share being higher than their respective shares in population and SDP. High income and special category states received less from market borrowing.

As for the investment on public enterprises by the Central Government, the share of only low income and special category states was higher than their income share. Middle income states' share in the investment by public enterprises was higher than that of high income states.

All-India financial institutions such as IFCI, ICICI, LIC, GIC, IDBI, SFCs and STDCs preferred to provide assistance to the higher income states at a level which is much higher than their income and population share. In fact, 42.4 per cent of the total disbursement by these institutions, were deployed in the high income states.

The share of disbursement clearly declined with the level of income. Special category states received only 2.5 per cent of their total disbursements. It is important to note that the disbursement by these financial institutions contributed more than one-fifth of the total fiscal transfers in absolute terms.

Similar observations can also be made on the flow of resources to the states in terms of paid-up capital of companies, both government and non-government companies. The shares of these companies stood at Rs.53,849 crore on March 31, 1992. Five high and five middle income states together cornered as much as 85 per cent of the total paid-up capital. On the other hand, low income states received only 13 per cent. while special category states together received no more than 2 per cent.

This type of highly skewed distribution is also observable in the case of foreign investment commitments, which stood at Rs.222,539 crore between January 1, 1991 and August 31, 1993. This has emerged as the singlemost important source of investment. The manner of distribution of these resources across states would greatly determine the level of investment in a state.

Even for Central assistance released for externally aided projects which come under plan assistance, the balance was highly titled in favour of the high income states.

From the analysis of the flow of resources from different sources, a general pattern is discernible : By and large, fiscal transfers from the Central Government favour the poorer and special category states while the financial institutions and market-oriented investment, which are at a much higher scale as compared to direct fiscal transfers favour the relatively advanced states.

This pattern of resource flows will in all likelihood get further accentuated under the new economic regime. For, the physical control instruments like licensing having been dismantled, the relatively more advanced states would inevitably attract much larger investment flows. For instance, Maharashtra and Gujarat, are reported to have received commitments of about Rs.100,000 crore and Rs.60,000 crore respectively in terms of foreign direct investment in the next two or three years. The expectation of such inflows of private investment would require these states to provide for higher level and world class infrastructures. This would be the beginning of a regressive vicious circle with the more advanced states building up better quality infrastructure matching the requirements of private investment while less developed states increasingly lagging behind in the growth process.

In order to arrest this trend, federal transfers would have to be reoriented. At one level, the equity-oriented fiscal transfers have to be enhanced so as to enable the less developed states to provide the level and quality of infrastructure that would attract private investment. And also larger loan assistances with softer terms have to be provided to them.

At the same time this policy of equity cannot be pursued at the expense of the developed states. To compensate these states in a manner that does not impair their growth prospects, the advanced states with higher capacity to utilize the borrowed fund productively, should be provided greater access to the capital market.

The observations made as above, raises one basic question : Is resource flow to an economy on government account by itself an effective instrument for generating economic growth? To put the question another way : Why have some states developed faster than others?

There does not seem to have a clear answer to this question since the economic development is a complex process influenced by interplay of multiple forces. Nevertheless, it can be hypothesized that the states which could evolve a clear development strategy with well-identified thrust areas seem to have achieved higher economic growth. Punjab and Haryana with clear thrusts on agriculture, Maharashtra and Gujarat on industry, Kerala on social sector, for example, provide some support to the hypothesis. Even the contrary cases of West Bengal and Tamil Nadu with initial advantage in industrial development but slided in the planning era for diffused thrusts in their successive plans lend credence to it.

It seems to work in the following process. When the government plays a pivotal role in the development process an identification of thrust areas or lead sectors and their uninterrupted pursuance over the years help improved monitoring of plan schemes and programmes and thus accountability. It is because the economic agents, once aware of the responsiveness of the system, tend to generate continuous pressures on the government machinery for better delivery. In the process formulation and implementation of go ernment schemes and agents' response and participation feed on each other thus leading to an increasingly higher level of performance. This is precisely what market mechanism ensures and power maximizing and risk averse bureaucracy frustrates.

But the question which still remains is : Why do some states succeed in evolving a development strategy with clear thrust areas and pursuing it continuously while others do not? The answer to this perhaps lie in the prevailing political economy and the characteristics of the dominant interest groups in a state economy. If the dominant group represents farming interest, they would inevitably generate pressure for larger allocation for agricultural development. Similarly, if the dominant group represents industrial interests, they would demand larger investment on activities which directly or indirectly contribute to industrial development. If no interest group holds a dominating position, the resource allocation is likely to be thinly spread with monitoring and accountability being weak. Needless to add, the initial conditions prevailing in an economy would inevitably determine the relative influence of different interest groups.

This analysis may be helpful in understanding sectoral resource flows, their effective monitoring and accountability as well as the resultant outcome in terms of income and employment generation in an economy. This also suggests that larger fiscal transfers to the poorer states, as argued earlier, do not necessarily ensure the expected outcomes. A proper monitoring and accountable system would be necessary for such outcomes. The Panchayat system and urban local bodies introduced recently as the third stratum of the Indian federal system would contribute, it is hoped, to unleashing productive forces and evolving a monitoring and feedback mechanism at a highly decentralized level, leading to higher growth.

Table 1
Aggregate Infrastructure Indices

States	*SDP Per capita*		*Infrastructure-I*		*Infrastructure-II*	
	1985	*1990*	*1985*	*1990*	*1985*	*1990*
High Income States						
Maharashtra	135.3	147.4	129.7	121.7	127.2	119.5
Gujarat	121.7	117.4	118.8	123.0	117.6	121.1
Haryana	137.2	144.7	154.5	158.9	151.3	155.1
Punjab	163.6	170.5	225.1	219.2	218.8	212.7
Goa	394.1	409.5	159.2	192.3	216.1	194.0
Middle Income States						
Andhra Pradesh	82.0	91.8	100.4	99.2	101.5	101.4
Karnataka	94.2	91.8	102.8	101.2	103.1	101.4
Kerala	87.4	80.8	192.6	205.4	190.6	202.2
West Bengal	96.8	95.5	137.3	131.7	138.5	133.1
Tamil Nadu	94.8	92.5	152.2	149.9	151.6	149.3
Low Income States						
Bihar	59.4	53.9	89.4	92.0	95.4	97.6
Madhya Pradesh	73.0	79.5	64.4	65.9	65.6	66.8
Orissa	71.5	69.8	72.9	74.5	73.7	75.2
Uttar Pradesh	72.8	70.8	113.2	111.8	112.1	110.6
Rajasthan	71.8	76.7	64.6	70.5	65.8	71.2
Special Category States						
Arunachal Pradesh	118.6	105.0	66.5	48.9	124.7	101.0
Assam	83.7	70.4	77.6	81.9	75.9	80.5
Himachal Pradesh	93.9	97.0	79.2	80.9	83.4	84.8
Jammu & Kashmir	105.9	84.9	77.3	76.1	77.5	76.3
Manipur	87.8	83.0	77.0	70.4	83.9	76.3
Meghalaya	82.1	84.1	71.4	73.8	78.5	80.0
Nagaland	95.6	96.2	65.7	70.9	97.8	102.7
Sikkim	111.5	95.2	93.3	104.6	100.5	102.2
Tripura	75.6	76.1	74.3	83.6	76.3	85.2
Mizoram	96.4	87.4	54.6	61.9	74.5	72.2
All India	100	100	100	100	100	100

Note: Infrastructure index I ignores administrative infrastructure, its correlation with SDP being low while infrastructure index II is constructed giving an arbitrary weight. For greater details see Anant, Krishna and Roy Choudhury, *op. cit.*

Source: Anant, T. C. A., Krishna, K. L. and Roy Choudhury, U. (1994) : *Measuring Interstate Differentials in Infrastructure*

Table 2
Index of Civil Administration

Sl.	*States*	*1985*	*1990*
	High Income States		
1.	Maharashtra	80.00	78.30
2.	Gujarat	89.30	87.20
3.	Haryana	84.70	82.20
4.	Punjab	95.00	88.80
5.	Goa	228.50	217.90
	Middle Income States		
6.	Andhra Pradesh	122.40	143.40
7.	Karnataka	103.40	101.60
8.	Kerala	149.70	152.40
9.	West Bengal	165.10	160.00
10.	Tamil Nadu	142.90	141.30
	Low Income States		
11.	Bihar	206.70	202.40
12.	Madhya Pradesh	81.80	78.30
13.	Orissa	87.40	87.20
14.	Uttar Pradesh	89.90	87.10
15.	Rajasthan	88.50	84.80
	Special Category States		
16.	Arunachal Pradesh	906.10	981.80
17.	Assam	44.70	52.60
18.	Himachal Pradesh	164.10	159.70
19.	Jammu & Kashmir	85.40	85.10
20.	Manipur	197.90	192.10
21.	Meghalaya	191.70	203.70
22.	Nagaland	710.60	709.80
23.	Sikkim	207.90	212.00
24.	Tripura	112.50	116.40
25.	Mizoram	346.70	335.50
	All India	100	100

Source: As of Table 1

Table 3
Social Infrastructure

Sl.	*States*	*1985*	*1990*
	High Income States		
1.	Maharashtra	170.90	145.30
2.	Gujarat	116.10	141.10
3.	Haryana	81.80	77.10
4.	Punjab	165.10	161.70
5.	Goa	316.90	258.50
	Middle Income States		
6.	Andhra Pradesh	78.70	73.40
7.	Karnataka	100.90	99.30
8.	Kerala	272.70	383.30
9.	West Bengal	184.60	164.90
10.	Tamil Nadu	140.90	143.10
	Low Income States		
11.	Bihar	70.40	76.80
12.	Madhya Pradesh	56.50	59.20
13.	Orissa	76.40	74.20
14.	Uttar Pradesh	90.40	86.70
15.	Rajasthan	68.10	65.50
	Special Category States		
16.	Arunachal Pradesh	160.00	112.50
17.	Assam	84.50	94.90
18.	Himachal Pradesh	120.00	109.90
19.	Jammu & Kashmir	86.80	100.60
20.	Manipur	127.00	85.70
21.	Meghalaya	104.50	107.00
22.	Nagaland	94.30	92.80
23.	Sikkim	228.00	224.50
24.	Tripura	117.00	122.80
25.	Mizoram	129.50	129.30
	All India	100	100

Source: As of Table 1

Table 4
Economic Infrastructure

Sl.	*States*	*1985*	*1990*
	High Income States		
1.	Maharashtra	121.87	117.20
2.	Gujarat	119.37	119.57
3.	Haryana	168.40	174.46
4.	Punjab	236.51	230.15
5.	Goa	184.63	172.97
	Middle Income States		
6.	Andhra Pradesh	104.54	104.10
7.	Karnataka	103.12	101.57
8.	Kerala	177.32	171.53
9.	West Bengal	128.26	125.34
10.	Tamil Nadu	154.28	151.15
	Low Income States		
11.	Bihar	93.06	94.95
12.	Madhya Pradesh	65.36	67.20
13.	Orissa	72.20	74.51
14.	Uttar Pradesh	117.55	116.59
15.	Rajasthan	63.87	71.40
	Special Category States		
16.	Arunachal Pradesh	31.14	33.91
17.	Assam	76.22	79.46
18.	Himachal Pradesh	71.42	75.42
19.	Jammu & Kashmir	75.48	71.39
20.	Manipur	61.24	67.46
21.	Meghalaya	63.32	67.42
22.	Nagaland	60.29	66.74
23.	Sikkim	58.78	66.04
24.	Tripura	66.18	76.07
25.	Mizoram	29.43	39.78
	All India	100	100

Source: As of Table 1

Table 5.1
Direct Resource Flow to States in 1990-91

(Per cent)

States	Population	SDP (Current prices)	F C Transfers: Share in taxes	F C Transfers: Grants	F C Transfers: Total	P C Transfers: Grants	P C Transfers: Loans	P C Transfers: Total
High Income States								
Maharashtra	9.45	15.12	6.95	3.85	6.54	4.20	5.18	4.70
Gujarat	4.94	6.73	1.97	1.26	1.87	1.86	3.12	2.50
Haryana	1.96	3.09	1.31	0.11	1.15	0.80	1.50	1.16
Punjab	2.42	4.66	1.74	0.00	1.51	1.45	15.16	8.42
Goa	0.14	0.26	0.37	1.56	0.53	0.59	1.14	0.87
Sub-total	**18.91**	**29.86**	**12.34**	**6.78**	**11.60**	**8.90**	**26.10**	**17.65**
Middle Income States								
Andhra Pradesh	7.97	8.21	8.05	7.44	7.97	5.39	5.54	5.47
Karnataka	5.38	5.82	4.64	0.24	4.06	2.40	3.15	2.78
Kerala	3.49	3.14	3.41	2.95	3.35	2.01	3.46	2.75
West Bengal	8.16	8.62	7.33	3.00	6.76	8.20	3.96	6.04
Tamil Nadu	6.68	6.77	7.04	0.62	6.19	4.52	6.44	5.50
Sub-total	**31.68**	**32.56**	**30.47**	**14.25**	**28.33**	**22.52**	**22.55**	**22.54**

(Contd.)

(Contd.)

States	Population	SDP (Current prices)	F C Transfers Share in taxes	F C Transfers Grants	F C Transfers Total	P C Transfers Grants	P C Transfers Loans	P C Transfers Total
Low Income States								
Bihar	10.37	5.94	11.35	11.71	11.39	4.51	7.83	6.20
Madhya Pradesh	7.94	6.28	7.65	1.02	6.77	7.76	4.90	6.31
Orissa	3.78	2.71	4.87	0.18	4.25	3.45	3.41	3.43
Uttar Pradesh	16.69	13.11	16.19	11.82	15.61	17.16	14.17	15.64
Rajasthan	5.27	4.79	5.33	6.01	5.42	6.32	3.96	5.12
Sub-total	**44.05**	**32.83**	**45.39**	**30.74**	**43.44**	**39.20**	**34.27**	**36.70**
Special Category States								
Arunachal Pradesh	0.10	0.11	0.58	2.99	0.90	2.57	0.24	1.38
Assam	2.68	2.32	3.42	8.67	4.12	4.57	7.05	5.83
Himachal Pradesh	0.61	0.67	1.32	5.28	1.84	4.04	0.37	2.17
Jammu & Kashmir	0.93	0.80	2.28	15.40	4.01	4.23	7.57	5.93
Manipur	0.22	0.19	0.79	3.45	1.14	2.65	0.82	1.72
Meghalaya	0.21	0.16	0.56	0.00	0.49	2.50	0.21	1.33
Nagaland	0.15	0.11	0.87	4.29	1.32	2.00	0.21	1.09
Sikkim	0.05	0.06	0.18	0.00	0.15	1.72	0.17	0.93
Tripura	0.33	0.26	1.10	4.67	1.57	2.79	0.26	1.51
Mizoram	0.08	0.08	0.70	3.45	1.06	2.31	0.18	1.22
Sub-total	**5.36**	**4.76**	**11.80**	**48.20**	**16.60**	**29.38**	**17.08**	**23.11**
Total	**100**	**100**	**100**	**100**	**100**	**100**	**100**	**100**

Table 5.1 Contd.

Table 5.1
Direct Resource Flows to States in 1990-91

(Per cent)

States	*Transfers from Centrally Sponsored Schemes*			*Discretionary Transfers*		
	Grants	*Loans*	*Total*	*Grants*	*Loans*	*Total*
High Income States						
Maharashtra	10.53	3.31	10.35	6.79	2.08	3.72
Gujarat	4.36	1.07	4.28	0.00	8.65	5.64
Haryana	2.23	0.99	2.20	2.22	0.86	1.33
Punjab	1.47	1.87	1.48	6.52	1.17	3.03
Goa	0.17	0.29	0.17	0.10	0.00	0.03
Sub-total	**18.76**	**7.53**	**18.48**	**15.63**	**12.76**	**13.75**
Middle Income States						
Andhra Pradesh	7.03	1.78	6.90	6.97	2.66	4.16
Karnataka	5.43	5.67	5.44	2.61	1.45	1.85
Kerala	3.51	8.82	3.64	5.18	3.46	4.06
West Bengal	3.43	10.26	3.60	8.47	4.88	6.13
Tamil Nadu	6.74	5.14	6.70	8.53	7.40	7.79
Sub-total	**26.14**	**31.67**	**26.28**	**31.77**	**19.85**	**23.99**
Low Income States						
Bihar	6.65	7.09	6.66	2.24	2.73	2.56
Madhya Pradesh	8.79	6.51	8.73	6.14	1.38	3.03
Orissa	5.53	11.93	5.69	20.94	16.47	18.03
Uttar Pradesh	19.26	10.19	19.04	7.71	2.88	4.56
Rajasthan	7.10	10.90	7.19	1.08	4.09	3.04
Sub-total	**47.33**	**46.62**	**47.31**	**38.11**	**27.55**	**31.22**
Special Category States						
Arunachal Pradesh	0.58	0.76	0.59	0.23	1.31	0.93
Assam	3.02	3.20	3.02	4.81	24.51	17.66
Himachal Pradesh	1.25	2.99	1.30	1.47	7.86	5.62
Jammu & Kashmir	0.00	0.00	0.00	4.22	0.02	1.48
Manipur	0.41	0.61	0.41	0.43	0.09	0.21
Meghalaya	0.34	2.27	0.39	0.74	0.08	0.31
Nagaland	0.99	2.46	1.03	0.90	2.94	2.23
Sikkim	0.00	0.86	0.02	0.00	0.02	0.01
Tripura	0.61	0.49	0.61	1.71	1.91	1.84
Mizoram	0.56	0.53	0.56	0.00	1.10	0.71
Sub-total	**7.76**	**14.17**	**7.93**	**14.51**	**39.84**	**31.00**
Total	**100**	**100**	**100**	**100**	**100**	**100**

Table 5.1 to be concluded.

Table 5.1
Direct Resource Flows to States in 1990-91

(Per cent)

State	*Transfers for Natural Calamities*	*Total Fiscal Transfers*	*Share in Small Savings*	*Market Borrowings Average of 1986-91*
High Income States				
Maharashtra	9.34	6.22	14.24	4.37
Gujarat	0.00	2.56	8.69	3.78
Haryana	0.00	1.27	2.69	2.10
Punjab	0.00	3.90	4.33	2.10
Goa	0.21	0.57	0.59	0.21
Sub-total	**9.55**	**14.52**	**30.54**	**12.56**
Middle Income States				
Andhra Pradesh	0.00	6.70	6.39	9.87
Karnataka	5.73	3.67	3.73	5.62
Kerala	6.58	3.26	2.27	6.01
West Bengal	0.00	6.05	12.15	6.55
Tamil Nadu	0.00	6.05	4.03	8.15
Sub-total	**12.31**	**25.73**	**28.57**	**36.20**
Low Income States				
Bihar	7.43	8.56	7.46	10.84
Madhya Pradesh	7.85	6.63	3.44	4.44
Orissa	16.16	5.07	2.73	5.84
Uttar Pradesh	19.09	15.40	16.60	18.26
Rajasthan	26.31	5.60	4.92	6.67
Sub-total	**76.84**	**41.26**	**35.15**	**46.05**
Special Category States				
Arunachal Pradesh	0.00	1.02	0.07	0.11
Assam	0.00	5.31	2.18	1.24
Himachal Pradesh	0.00	2.09	1.47	0.74
Jammu & Kashmir	0.00	4.01	0.88	0.77
Manipur	0.21	1.19	0.14	0.39
Meghalaya	0.25	0.75	0.19	0.15
Nagaland	0.00	1.25	0.31	0.59
Sikkim	0.00	0.39	0.02	0.17
Tripura	0.64	1.44	0.41	0.98
Mizoram	0.21	1.03	0.07	0.05
Sub-total	**1.31**	**18.48**	**5.74**	**5.19**
Total	**100**	**100**	**100**	**100**

Note: SDP = State Domestic Product, FC = Finance Commission, PC = Planning Commission

Table 5.2
Other Resource Flows to States

State	Population	SDP (Current Prices)	Central Government Public Enterprises Investment on		Assistance Disbursed by AFI's* Average
	1991	1990-91	1- 4- '85	31-3-'91	of 1987-91
High Income States					
Maharashtra	9.45	15.12	17.72	19.03	21.98
Gujarat	4.94	6.73	4.13	5.33	13.04
Haryana	1.96	3.09	0.96	0.93	2.79
Punjab	0.14	0.26	0.04	0.20	3.84
Goa	2.42	4.66	1.31	0.77	0.74
Sub-total	**18.91**	**29.85**	**24.16**	**26.26**	**42.39**
Middle Income States					
Andhra Pradesh	7.97	8.21	9.46	11.21	9.19
Karnataka	5.38	5.82	3.09	2.33	5.17
Kerala	3.49	3.14	1.94	1.60	2.00
West Bengal	8.16	8.62	7.80	7.60	4.69
Tamil Nadu	6.68	6.77	5.94	6.17	9.59
Sub-total	**31.68**	**32.56**	**28.23**	**28.91**	**30.64**
Low Income States					
Bihar	10.37	5.94	13.60	9.25	1.99
Madhya Pradesh	7.94	6.28	12.58	11.16	6.01
Orissa	3.78	2.71	6.99	5.97	2.55
Uttar Pradesh	16.69	13.11	5.90	8.85	10.19
Rajasthan	5.27	4.79	1.51	1.92	3.69
Sub-total	**44.05**	**32.83**	**40.58**	**37.15**	**24.43**
Special Category States					
Arunachal Pradesh	0.10	0.11	0.00	0.07	0.01
Assam	2.68	2.32	5.71	4.72	0.67
Himachal Pradesh	0.61	0.67	0.49	1.20	0.89
Jammu & Kashmir	0.93	0.80	0.11	1.10	0.58
Manipur	0.22	0.19	0.31	0.14	0.07
Meghalaya	0.21	0.16	0.00	0.00	0.12
Nagaland	0.15	0.11	0.17	0.11	0.06
Sikkim	0.05	0.06	0.00	0.01	0.04
Tripura	0.33	0.26	0.22	0.31	0.04
Mizoram	0.08	0.08	0.00	0.02	0.06
Sub-total	**5.36**	**4.76**	**7.01**	**7.68**	**2.54**
Total	**100**	**100**	**100**	**100**	**100**

Table 5.2 continued.

Table 5.2
..er Resource Flows to States

(Per cent)

State	*Credit from Public Sector Banks*		*Credit Deposit Ratio in Public Sector Banks*		*Companies Limited by Shares (Paid up Capital as on)*		
	1969	*1991*	*1969*	*1991*	*All Companies 31-3-'92*	*Govt. Companies 31-3-'92*	*Non-Govt. Companies 31-3-'92*
High Income States							
Maharashtra	33.76	23.65	1.01	0.80	17.07	8.34	32.74
Gujarat	7.22	6.94	0.49	0.61	7.19	6.37	8.65
Haryana	0.86	2.25	0.47	0.59	0.80	0.55	1.25
Punjab	1.86	4.30	0.27	0.44	0.78	0.18	1.86
Goa	NA	NA	NA	NA	0.51	0.17	1.13
Sub-total	**43.70**	**37.14**	**0.77**	**0.68**	**26.35**	**15.61**	**45.63**
Middle Income States							
Andhra Pradesh	4.52	8.23	1.01	0.83	10.80	13.28	6.35
Karnataka	5.30	7.32	0.76	0.89	5.67	5.31	6.33
Kerala	2.85	3.52	0.66	0.59	2.44	2.82	1.75
West Bengal	19.47	8.38	1.15	0.52	21.97	26.56	13.72
Tamil Nadu	11.53	11.36	1.33	0.98	8.13	6.53	10.99
Sub-total	**43.67**	**38.81**	**1.06**	**0.75**	**49.01**	**54.50**	**39.14**

State	Credit from Public Sector Banks		Credit Deposit Ratio in Public Sector Banks		Companies Limited by Shares (Paid up Capital as on)		
	1969	1991	1969	1991	All Companies 31-3-'92	Govt. Companies 31-3-'92	Non-Govt. Companies 31-3-'92
Low Income States							
Bihar	1.93	3.33	0.31	0.39	5.32	7.68	1.08
Madhya Pradesh	2.34	5.39	0.59	0.75	5.46	7.38	2.01
Orissa	0.52	1.92	0.48	0.78	3.93	4.99	2.05
Uttar Pradesh	5.69	8.64	0.46	0.48	5.20	4.76	6.01
Rajasthan	1.41	2.71	0.52	0.58	1.85	1.66	2.19
Sub-total	**11.89**	**21.99**	**0.45**	**0.54**	**21.76**	**26.47**	**13.34**
Special Category States							
Arunachal Pradesh	NA	NA	NA	NA	0.02	0.02	0.03
Assam	0.48	1.00	0.39	0.49	1.21	1.10	1.42
Himachal Pradesh	0.13	0.48	0.28	0.36	0.52	0.70	0.21
Jammu & Kashmir	0.03	0.27	0.05	0.32	0.19	0.24	0.11
Manipur	0.01	0.07	0.14	0.72	0.05	0.07	0.01
Meghalaya	0.09	0.06	0.28	0.18	0.69	1.03	0.08
Nagaland	0.00	0.08	0.06	0.38	0.13	0.17	0.05
Sikkim	NA	NA	NA	NA	0.00	0.00	0.00
Tripura	0.01	0.10	0.04	0.45	0.05	0.08	0.00
Mizoram	NA	NA	NA	NA	0.02	0.03	0.00
Sub-total	**0.75**	**2.06**	**0.26**	**0.40**	**2.88**	**3.44**	**1.91**
Total	**100**	**100**	**100**	**100**	**100**	**100**	**100**

Note: Credit-deposit ratio is not in per cent

Table 5.2 to be concluded.

Table 5.2
Other Resource Flows to States

(Per cent)

State	*Special Compensation to Farmers on Decontrolled Fertilizer Rubi 1992-93*	*Distribution of Foreign Investment of IEMS** from 1-8-'91 to 31-8-'93*	*Central Assistance Released for Externally added Projects (Rs. Cr.) 1980-85*	*1990-91*	*Plan Expenditure for Irrigation & Flood Control 1988-89*
High Income States					
Maharashtra	4.96	19.72	20.68	12.07	15.92
Gujarat	4.33	15.20	13.45	14.92	7.05
Haryana	5.94	3.99	5.25	3.04	3.21
Punjab	13.07	4.06	4.22	0.35	2.01
Goa	0.03	0.48	0.00	0.00	0.56
Sub-total	**28.33**	**43.45**	**43.60**	**30.38**	**28.75**
Middle Income States					
Andhra Pradesh	7.87	8.29	7.06	5.87	9.94
Karnataka	5.17	4.87	6.14	5.00	4.90
Kerala	2.90	1.03	2.85	3.98	2.22
West Bengal	8.28	3.01	5.87	3.55	2.86
Tamil Nadu	10.13	4.90	5.42	12.30	1.81
Sub-total	**34.35**	**22.10**	**27.34**	**30.70**	**21.73**

State	*Special Compensation to Farmers on Decontrolled Fertilizer Rabi 1992-93*	*Distribution of Foreign Investment of IEMS** from 1-8-'91 to 31-8-'93*	*Central Assistance Released for Externally added Projects (Rs. Cr.)*		*Plan Expenditure for Irrigation & Flood Control 1988-89*
			1980-85	*1990-91*	
Low Income States					
Bihar	6.41	1.30	2.22	1.71	11.19
Madhya Pradesh	5.38	11.65	7.72	4.12	10.36
Orissa	0.81	1.17	6.16	4.05	5.40
Uttar Pradesh	19.29	12.89	7.32	25.25	13.87
Rajasthan	4.33	5.17	4.03	1.07	4.09
Sub-total	**36.22**	**32.18**	**27.45**	**36.20**	**44.91**
Special Category States					
Arunachal Pradesh	0.00	0.00	0.00	0.00	0.16
Assam	0.41	0.17	0.60	0.23	1.51
Himachal Pradesh	0.27	1.63	0.77	1.90	0.55
Jammu & Kashmir	0.30	0.00	0.24	0.60	1.05
Manipur	0.00	0.00	0.00	0.00	0.61
Meghalaya	0.01	0.00	0.00	0.00	0.08
Nagaland	0.00	0.00	0.00	0.00	0.08
Sikkim	0.02	0.01	0.00	0.00	0.06
Tripura	0.06	0.47	0.00	0.00	0.45
Mizoram	0.01	0.00	0.00	0.00	0.06
Sub-total	**1.08**	**2.28**	**1.61**	**2.73**	**4.61**
Total	**100**	**100**	**100**	**100**	**100**

* AFI's includes IDBI, IFCI, ICICI, LIC, GIC, IRBI, SFCs and STDCs.

** Industrial entrepreneurial memoranda.

10

A Perspective on Centre-State Relations in the Context of India's Economic Reforms

V.V. Bhanoji Rao

INTRODUCTION

Since 1991, significant reforms have been introduced in practically every sphere of economic policy to bring about a fundamental change in the framework within which the Indian economy operates. The policy reforms included virtual elimination of industrial licensing and open-door policy toward foreign direct and portfolio investment, substantial reduction of import duties, current account convertibility of the Indian rupee, streamlining direct and indirect taxation, moving towards a vastly increased role for the private sector including a role in infrastructure and banking and divestiture of state enterprises. Clearly, the Indian economy as a whole and the various constituent regions are now operating in an environment that has hardly any resemblance to the regime that existed for four and a half decades since independence. Centre-state relations also cannot be on the same basis as before.

The opening up of the Indian economy to foreign direct investment has propelled various initiatives from the states. Karnataka, Gujarat and Maharashtra have been particularly successful in attracting FDI. The governments of Bihar, Rajasthan, Tamil Nadu and West Bengal have also been in the forefront to attract FDI. The hope is that, as a result of all these additional investments, the national economic growth rate will soon be in the 6.5 to 7 per cent range and will become the basis for employment growth and poverty alleviation.

REGIONAL DISPARITIES : RETROSPECT AND PROSPECT

India is like a mega nation of several nations; in population size, some of the states are comparable to the major countries in the world. Uttar Pradesh (Population; 138.8 million in 1991) has more people than Japan, Bangladesh or Pakistan. Bihar (86.3 million) is comparable to Mexico. The states of Maharashtra, West Bengal, Andhra Pradesh and Madhya Pradesh (each with population in the range 66 to 80 million) are larger than West Germany, Philippines, Italy, United Kingdom and France. Tamil Nadu (55.6 million) is about the size of Thailand, Turkey and Iran, while Karnataka and Rajasthan (44-45 million) are comparable to South Korea. There are also seven 7 smaller states with less than 2 million people each and most union territories have population size of less than a million each.

Based on Table 1, it can be seen that the per capita regional net domestic product varied from Rs. 2122 in Bihar to Rs. 7081 in Punjab in 1989-90. The World Bank classified low income countries as those with a GNP per capita of less than \$580 (Rs. 9686) in 1989. All the Indian states, therefore, fall under the low income category. As many as eight states had net domestic product per capita of less than \$200, while 11 were in the \$200-\$300 category and four in the \$300-\$400 range. Punjab and Goa have per capita NDP higher than \$400. There is no systematic variation in per capita NDP in relation to population size, although some of the relatively large states (in population) do come under the low NDP per capita group. (The correlation coefficient between population and NDP per capita is -0.21, too low, though negative).

Growth rates of regional per capita NDP for the 1960s, 1970s and 1980s are also shown in Table 1. India's largest state, Uttar Pradesh recorded a 2.4 per cent growth in the 1980s as against 0.8 and 0.9 in the 1960s and 1970s respectively. The other large regions that have improved their growth performance in the 1980s compared to the 1960s and 1970s are Andhra Pradesh, Bihar, Madhya Pradesh, Maharashtra and West Bengal. The good performance of the large regions had greatly contributed to the relatively high growth rate of the country as a whole in the 1980s. The correlation between per capita NDP and its growth rate is only 0.16 while the correlation between population size and per capita NDP growth rate is almost zero (-0.03). Rates of economic growth are thus not biased in favour of either the rich or the populous states.

The coefficient of variation (mean upon standard deviation) of regional per capita product remained constant at around 32 per cent in 1970-71, 1980-81 and 1989-90 indicating no change in regional inequalities in product per capita. But, the coefficient of variation has increased to 36 per cent in 1992-93. (Data on regional product per capita and infant mortality rate for 1992-93 and female literacy rate for 1991 are given in Table 2).

PROSPECTS

Of much significance than the slight rise in the coefficient of variation (c.v.) of regional product per capita is the relatively high c.v. values of infant mortality (c.v. 30 per cent) and female literacy (c.v. 40 per cent). It should be of much greater importance to reduce the regional variations in infant mortality and female literacy than the reduction in the variations in product per capita.

Achieving substantial reductions in the inequalities in regional per capita product levels will be difficult, given the difference in regional resources (physical and human) and capabilities. In addition, while in the past, the states went along with the overall Indian legacy of slow growth, the new economic policy is most likely to unleash growth impulses in the states with unequal rates of economic growth, in all likelihood widening regional disparities in product per capita.

It is therefore important to recognise that reducing regional differentials in product per capita may not be the priority development objective for the future. Instead, the top development objectives for each and every state must be eradication of poverty and illiteracy, achieving full employment, eliminating the various dimensions of gender inequality and raising life expectancy to levels close to 75-80 which are all important facets of human and social development. Significantly, their achievement will also be manifest as a reduction in the regional variation in social indicators such as female literacy. However, none of these objectives has any intrinsic relationship with eliminating inequalities in regional product per capita. Furthermore, since the accomplishment of almost all the objectives of human and social development, and most notably poverty reduction, will be facilitated when high rather than low economic growth rates prevail, it is most likely that a narrowing of regional inequalities in social and human development may co-exist with a widening of inequality in regional product per capita.

IMPLICATIONS FOR CENTRE-STATE RELATIONS

In the final analysis, economic reforms will be judged on the basis of whether or not they have helped to achieve (i) the immediate objectives of a higher national economic growth rate and the accompanying reduction in poverty, requiring the state to achieve economic growth commensurate with their potentials as well as (ii) the ultimate objective of the highest standard and quality of life for each and every Indian while safeguarding the unity and territorial integrity of the country. Furthermore, given that economic growth will increasingly be private sector driven, states' attention on social development goals will have to be significantly raised. From the point of view of economic and social development of the regions, two aspects of centre-state relations are of much significance : division of functions between the centre and the states and the conduct of centre-state fiscal relations. The relevant issues are addressed in the rest of the paper.

DISTRIBUTION OF POWERS BETWEEN THE CENTRE AND STATES

Prevailing Situation

The Constitution of India provides for an exhaustive listing of the functions of Centre and states. The Seventh Scheduled (relating to Article 246) has - List I - Union List, List II - State List, and List III - Concurrent List (There is no specified list of functions for and responsibility to the local governments).

The Union List, as one would expect, includes functions which have a direct bearing on national unity and security foreign affairs, defence, communications, currency, central banking, patents, weights and measures, quality standards, fishing and fisheries beyond territorial waters, sanctioning of cinema film for exhibition, industrial disputes concerning Union employees, national libraries and museums, elections, central services, Parliament matters, audit of accounts of the Union and the states, Supreme Court and High Courts. Over and above these, the Union List has a number of functions which embody the spirit of an interventionist state and/or a strong central government. In this regard, of the more than 90 functions in List I, the following may be mentioned; railways, national highways, ports, airways, aircraft and aerodromes, foreign loans, lotteries, incorporation, regulation and winding up of trading corporations, including banking, insurance and financial corporations the control of which by the Union is declared by Parliament by law to be expedient in the public interest, regulation and development of oilfields and mineral oil resources and other dangerously inflammable substances, mines and mineral development declared by Parliament to be under the Union, regulation and control of salt manufacture, scientific and technical education institutions financed by the Government of India and declared by Parliament by law to be institutions of national importance, and any matter not enumerated in List II or List III including any tax not mentioned in either of those lists.

The State List has a total of 66 items. Ignoring such items as burials and burial grounds, the relatively more important items are the following : public order, prisons and reformatories, public health and sanitation, hospitals and dispensaries, production, manufacture, transport, purchase and sale of intoxicating liquors, relief of disabled, communications not specified in List I, agriculture including agricultural education and research, water projects not in List I, land rights, land tenure, rents etc., fisheries, trade and commerce within the state, markets and fairs, land revenue and land records, taxes on agricultural income, and other state taxes and municipal taxes.

List III, the Concurrent List, has a total of 47 items. They include criminal law and procedure, preventive detention, inter-state transfer of prisoners, and marriage and divorce. Some of the items of significance to economic and social development are : economic and social planning. trade unions, industrial and labour disputes, social security and social insurance, employment and unemployment, labour welfare, education except those relating to items in List I, legal, medical and other professions, production, supply and distribution of production outside the Union sphere, food stuff including edible oils, cattle fodder, raw cotton, and raw jute, factories, electricity and acquisition of property.

Historically, political evolution has been from less to more decentralization and federalism (Basu, 1987; 2). The trend in India over the past four and a half decades, however, has been towards more centralization:

> .... We have today entrenched bureaucracies at the Centre in the name of education, health, nutrition, family planning, water supply, sanitation, shelter, women's development, child development, social welfare — with no substantial contribution to make to those fields apart from channelling centrally controlled funding. And each of these fields happens to be the direct constitutional responsibility of the state governments. Rather than further devolve the related functions to the level of the local community, who alone can perceive the need and preserve the aims of the social sectors, the trend in recent years has been to delegate upward and centralise control (Matthew, 1990;8).

CHELLIAH'S REFORM PROPOSALS

Raja Chelliah (1991 a) in his L.K. Jha Memorial Lecture outlined a proposal for a decentralized polity. In the introductory remarks, after pointing to the diversities of language and culture in India, he notes that the Indian people were and still are ideal candidates for being governed under a truly federal constitution. "As in the case of the United States of America, for example, such a constitution would have had the necessary minimum provisions to safeguard the unity of the country and to foster a national economy with a common market; its other provisions would have largely been designed to enable and support the autonomous actions of the state governments, subject to the fundamental principles of the Constitution being observed". (*ibid.* 2).

The basic premise to move towards a decentralized polity is stated as follows : "In order to move towards a decentralized polity, there is need to transfer much of the allocation decisions from the Planning Commission and the Central Government (and to an extent from the State Governments also) to the market". (*ibid.* 14). Within this framework, Chelliah formulated a number of proposals (*ibid.* 14-22). Those relating to overall liberalization and marketisation have already been implemented since 1991. Others which are still relevant are noted below:

(a) *Transfer of some subjects from the Union List and the Concurrent List to the State List* : A number of suggestions were made in this matter, among others, by the Centre-State Relations Committee appointed by the Tamil Nadu Government (The Rajamannar Committee). More recently, the Sarkaria Commission "which basically accepted the existing framework and the centralized economic policy regime has suggested the partial shifting of one entry (97 in the Union List)." The Entry gives the residual powers to the Union. Chelliah says (*ibid.* 15), "I believe that the Sarkaria's recommendation in this regard that all residuary powers except in the field of taxation be given to the states should be accepted. Another good case for transfer is Education - Entry 25 in the Concurrent list. Education except higher education should be transferred back to the State List. Other important Entries could be identified for the transfer."

(b) *Stipulating that in respect of specified subjects in the Concurrent List, the Centre would only set the standards and the basic pattern* : Chelliah suggests that the Inter-State Council, established under Article 263 of the Constitution, should discuss the whole matter of transfer of Entries and restricting the use of Concurrent Powers by the Centre.

(c) *Re-defining the role of the Planning Commission and re-designing the planning process* : The role of the Planning Commission is envisaged as follows : long term policy planning, reviewing the efficiency of resources and identifying ways of raising it, preparation of the macro-economic framework for the five year plans, allocation of resources for the Plan in a few non-enterprise areas in the Central public sector (investment in which will be out of the budget), allocation of capital funds to the states for meeting a part of their Plan investments, etc.

(d) *Introducing safeguards to prevent the misuse of special overriding powers given to the Centre such as Article 356* : Here, Chelliah suggests that in the light of experience it is necessary to prevent or at least minimize the misuse of certain special provis-ions by the party in power at the Centre such as Article 356. The Article refers to the imposition of President's rule in a state.

DIRECTIONS FOR REFORM

Many of Chelliah's recommendations are sound and should be acceptable. However, Chelliah does not seem to go far enough in the matter of states obtaining reasonable political decentralization, and economic autonomy within the framework of a strong and united nation.

Towards a High Degree of Decentralization. The long-term direction here should be for the Constitution to specify only one Union list of subjects and leave all residuary subjects and powers to the states. The Union list need not be limited to defence, currency and foreign affairs. However, it should not be a long list of 97 subjects (including the residuary powers). The issue should be looked at as what the minimum Union list should contain rather than what should be transferred from the Union list to the states. This is important for the states' overall development via decentralized decision making.

Decentralization becomes a necessary complement to economic liberalization of the recent years, aimed at marketisation and globalization. "In a federal setting there is a close link between the ideological stance of a regime and the concept of 'levels' of government. The more a regime is positively oriented to welfare statism and regulated growth, the more there is a strong possibility for the central level to grow powerful and the more there is a chance for a sort of hegemonic federalism to emerge. And, the more a regime is liberal and is related to the instrumental value of a market economy, the more there is a possibility of inter-governmental relations being based on decentralized networking rather than hierarchical control." (Ray, 1992; 147).

Since there is an Inter-State Council in place to deliberate on matters concerning centre state relations, the Council should take up the issue of how the present system of Union, State and Concurrent lists can change smoothly and move towards a system comprising only one Union List along with a Constitutional provision that delegates all residuary functions and powers to the states. The Council could also examine the desirability of applying the same principle in regard to the local governments.

CENTRE-STATE FISCAL RELATIONS

Constitutional Provisions

Of all the powers exercised at the various levels of government, the most important ones relate to the fiscal realm. International experience shows two essential approaches to the distribution of tax revenues : first, as in Germany and Brazil where the constitution stipulates the distribution, and second, as in Malaysia and Pakistan, where a commission meets periodically to deliberate and decide on the sharing of revenue between the central and provincial governments. India followed the second approach.

The assignment of tax powers in the Indian Constitution appears to be based on two considerations; (i) any one tax should be assigned to only one level of government, and (ii) taxes which have economy-wide implications or which can be collected efficiently and economically only by the Central Government should be assigned to the Centre (Sinha, 1987 :172 and Chelliah, 1991b; 6-7). The resulting system gave the Centre the power to levy taxes on non-agricultural income and wealth, and excise (except on liquor) and foreign trade taxes. States are empowered to levy taxes on land (land revenue) and agriculture (agricultural income tax), sales taxes (except taxes on inter-state trade), excise on liquor, and taxation of inland transport except railways.

In addition, local governments have the power to levy property tax and entry tax.

The Constitution (Article 269), provides for a number of duties and taxes levied and collected by the Union and assigned to states (instead of forming part of the Consolidated Fund of India). Such duties and levies include duties in respect of succession to property other than agricultural land; estate duty in respect of property other than agricultural land; terminal taxes on goods or passengers carried by rail, sea or air, taxes on railway fares and freights; taxes on other than stamp duties on transactions in stock-exchanges and futures markets; taxes on the sale or purchase of newspapers and on advertisements published therein; taxes on sale or purchase of other goods (other than newspapers) where the sale/purchase takes place in the course of inter-state trade or commerce; taxes on the consignment of goods (whether the consignment is to the person making it or any other person), where such consignment takes place in the course of inter-state trade or commerce.

Article 270 of the Constitution relates to the distribution of taxes levied and collected by the Union. A prescribed percentage of revenue from taxes on income (other than agricultural income) will be assigned to the states. This percentage will be determined by the Finance Commission. If any surcharge were to be levied on income, revenue from such surcharges will form part of the Consolidated Fund of India (Article 271). Revenue from Union Excise (levied and collected by the Union), may be distributed between the Union and the states (Article 272). Grants-in-aid are also provided for to be paid to states from the Consolidated Fund of India (Article 275). Article 280 refers to the five-yearly appointment of a Finance

Commission and its terms of reference. (In passing, it may be noted that Article 293 restricts the borrowing power of the states to borrowing within the territory of India). The Finance Commission thus plays an important role in the distribution of fiscal resources between the Centre and the states.

Resources for the State Plans were made available by the Planning Commission in the form of grants and loan. Since 1969, the assistance is allocated on the basis of a formula (known as the Gadgil formula). The latest (modified) version of the formula of October 1990 works as follows. After earmarking the assistance for the special category states, the resources available for distribution are allocated to the major states with weights assigned to various factors; 55 per cent to population, 25 per cent to per capita state domestic product, 5 per cent to fiscal management and 15 per cent to the special problems of the states (Govinda Rao and Chelliah, 1990; 42). The major states obtained grants and loans in the ratio of 30 to 70 while the ratio for special category states was 90 to 10.

Problems and Issues

As the most productive and progressive taxes are in the Central sphere, and as the states have the responsibility to deliver key social and economic services, there arises a vertical fiscal imbalance (Govinda Rao and Chelliah, 1990; 14-15). The various Finance Commissions tried to counter the imbalance via the distribution of tax revenues and grants-in-aid. Over the years, the states' share of Central taxes rose from "50 per cent of income tax in 1950-51 to 85 per cent of income tax and 45 per cent of Union excise duties in the period 1985-86 to 1989-90...." (Chelliah, 1991b; 15). In spite of this, the financial position of most states was not sound and there were constant demands for higher states' share in Central taxes. The Centre's finances too were in no better shape as evidenced, for instance, in fiscal crisis by the turn of the 1980s.

There were also problems in regard to the loans and grants provided for State Plans. Because incremental recurrent expenditure during a Plan period is financed from the Plan resources, at the end of the Plan period, the Central and state Governments faced a rise in recurrent expenditures. If Plans achieved rapid economic growth and if this in turn lead to substantial increase in tax revenues, the rise in recurrent expenditure would not be burdensome. In actual practice, however, states' growing recurrent expenditures have to be financed from increased Central allocations to states. The loans to states, which are for development purposes, have been used at times to cover current expenditures. "In the event, part of the of the loans has been used to cover revenue deficits and whatever was invested did not bring sufficient returns to cover interest and amortization. Hence the states have been hard put to repay loans. To ease the situation, the Finance Commissions rescheduled debt repayments of the states to the Centre and also wrote-off some loans.

Since the Centre has been borrowing to give loans to the states, the rescheduling and write-off by the Finance Commission led to a faster growth of the debt and larger interest burden at the Central level" (Chelliah, 1991b; 19). The Ninth Finance Commission, however chose to make the terms of Central loans to the states more reasonable rather than recommend rescheduling and write-off of existing debts. Despite this recent trend in fiscal prudence, the cumulative experience in regard to Centre-state fiscal relations, has only added to the overall fiscal imbalance of the country.

Two general problems have cropped up in the overall working of inter-Governmental transfer in India (Govinda Rao and Chelliah, 1990: 44-46). First, resource transfers by Planning and Finance Commissions for Plan and non-Plan purposes respectively have posed difficulties in the clear pursuit of objectives of the transfer due to overlapping roles and duplication of functions. The two Commissions' process has also induced the states to adopt diverse strategies : overestimating resources to get larger plans approved by the Planning Commission and underestimating state revenues to obtain large transfer from the Finance Commission. Second, the transfer by the two Commissions did not always address horizontal equity across the states.

The distributive criteria used by the Finance Commission also came under criticism. In the very nature of things, it is difficult to arrive at a fool-proof formula for distribution, given the multiple objectives of such distribution and the diverse levels of economic, social and administrative development of the states.

Over the years, the states have been critical of the functioning of the present system of Centre-state fiscal relations. For instance some of the states complained of the absence of their representatives on the Finance Commissions. They also complained about the Central levies of additional excise duties and surcharges. On three occasions, when the Central Government did not accept the recommendations of the Finance Commission, there were protest by the states (Fadia and Manaria, 1990; 136). There were also complaints from time to time about the Centre having far too much access to capital resources. The states wanted a higher share of plan transfers in the form of grants. States also have grouses about the transfer of external loan/grant funds for state projects : the full amount may not be transferred or terms may be more stringent than the original terms governing the loan/grant.

SOME EARLIER REFORM SUGGESTIONS

Sarkaria Commission Recommendations : The Commission made a large number of recommendations. Some of the important ones are (i) in-depth and comprehensive consideration of agricultural income taxation, (ii) constitutional provision for sharing of Corporation Tax between the Centre and the states (and consequently bringing down the shares of states in Income Tax and Union Excise duties), (iii) a Finance Commission Cell/Division to be located in the Planning Commission for monitoring the behaviour of states' finance, (iv) legislation for the levy of a Consignment Tax, (v) constitutional amendment to add the subject of taxation of radio and television advertisements (in Article 269), (vi) introduction of tax from municipal bonds, and (vii) Union Government to consider placing at the disposal of a state, free foreign exchange to the extent of a small fraction of its annual budget. After an examination of the recommendation of the Sarkaria Commission, Gulati (1991) concludes that the recommendations simply add up the maintenance of status quo.

Chelliah' s Proposals : Having regard to the complaints of the states about the present arrangements and the difficulties faced by successive Finance Commissions in coping with the pressure from states for increasing fiscal devolution, Chelliah says that the solution may be to constitutionally fix the percentage share of tax revenue of the Centre which should go to the states. It could be specified, in his view, that the Centre would share 25 per cent of its total tax revenues with the states. The role of successive Finance Commissions would then be to look at the requirements of backward or poorer regions and recommend equalization grants-in-aid. If these are put into operation, the states will be largely on their own and there is no question of filling their deficits. The states will have to manage their finances.

NEED FOR REFORMS

Comments on the Devolution Recommendations of the Tenth Finance Commission : The Commission has "recommended a basic change in determining the devolvable tax revenues of the Centre by pooling the proceeds of all taxes instead of going tax by tax accepting a long standing advice from experts". (Bagchi, 1995: 1985). Despite this complement, a number of limitations of the recommendations have been noted in the recent reviews and critiques of them (Bagchi, *ibid.*, for instance). For the purpose of this paper, the following correlation are of relevance. The one and only high and significant negative correlation coefficient happens to be the one between per capita transfer and state per capita GDP. The devolution package is thus concerned with giving more to the less developed regions in the hope that they will benefit from this. Though this has been the practice all these years since the Finance Commissions have been in existence, one may say that such a practice has meant providing incentives for not moving up the economic ladder. Even if such an allegation may not hold water, the fact remains that the devolutions have no significant correlation with social development indicators.

Selected Correlation Coefficients Based on States Data

Item	*State per capita GDP (92-93)*	*Infant mortality rate*	*Female literacy rate*
Grants per capita	-0.22	-0.16	-0.26
Total Transfers per capita	-0.89	-0.37	-0.26

Economic Autonomy, Responsibility and Accountability: The growth of centrally sponsored projects, annual Plan consultations and the numerous trips of state ministers and officials to New Delhi provide a window for the states to safely blame the Centre for lapses in their own economic and social development performance. For instance, it is not uncommon for state ministers to promise to their people, projects of popular appeal and then point to the lack of central assistance or approval as the cause for delays or deferment. The situation can lead to the states only looking at the expenditure side of economic performance without regard to state level resource mobilization, productivity of expenditure and economy and efficiency in resource allocation.

In the case of the burden of external indebtedness, the lack of states' concern is most conspicuously visible. Since external borrowing and international trade are Central subjects, states may naturally be unmindful of the debt service and export obligations of the country, even though they are eager to obtain externally funded projects. Because of its external trade and debt responsibilities, the Centre is obliged to have a hold on all activities even remotely connected to them. Thus, scientific and, industrial research, higher education, mineral exploration, export promotion, foreign investment approval and similar subjects are all under central control. However, with controllers (bureaucrats) stationed in Delhi close to the offices of the Centre, and the activity located in one state or the other, the costs of coordination and control will be ever increasing.

DIRECTIONS FOR REFORMS

Medium Term : The need of the hour is bridging the gaps in social and human development across the states in order to lay the groundwork for economic growth in line with their potentials. This would require an approach to Centre-state fiscal relations broadly in line with the proposal of Chelliah, comprising (1) a constitutional provision for sharing all tax revenues as per a fixed proportion and (2) re-defining the role of the finance commissions to allocating grants to states for education and health in line with state-wise targets to be achieved. The second is analogous to the Indonesian practice or allocating presidential funds (known as *inpres* funds) to provinces and even lower level regions exclusively for specific social development objectives. Use of the funds received under (1) need not be a matter of concern to the Centre at all. States could do what they like as per their own economic and social development goals and aspirations. In regard to (2), the grants should be exclusively for the first 10 years for education and essential health and nutritional provisions. There should be no need whatsoever for central supervision and control here also. Instead, the finance commissions could review the results achieved against the targets set. Grant allocations should be strictly in accordance with the needs of each state in regard to achieving highest desirable goals (e.g. life expectancy of 70 years and 100 per cent female enrolments in the first 10 years of education).

Long-term : In the long term, that is after a desirable level of social development has been achieved in the whole country, and when international trade taxes cease to be of importance due to the globalisation of the country, the states alone could levy and collect indirect taxes (hopefully in the form of value added taxes) within the framework of the common market, while taxes are levied and collected by the Centre. In this approach it should be possible to do away with the Finance Commission and provide in the Constitution the sharing percentages for direct taxes. One could even envisage a time when direct taxes would just about be enough to sustain the central expenditures which by then could be limited to those essential to safeguard the unity and territorial integrity of the nation.

IN SUM

The states in India are of all sizes and potentials in terms of resources-both physical and human. Economic autonomy, responsibility and accountability at the state level, therefore, can produce India's own Indonesia, Korea and Taiwan. This can only be done by the states' own efforts and by their exposure to the rest of the world. Seen in this light it is not difficult to endorse the recommendation of Ashok Mitra (1975, quoted in Chelliah, 1991a) "to transfer the primary responsibility for economic management to the federating sates themselves." He envisages that the Centre "will no longer be directly responsible for economic management and growth. The prerogative will be transferred to the states."

REFERENCES

Bagchi, Amaresh (1995). Tenets of Tenth Finance Commission : A Critique. *Economic and Political Weekly,* 30(31,32), August 5-12, 1985-1992.

Basu, Durga Das (1987). *Comparative Federalism,* New Delhi : Prentice Hall of India.

Chelliah, R.J. (1991). *Intergovernmental Fiscal Relations and Macroeconomic Management in India,* New Delhi; National Institute of Public Finance and Policy (Mimeo).

Chelliah, R.J. (1991a). *Towards a Decentralised Polity,* New Delhi : The Fiscal Research Foundation

CMIE (1991a). *Basic Statistics Relating to the Indian Economy.* Volume I : All India.. Bombay: Centre for Monitoring the Indian Economy

CMIE (1991b). *Basic Statistics Relating to the Indian Economy. Volume 2: States.* Bombay : Centre for Monitoring the Indian Economy

EPW Research Foundation (1995). National Accounts Statistics of India : Net State Domestic Product, *Economic and Political Weekly*, 30(51), December 23, 3321-3328

Fadia, B.L. and Menaria, R.K. (1990). *Sarkaria Commission Report and Centre State Relations.* Agra: Sahitya Bhavan

Gopalan, C (1995). Towards Food and Nutrition Security, *Economic and Political Weekly,* 30(52), December, 30, A. 134-A.142

Govinda Rao, M. And Chelliah, R.J. (1990). *Survey of Research on Fiscal Federalism in India.* New Delhi : National Institute of Public Finance and Policy.

Govinda Rao, M. and Das-Gupta, Arindam (1991). *Intergovernmental Transfers as an Instrument to Alleviate Poverty.* New Delhi : National Institute of Public Finance and Policy.September (Mimeo).

Gulati, I.S. (1991). State Level Planning - A Critique of. Sakaria Commission's Recommendations. In Kurien *et. al.* (1991).

Inamdar, N.R. (1991). Distribution of Powers between the Union and the States. In Nadkarni *et. al.* (1991)

Kurien, C.T., Prabhakar, E.R., and Gopal, S. (1991). *Economy, Society and Development.* New Delhi : Sage Publications.

Nadkarni, M.V., Seetharamu, A.S. and Aziz, A. (eds.) (1991) *India : The Emerging Challenges.* New Delhi; Sage Publications.

Nanjundappa, D.M. (1991). Fiscal Devolution and its Redistributive Role. In Nadkarni *et. al.* (1991)

Peaslee, Amos J. (1968). *Constitutions of Nations. Volume III – Europe, Volume IV: Americas.* 3rd Edition, The Hague; Martinus Nijhoff.

Peaslee, Amos J. (1985). *Constitutions of Nations: Volumes I and II; Asia, Australia and Oceania* 4th Edition, Dordrecht; Martinus Nijhoff.

Rao, V.V. Bhanoji (1993). *India's Economic Future: Government, People and Attitudes.* Delhi: Tata McGraw-Hill.

Ray, Amal (1992). New Economic Policy and Indian Federalism, *Economic and Political Weekly,* January 25, 147-150

Shiva Rao, B. *et. al.* (1968). *The Framing of India's Constitution.* New Delhi; The Indian Institute of Public Administration.

Sinha, R.K. (1987). *Fiscal Federalism in India.* New Delhi: Sterling Publishers.

World Bank (1991). *World Development Report,* 1991, Washington, D.C. : The World Bank.

World Bank (1993). *World Development Report* 1993, Washington, D.C. : The World Bank.

TABLE 1
Regional Economic Indicators

State	*Population (Million) 1991*	*State domestic product*		*Average annual growth of per capita SDP*		
		Per capita (Rs.) 1989-90	*Per capita ($) 1989-90*	*1960-61 to 1970-71*	*1970-71 to 1980-81*	*1980-81 to 1988-89*
Andhra Pradesh	66.3	3211*	222	1.0	1.2	2.6
Arunachal Pradesh	0.8	4176	251	n.a.	n.a.	5.7
Assam	22.3	3179	191	n.a..	0.1	3.3
Bihar	86.3	2122	127	0.4	0.8	2.3
Goa	1.2	6939	417	n.a.	4.4	1.4
Gujarat	41.2	5404	325	1.9	1.8	3.1
Haryana	16.3	6265	376	7.1	1.9	3.4
Himachal Pradesh	5.1	4005	241	n.a.	0.9	2.0
Jammu & Kashmir	7.7	3420	205	1.2	1.3	1.1
Karnataka	44.8	4075	245	2.0	0.7	3.0
Kerala	29.0	3389	204	1.4	0.4	0.1
Madhya Pradesh	66.1	2878	173	0.0	1.1	3.5
Maharashtra	78.7	6184	371	0.2	2.0	2.5
Manipur	1.8	3502	210	0.9	3.7	2.6
Meghalaya	1.8	3250	195	n.a.	n.a.	1.2
Mizoram	0.7	4077 @	314	n.a.	n.a.	n.a.
Nagaland	1.2	3464 *	239	n.a.	n.a.	n.a.
Orissa	31.5	3066	184	7.4	0.5	2.1

(Contd.)

State	*Population (Million) 1991*	*State domestic product*		*Average annual growth of per capita SDP*		
		Per capita (Rs.) 1989-90	*Per capita ($) 1989-90*	*1960-61 to 1970-71*	*1970-71 to 1980-81*	*1980-81 to 1988-89*
Punjab	20.2	7081	425	3.5	2.2	3.4
Rajasthan	43.9	2923	176	3.0	1.8	3.8
Sikkim	0.4	4396	264	n.a.	n.a.	6.5
Tamil Nadu	55.6	3894	234	0.7	0.3	3.9
Tripura	2.7	2866	172	- 0.7	2.3	0.8
Uttar Pradesh	138.8	3072	184	0.8	0.9	2.4
West Bengal	68.0	3963	238	- 0.5	0.9	2.3

Source: (i) *Economic Survey, 1991-92*
(ii) CMIE (1991b)
(iii) Government of India, Central Statistical Organisation, *Estimates of State Domestic Product, 1960-61 to 1983-84,* New Delhi : CSO. November 1985
(iv) Government of India, Central Statistical Organisation, *Estimates of State Domestic Product, 1970-71 to 1987-88,* New Delhi : CSO. 1989

* for 1988-89, @ for 1987-88

Table 2
Tenth Finance Commission Transfers to Major States and Latest Data on State Per Capita GDP, Index of Social Development, Infant Mortality and Female Literacy

State	*TFC Grants per capita*	*TFC Total Transfers per capita*	*State per capita GDP (1992-93)*	*INSD 1992-93*	*Infant Mortality Rate 1992-93*	*Female Literacy Rate 1991*
Andhra Pradesh	255.8	2,635.9	5,767	0.4702	70.4	32.7
Bihar	151.5	2,761.0	3,084	0.3779	89.2	22.9
Gujarat	203.1	2,093.4	7,175	0.5525	68.7	48.6
Haryana	140.8	1,652.7	9,171	0.5717	73.3	40.5
Karnataka	105.2	2,277.3	6,443	0.5128	65.4	44.3
Kerala	170.6	2,608.8	5,768	0.7406	23.8	86.2
Madhya Pradesh	119.1	2,342.7	4,733	0.4359	85.2	28.9
Maharashtra	104.0	1,680.0	9,628	0.5484	50.5	52.3
Orissa	284.9	2,996.0	4,097	0.4559	112.1	34.7
Punjab	206.3	1,725.5	11,106	0.5719	n.a.	50.1
Rajasthan	251.3	2,500.2	5,086	0.4557	72.6	20.4
Tamil Nadu	129.7	2,348.2	6,663	0.5585	67.7	51.3
Uttar Pradesh	182.7	2,509.3	4,273	0.4146	99.9	25.3
West Bengal	124.4	2,217.8	5,901	0.5010	75.3	46.3

Source: Bagchi (1995), *EPW* (1995), Gopalan (1995) and *Economic Survey* (1994-95).

11

Regional Inequality in India With Reference to Assam

A.K. Neog[1]

INTRODUCTION

The concept of Indian economy is not homogeneous as it encompasses regions and states with different levels of development. On Independence, India inherited an economy which was unbalanced both inter-regionally and intra-regionally. The economy was wedded to planning with the launching of the First Five Year Plan from 1951-52. Balanced regional development was accepted as one of the objectives of planning. The industrial policy Resolution of April 1956 has mentioned : "In order that industrialisation may benefit the economy of the country as a whole, it is important that disparities in levels of development between different regions should be progressively reduced." It was also recognised that only by securing a balanced and coordinated development of the industrial and agricultural economy in each region, can the entire country attain a higher standard of living.

This paper aims at exploring factors, levels and trend of equality and inequality in development over time and space in the Indian economy across 14 major states (state with population above

---

[1] The paper is prepared in the individual capacity of the author and has nothing to do with the service or the organisation to which he belongs. The author is grateful to Dr. B.C. Barah, Senior Consultant, National Institute of Public Finance and Policy, New Delhi, for his preliminary comments.

two per cent of all-India) during the period 1950-51 to 1993-94. These 14 states together (Table 1) account for about 94 per cent of the country's population and 93 per cent of the Net National Product (NNP).

CONCEPT OF EQUALITY

Before understanding the concept of equality or inequality in development it is necessary to understand the concept of development. Development is a multi-dimensional concept encompassing economic, demographic, technological, social, political, cultural, environmental and other aspects. Economic development, however, can be defined as a process whereby the real per capita income of the people increases over a long period of time, subject to the conditions that the percentage of people below a poverty line does not increase and that the distribution of income does not become more unequal in the process. The concept of per capita income has its own limitations. It is possible that its measure could be partly influenced by extra-economic considerations. Even if the measure is comparable between states in terms of concepts, definitions and methodology adopted, its relevance in the context of measurement of real value of production is still questionable. This is because inter-state prices not only differ but also their movements are not uniform. Despite these limitations, per capita income concept remains a common denominator for measuring development.

Regional economic equality implies not only equal level of per capita income among the regions or slates vis-à-vis the nation, but also equal rates of growth for all. It is both vertical and horizontal. Total economic inequality is the sum of inter-regional inequality i.e. inequality between regions and intra-regional inequality i.e. within region inequality. Income distribution among the states would be regarded as 'equal' if the shares in national income for every state are identical with their population shares in the country's population. Table 1 presents the scenario of this kind of inequality.

Concept of equality is a controversial one as it is as it is used interchangeably with equity, even though the former is positive and the latter is normative. Equity is concerned with the fairness of distribution which can be real as well as perceived. Martin Rein and S M Miller in their paper 'Standards of Income Redistribution' (1974), have presented as many as nine kinds of equality. These are : (i) one-hundred-percentism, e.g. equal pay for equal work, allowing no discrimination; (ii) the social minimum or the floor of protection, i.e. none should fall below some minimum level of income and service; (iii) equalisation of lifetime income profiles i.e. everyone should have an upward-sloping age-income profile, income differentials among different earning groups should not widen and people should have greater freedom to distribute lifetime earnings as they choose; (iv) stratum mobility i.e. narrowing down of income differentials among occupational groups; (v) economic inclusion i.e. reduce the contribution of income differences to the feelings of exclusion from society through measures like access to equal opportunity and equal treatment; (vi) income shares i.e. influence the share of national income that goes to particular segments of the society, usually defined in terms of deciles or quartiles; (vii) lowering the ceiling i.e. narrow the spread of incomes by reducing concentration at the top; (viii) avoidance of income and wealth crystallization i.e. reduce the advantage that high income and wealth give in the field of education, medical services, etc.; and (ix) international yardsticks i.e. a nation should have as equal an income distribution as that achieved by similar nations. The above concepts also embodies in them the measures to reduce inequality.

Inequality carries with it the notion of inequity. Welfare theorists regard inequality as undesirable. Bibek Debroy presents five notions of equity. These are: (i) identification of equity with equality as income inequality is undesirable because it is inequitable; (ii) a situation is equitable provided that every individual's income is proportional to his needs; (iii) a distribution of income is equitable only if each individual has the same marginal utility of income i.e. the utilitarian notion; (iv) a distribution of income is equitable only if each individual's income is proportional to his productive contribution (marginal or otherwise); and (v) distribution is equitable only if each individual has an income that is sufficient to meet minimum needs.[2]

---

2. 'Reducing Income Inequality – A Skeptical View', *The Economic Times,* November 5, 1986.

It is noticed that the above concepts of equality and equity are conflicting and none can be foolproof. It is however clear that equality and equitability are not identical. It is evident that there cannot be universally accepted optimum distribution of income, though one may agree that the positions of worst-off individuals amid regions need to be improved in absolute terms, not necessarily in relative terms.

A PRIORI RELATION BETWEEN INEQUALITY AND GROWTH

According to a hypothesis, inequality leads to more growth. This is beca-use propensity to save of the rich is higher than that of the poor. Saving is a sine-qua-non for growth. Because of larger savings the rich are able to accumulate wealth at a rate higher than the poorer class. This will accelerate growth that will "trickle down" to the poor. In other words, if the richer classes are doing well, the poor are also bound to fare better. Some even suggest that unequal distribution of income and wealth is to be welcomed because that alone can spur the idle amid the spend-thrift to change their habits. It is to be noted that all the rich are not always savers as more often they indulge in conspicuous consump-tion, wasteful expenditure and invest in non-performing assets.

Hidden in the above hypothesis is a sub-hypothesis that suggests that the larger the regional inequality, the larger would be national income growth. It is argued that a faster growth in the regional disparities will create more opportunities for the poor in the backward areas in the short run. It also draws support from the exponents of unbalanced growth thesis. If this is accepted then it will lead to perpetual pauperization of backward regions as the initial unequal distribution would be further accentuated. However, 'a posteriori' relation between income inequality and growth would depend on the state policy and its objectives. As for instance, historically, Republic of Korea has been experiencing higher rates of growth with higher degree of equality. Simon Kuznets has generalised that relative income inequality tends to rise during the early stages of development, reaches a peak and then declines in the later stages. It is however not the intention of this paper to test this.

Income is only a means, a means to buy goods and services. If income is unequally distributed then purchasing power is also unequally distributed. Consumption is a function of income. Consumption inequality is therefore linked to income inequality. Owners of assets are rewarded with income. Hence inequality in the distribution of assets, like land, is associated with income inequality. Assets and income are two sides of the same coin. Likewise employment inequality is associated with income inequality.

MEASUREMENT OF INEQUALITY

Inequality measures are classified into cardinal or positive and ordinal or normative. In his book *'On Economic Inequality'*, Amartya Sen presents six measures of positive inequality. However, commonly used measures are the range, index of decile inequality (also called Oshima index), standard deviation, coefficient of variation and the Gini coefficient. Some of these are applied in testing our hypotheses. It is to be noted that inequality trends are highly sensitive to the choice of the measure, the income recipient unit, the time period, the definition of income and the quality of data. Data limitations, like non-coverage of earnings from unorganised activities, barter and black money are well-known in backward regions.

EMPIRICAL ESTIMATES OF INEQUALITY

Per capita income data at current prices for 14 states presented in Table 2, show that the levels and trend of growth are unequal across the states vis-a-vis the per capita NNP for all-India. The 1950-51 data show higher levels than 1960-61 for West Bengal, Punjab, Gujarat, Assam, Kerala, Uttar Pradesh and Orissa, which were compiled by the National Council of Applied Economic Research (NCAER). The data for 1960-61 onwards are as prepared by the CSO. The 1950-51 data also give the ranking. West Bengal topped the states in per capita income with Rs. 471.40, while Bihar was at the bottom with Rs. 180.60, the range being Rs. 290.80. Assam ranked fifth in the per capita income ladder with Rs. 334.60, ahead of all-India average by Rs. 95.80, i.e. by over 40 per cent in 1950-51.

The ranking matrix has changed over time where some states have caught up while others lagged behind. For instance, in 1990-91 Punjab was at the top (even earlier), while West Bengal's position slided to fifth and Assam to eleventh. The range between the most developed Punjab and the least developed Bihar, widened to Rs. 5718. The gap between Assam and per capita NNP also widened to Rs. 968.8 i.e. by 19.4 per cent in 1990-91 compared to a marginal 4 per cent in 1960-61. Like Alice in Wonderland, Bihar is running and running to arrive at the same place, while Assam is playing a game of the hare and the tortoise.

Table 2 suggests that all the states are growing but some are growing faster than the others. Hence the argument that backward regions are getting poorer because of increasing disparities should be examined intrinsically.

Whether regional inequality is showing an increasing or decreas-ing trend can be examined by estimating the Gini coefficient (or ratio) and the coefficient of variation. Estimates of these two coefficients on the basis of per capita income data given in Table 2 for the 14 states are presented in Table 3.

Table 3
Inequality in per capita income distribution of 14 states during 1950-51 to 1993-94.

Item	*1950-51*	*1960-61*	*1970-71*	*1980-81*	*1990-91*	*1993-94*
Gini Ratio	0.1387	0.1124	0.1427	0.1616	0.1649	0.1765
Coefficient of Variation	0.2515	0.1981	0.2668	0.3 110	0.3140	0.3413

Both the indices in Table 3 show that after an initial decline in the concentration of per capita income during the first development decade (1950-60), inequality has been gradually rising thereafter. In 1960-61, the Gini concentration ratio was 0.1124 which rose to 0.1765 in 1993-94, while the coefficient of variation rose from 0.1981 to 0.3413 during the same period. These evidences show that regional inequality has remained undiminished despite economic growth over the last four decades or so.

CONSUMPTION INEQUALITY

The reports of NSS furnish evidence of consumption inequality. The concentration ratio of per capita consumer expenditure at the all-India level, in the rural sector for the total population, has marginally increased from 0.283 in NSS 25th round (1970-71) to 0.297 in its 38th round (1983). During the same period in rural India, the percentage of the total consumer expenditure shared by the bottom decile (10%) group fell from 3.91 per cent to 3.79 per cent compared to rise from 23.26 to 24.64 per cent for the top 10 per cent. However, for the period between 1987-88 and 1990-91 examining NSS data, Kaushal and Swaminathan, have shown that inequalities were declining as the share of the top 20 per cent in consumption decreased and of the bottom 20 per cent rose.[3] Hanumantha Rao points out that between 1990-91 and 1992, the distribution of consumption both in the rural and urban areas has deteriorated.[4] However, NCAER surveys indicate that majority of the people have not moved up high along the Engel curve, the vast rural population still spending mostly on food items.

LAND INEQUALITY

Concentration ratios for household ownership holdings, a measure of inequality in the distribution of land in India, prepared by the NSSO show a declining tendency from 0.75 in 1953-54, to 0.73 in 1961-62, to 0.71 each in 1971-72 and 1982. Our estimates, based on Agricultural Census data, however show the ratio at 0.60 in 1980-81 and 0.59 in 1985-86.

IDENTIFICATION OF CAUSES OF INEQUALITY

At the beginning of the First Plan, the different states were varying in levels of development, partly because of historical factors as population, soil condition, climate and natural resources. Hence the causes were hereditary.

Resources flowed to the states from four sources viz., plan allocation, Finance Commission award, central sector programmes

3. Neeraj Kaushal and Swaminathan S.A. Aiyar, *The Economic Times,* January 21, 1995

4. Hanumantha Rao, C.H., *The Economic Times,* February 11, 1995

and institutional finance from the banking sector. It has been noticed that financial assistance rendered up to March 1994, by financial institutions had been much higher than the population share or NNP share in respect of the developed states such as Maharashtra, Gujarat, Tamil Nadu and Karnataka and to some extent Punjab. It has been much lower in the rest. The concentration ratio or coefficient of variation in the per capita disbursement of financial assistance by the said institutions have considerably increased as can be seen from Table 4, suggesting that uneven flow of such resources could be a cause. While plan and finance awards are subject to some comprehensive criteria, there does not seem to be such criteria behind flow of institutional finance.

It may be added that the concentration ratio in the credit-deposit ratio of the public sector banks has declined in the 14 states from 0.2612 in 1969 to 0.1545 in 1991 and further to 0.1498 in 1993. The coefficient of variation also showed a downward trend.

Table 4
Index of Inequality in Per Capita Disbursement of Financial Assistance by All India Financial Institutions to the 14 States in the Given Years

Index	*1980-81*	*1989-90*	*1990-91*	*1993-94*
Gini Ratio	0.36	0.35	0.37	0.42
Coefficient of variation	0.65	0.65	0.69	0.83

Source: IDBI Reports on Development Banking in India (1989-90) and (1993-94)

Investment is only a necessary but not sufficient condition for growth or inequality. Much depends on the absorptive capacity or entrepreneurial ability, which in turn depends on other factors such as infrastructure, market, etc. Availability of adequate infrastructural facilities is a basic prerequisite for sustained development. The same has to be created before growth as it cannot be borrowed, imported, deferred or had on hire purchase. Hence lack of infrastructure is a kingpin behind regional disparity.

MARKET MECHANISM AND INEQUALITY

Market reform has been introduced in Indian economy from the Eight Plan (1992-97). Planning is now more indicative and the private sector has a greater role to play in development. The Government now has to depend more on market forces for price corrections than on regulations, which would adjust themselves according to rates of return and relative scarcity of inputs and outputs. Under market regime, the factors of production like capital, labour and technology can move freely across the regions, resulting in a secular tendency towards income equalisation.

Market is said to be a good servant but a bad master. One must therefore put some caveats. It excludes those who lack purchasing power and are backward. The market exacerbates disparities because the more the rich have, the greater the interest the market takes in them due to profit motive. In an economically unequal society the market unduly favours the production of goods and services for the rich and puts a low price on labour where the poor are without assets and lack bargaining power. When the economy is left to the full play of market forces, it distorts the distribution of income. Markets can be expected to perform the efficiency function without harming equity only when the initial distribution of income and wealth is equal, or when efforts are made consciously to turn the markets friendly towards the poor by widening freedom of choice, opportunities and capabilities for them. Under competitive regime, therefore, markets can achieve efficiency in production but not distributive justice. Market also fail in promoting non-price variables such as skill formation, technology, innovation, culture and institutional reform.

There is no mechanism in the law of markets that can automatically equalise fruits of development in all the regions. In backward areas, like tribal North East India, markets are either non-existent or highly imperfect or are underdeveloped. Suitable social norms and legal framework are prerequisites for an efficient market, which however are lacking in backward areas. The success of market forces as an integrating mechanism requires that no state or region be in a position to siphon off savings and resources from the scarce regions and appropriate all the benefits to itself, at the cost of others. One can therefore argue that market is for the developed areas and planning for the backward areas.

Symbiotic relationship between state and market is needed to combine market efficiency with social justice. Individualism, promotion of enterprise and market economy are quite compatible with a substantial state sector and government intervention. Reduction in government intervention is not a sufficient condition but better governance is, for the success of market. The government has a significant role in promoting market efficiency and growth, expanding public investment in infrastructure and social expenditure, reducing poverty and illiteracy and improving equity besides producing public goods. In addition, government intervention is also necessary to take counteractive measures to neutralise the gravitational and centrifugal forces associated with market in centralisation of activities, thereby reducing spatial disparities.

NORTH EASTERN SCENARIO

Situated in the mountain zone, the North Eastern region comprising Arunachal Pradesh, Assam, Manipur, Meghalaya, Mizoram, Nagaland and Tripura, accounting for 7.7 percent of the national geographical area, with 3.72 per cent population, producing above three per cent of national product is a declared backward region, categorised as special category states for plan finance. There is however considerable intra-regional heterogeneity in terms of production, demography and topography. As for instance, Assam alone accounts for over 71 per cent of the region's population with 30.7 per cent of the region's area, and 70.4 per cent of the regional State Domestic Product. Though a major portion of land in Assam is plain, in Manipur and Tripura it is marginal and extremely negligible in the hill states. Low level of infrastructure and outmoded production technology are responsible for the region's backwardness. While majority of the population in Assam, Manipur and Tripura are non-tribal, the tribal population in the rest ranges from minimum 70 per cent in Arunachal to 94 per cent in Mizoram. The literacy rate as per 1991 census ranges for males from 51.1 per cent in Arunachal to 84.06 in Mizoram compared to national average of 63.86 per cent, and for females from 29.37 per cent to 78.09 per cent each for the same states, compared to national average of 39.42 per cent. The region is rich in natural resources but backward economically and is over dependent on Central assistance. Its viability is persistently weak.

It is worth noting that in 1990-91, the per capita income of Arunachal Pradesh (Rs. 5479) and Nagaland (R.s. 5006) are higher than the national per capita income (Rs. 4982.8); while that of Meghalaya (Rs. 4530) and Mizoram (Rs. 4451), the states that were carved out of erstwhile Assam, are higher than that of Assam (Rs. 4014). Per capita income of Manipur and Tripura in the above year was Rs. 3893 and Rs. 3420 respectively. High levels of per capita income in Arunachal and Nagaland may be due to low population denominator, they do not reflect regional inequality in income terms even though there may be imbalance otherwise. The estimated growth rates (in annual percentage) of per capita income of Assam and of per capita NNP (at current prices), alongwith the growth of regional inequality measured as the growth in the difference gap between the state per capita income and per capita NNP with the help of exponential regression over time during the period 1980-81 to 1993-94 are presented in Table 5. The estimates of correlation coefficient between dependent variable viz., per capita income and the independent variable viz., time show that there is almost perfect relationship. Confining to the decade 1980/81 to 1990/91, it is seen that the per capita income gap was growing (10.06 per cent) annually almost at the same rate as in per capita growth of Assam (10.93 per cent) and of NNP (10.74). However, if the period is extended i.e. 1980/81 to 1993/94, then the growth rate in the 'gap' declines to 9.7 per cent. This decline together with the marginally higher growth rate of Assam than the NNP, is a silver lining for the inequality decline. This is pertinent, otherwise, according to the law of exponential growth when initial difference exists in the intercepts then the gap grows at the same rate as the growth rate in the per capita income or per capita NNP. This characteristic is analogous to the fact that two parallel lines or curves never intersect.

Table 5
Annual Growth (per cent) of per capita income of Assam and per capita NNP, of inequality gap and values of intercept and correlation coefficient.

Per capita Income	*Period*	*Growth*	*Intercept*	*Correlation (r)*
Assam	1980/81-90/91	10.93	1153.0	0.9865
	1980/81-93/94	11.51	1122.7	0.9928
NNP	1980/81-90/91	10.74	1461.2	0.9966
	1980/81-93/94	11.13	1435.4	0.9979
Gap	1980/81-90/91	10.06	298.1	0.8233
	1980/81-93/94	9.70	303.8	0.8895

Source: GOI, *Economic Survey*, 1994-95

The above exercise is carried out at current prices. When carried out at constant prices or adjusted for rate of inflation (implicit inflation rate at 8 to 9 per cent), the growth rates would be of lower order. Inequality gap has also a time dimension. Elsewhere, this author estimated that in 1984-85, the per capita income of Assam (at constant 1970-71 prices) was lagging the all-India average by a big margin. A real growth rate of 13.98 per cent in per capita income (really a Hanuman jump) was projected for Assam to catch up with national average by 2000 AD. This, in other words, calls for quantum jump in investment.

MEASURES TO PROMOTE EQUALITY

Measures must be taken to open the regional economy. This is a necessary condition. Low levels of farm productivity remains critical to the health of the regional economy, particularly of the North East. Both efficiency and equity considerations demand land reform particularly in the hill states, where land is unequally distributed. The link between higher agricultural productivity and local economic growth is direct. A more productive farm sector also means more food at lower prices. The fact that regional inequalities are associated with regional differences in agricultural productivity also calls for developing agriculture. Rapid technological progress in agriculture is needed.

The North East needs substantial investment in education, health and infrastructure. But the financial position of the states is so precarious that they are not in a position to meet these from their own resources. On the other hand, due to law and order problems entrepreneurs may not be attracted to invest in these areas in spite of tax-subsidy package. Hence Government investment particularly Central assistance, will have to come not only in infrastructure development but also in others, to wipe out the regional backlog, thereby enlarging the scope to catch up with the rest of the country. This will usher in cost-effectiveness and scale economies to the region to become competitive.

A long term regional perspective plan is needed to provide a general design of development that takes into account the strength, weakness, opportunities and threat perspectives of the region so as to spread the benefits of development as evenly as possible without slowing down the growth momentum elsewhere. The government should identify potentialities on the basis of inflow and outflow of resources viz. inside resource-inside market, inside resource-outside market, outside resource-inside market and outside resource-outside market. It should choose that strategy which optimises regional benefits.

The region has vast natural resources (like water, power, gas, etc.) and here lies the strength. New opportunities are coming up with the opening of trade frontiers with the bordering countries such as Bangladesh and Myanmar. Extending the same to Bhutan and China can augment the export activity. But infrastructure remains a weakness. Needless to say, industrialisation in the North East can not be sustained without infrastructure. The various export promotion councils of the country can mitigate this weakness by opening up offices within the region.

Regarding poverty removal measures, it is worth while to quote from L.C. Jain : "The North-East has its own traditional local institutions, and the starting point for a poverty-removing growth endeavour must be to allow the ideas, innovations and resources of these institutions to lead and direct development village by village - the Centre only supplementing their efforts rather than imposing a standard format from far away. This is by no means a sufficient condition, but certainly a necessary first step."[5]

---

[5] Jain, L.C., 'Poverty Alleviation through Growth : Policy Options for the North East', Seminar paper, NIRD (Guwahati) Seminar, March 17-19, 1993.

CONCLUDING REMARKS

Indian economy is at crossroads with launching of reforms in June 1991. The regional economy cannot remain insular. It has to launch institutional reform, create infrastructure, improve skill, technology and productivity of land and labour. Development is the best remedy to reduce regional inequality. Horizontal and vertical equality in development is a far cry. It can be possible only under the unlikely circumstances that all regions enjoy an equal and homogeneous share of resources, that all productive activities are subject to constant returns to scale and the society is homogeneous. The chances of such a configuration is rare and rarer still is the phenomenon that each state will display parallel rates of growth. Correction of inequality however cannot be delayed. The planners must design such strategies that can minimise inequality within a defined time horizon.

Table 1

Percentage Shares of major states in India's total population (1991) and Net National Product (NNP) at factor cost in 1990-91.

States	*Population share*	*NNP share*
Uttar Pradesh	16.5	11.6
Bihar	10.2	5.4
Maharashtra	9.3	13.7
West Bengal	8.1	7.7
Andhra Pradesh	7.9	7.5
Madhya Pradesh	7.11	6.5
Tamil Nadu	6.6	6.7
Karnataka	5.3	5.0
Rajasthan	5.2	4.3
Gujarat	4.9	5.6
Orissa	3.7	2.3
Kerala	3.4	2.9
Assam	2.6	2. 1
Punjab	2.4	4.0

Source: Government of India, *Economic Survey,* 1991-92 and 1994-95.

Table 2
Per capita income (Rs.) at current prices for 14 states for given years.

State	*1950-51*	*1960-61*	*1970-71*	*1980-81*	*1990-91*	*1993-94*	*Rank (1993-94)*
West Bengal	471.4	390	722	1564	4753	6055	(8)
Punjab	404.4	366	1070	2675	8373	12319	(1)
Gujarat	381.0	362	829	1951	5687	7600	(3)
Maharashtra	373.3	409	783	2427	7316	10984	(2)
Assam	334.6	315	535	1200	4014	5916	(9)
Kerala	303.9	259	594	1494	4207	6242	(7)
Karnataka	286.8	296	641	1596	4696	7029	(5)
Uttar Pradesh	270.5	252	486	1286	3516	4744	(12)
Andhra Pradesh	257.5	275	585	1380	4728	6489	(6)
Rajasthan	256.3	284	651	1222	4113	5220	(11)
Orissa	251.8	216	478	1231	3077	4726	(13)
Tamil Nadu	244.7	334	581	1498	5047	7352	(4)
Madhya Pradesh	235.8	260	484	1183	4149	5485	(10)
Bihar	180.6	215	402.	878	2655	3650	(14)
All-India	238.8	328.2	674.7	1630.1	4982.8	6929	

Sources: (i) For 1950-51 see NCAER, *Estimates of State Income* (1967)
(ii) Government of India, CSO
(iii) Parliament Question for 1993-94 data

SELECTED REFERENCES

Bhagwati, J. and Srinivasan, T. : *India's Economic Reforms* (July 1993)

Choudhury, R.A. et. al. : *The Indian Economy and its Performance since Independence*, OUP (1990). See the paper by Raj Krishna

Das, H.N. : A New Paradigm of Development – Regional Imbalance and Assam

Deb, Bimal J. (ed.) : *Regional Development in North-East India*, Reliance Publishing House (1995). See the paper by A.K. Neog

FAO : The Dynamics of Rural Poverty

Goswami, Atul (ed.) : *Land Reforms and Peasant Movement* (1986). See paper by Neog and Bardoloi

Heilbroner, R.L. and Ford, A. : *Economic Relevance – A Second Look*, Goodyear Publishing (1976). See paper by Rein and Miller

Jain, L.C., : *Report on Agricultural Development of North Eastern India*, Planning Commission, GOI (1990)

Jalan, B (ed.) : *The Indian Economy – Problems and Prospects*, Viking (1992)

Mathur, A. : "Why Growth Rates Differ" within India –An Alternative Approach, in *Journal of Development Studies* (January, 1987)

Ministry of Planning, GOI : *Sarvekshana* (Jan-March 1989)

ibid. : NSSO 37th Round, Report No. 330 (1987)

Needleman, L. (ed.) : *Regional Analysis*, Penguin (1968)

Oshima, H.T. : Income Inequality and Economic Growth – The postwar experience in Asian countries, *Malayan Economic Review* (Oct. 1970)

Planning Commission, GOI : Economic Development in Different Regions (Aug. 1962)

Sen, Amartya : *On Economic Inequality*, OUP (1989)

Thakur, P. (ed.) : *Profile of a Development Strategy for India's North East* (1988). See the article by A.K. Neog

12

Proposals to Promote Equality and Development in India's Far East

Sanjoy Hazarika

One of the major reasons for disparities and tensions in India's Far East which is how I would prefer to call what is usually known as the Northeast is the pressure on resources, causing both environmental scarcity and the overspill into social conflict that is so visible in every part of the region.

It would be too ambitious in a limited paper such as this, to enumerate and analyse the various aspects of these pressures. Therefore, one would seek to limit one's focus on an issue that caused much confrontation and trouble in the 1980s, and which is rising again as a major source of potential conflict.

One is referring here to the question of migration from Bangladesh and Nepal (and to a very limited extent from the Nepalese-speakers in Bhutan), that is leading to economic and other imbalances in the area, especially in Assam.

Migration is not a new phenomenon in this region or to any other part of the world. There are historic, political, traditional and geographical as well as economic and ecological reasons behind these movements of people.

Yet, for centuries, India's North-east has been a frontier land that has drawn communities from as far away as present-day Kampuchea and Thailand, Burma and Bangladesh, Nepal and North India. In addition, the British transported Adivasis and other groups from Central and Eastern India to work in the tea plantations in the 19th century.

But over the past half a century, migration has flowed especially from what is now Bangladesh but what was earlier the province of East Bengal and later East Pakistan.

For purposes of brevity, one does not propose to go into the reasons for these migrations : they were induced by the Muslim League Government in the 1930s and 1940s, and opposed by the Congress under Gopinath Bardoloi. This attitude of the Congress changed after Bardoloi's demise - as did that of other political parties - who saw the settlers and immigrants as potential vote banks.

One is only too familiar with the pattern of unrest, confrontation, violence and fractured peace that has existed in the Assam Valley since 1979 over this question. But one must look deeper to the roots of the crisis and look beyond the present, to develop a broad yet deep enough perspective of the future.

ROOT CAUSES

Why do migrants from Bangladesh and earlier from East Pakistan come? What are the push and pull factors? Is land scarcity a major problem? Where do they come from? And where do they go?

In numerous respects, Bangladesh represents the Malthusian nightmare : too many mouths to feed and too little food, or too many people on too little land. The population of 115 million continues to grow at an estimated pace of between 2.2 and 3 per cent a year. It has doubled in the past 30 years. The country's population density of over 800 per sq. km. is the world's highest. Bangladesh is one of the poorest nations in the world, with a per capita income of less than 170 dollars a year. Less than one-third of the adults were literate, and although three-quarters of the children enrolled in primary school, two-thirds dropped out before secondary school.

Nearly 80 per cent of the agricultural land is already covered by rice, and nearly 60 per cent of the country's investments are financed by foreign aid. The growth in population has led to a situation where the average farm holding is less than one hectare (or less than two acres). Despite their lower costs, high-yielding modern varieties of foodgrains have not been introduced to all areas. By one estimate, such varieties now cover 40 per cent of the cereal-growing areas, but their potential remains largely unexploited because of flooding. Estimates indicate that if irrigation were extended to 62 per cent of the cultivated area, foodgrain production would reach the level of 30.7 million tonnes, a vast leap over the current level of 18 to 19 million tonnes. This output could feed an estimated 185 million people at the current levels of food intake.

The attractions to migrate to more lightly populated lands across the borders are immense. Bangladesh has a high population density. The density of population in India's North East is far less. In Assam it is 284 per sq. km.; the figures are 78 for Meghalaya, 262 for Tripura, and 33 for Mizoram. West Bengal, however, has a reported density almost on par with Bangladesh : 766 per sq. km., the highest among all major states.

Bangladesh officially maintains that its nationals prefer to go to the Gulf where there are opportunities, rather than to India which can offer little. Yet, most come to India because as unskilled labourers, they find a ready market in the subcontinent for maids, construction workers, and porters. Bangladesh journalists and officials privately acknowledge the fact of continuing emigration. While economic conditions in the bordering Indian states of West Bengal, Assam and Meghalaya may not be ideal, they are better than in Bangladesh. Land and work are available.

There are two basic factors that favour an immigrant moving from Bangladesh to North-Eastern India. One is that the migrant speaks Bengali, a language that is spoken by more than 170 million people in the region, making the Bengalis one of the largest linguistic groups in the world. Language gives access to jobs, property and education. A second factor is that many migrants have relatives on the other side of the border.

Emigration has been a perennial feature of East Bengal long before the British Raj ended; it continued through the years of East Pakistan and post-partition; and it continues today from Bangladesh across the borders of eastern India. More than anything else, the emigrants are fleeing from the poverty and degradation that give them little choice but to leave their homes for another land.

According to one estimate, population growth in Bangladesh will slash in half the amount of cropland available per capita by the year 2025. This crisis is worsened by the fact that all of the country's good farmland has already been heavily exploited. "At about 0.08 ha. per capita, cropland is already desperately scarce," says the study. "Flooding and inadequate national and community institutions for water control exacerbate the lack of land and the brutal poverty and turmoil it engenders."

The poverty in Bangladesh, is in no small way attributable to the region's vulnerability to natural disasters. Bangladesh seems to move through an unending cycle of floods, cyclones, devastation, death, drought and famine. Marauding rivers burst their banks and change course with impunity, and heavy silting raises the level of river beds and increases the size of the flood plains, wiping out entire villages and reducing even the moderately affluent to penury. More than one million people have been killed by floods since 1961. And the 1988 floods, the worst in recent memory, reduced rice production by 1.6 million tonnes and caused 1.3 billion dollars worth of damage to roads, railroads, houses and industrial machinery.

Floods, however, are a necessary evil. They renew the land. Bangladesh's intensive cultivation depends on silt deposited on the flood plains by water-gorged rivers in the rainy season.

DEMOGRAPHIC DATA

We also need to look at data that will enable us to see the other side of the demographic road and see if it supports the views expressed above.

Rough estimates are available of the numbers of migrants moving over the years out of Bangladesh and into North East India. A significant study by Sharifa Begum, of the Bangladesh Institute of Development Studies in Dhaka, represents the first semi-official acknowledgement by Dhaka of the size of the migration problem. According to Begum, between 3.15 and 3.5 million people migrated from East Pakistan to India between 1951 and 1961. And between 1961 and 1974, another 1.5 million migrated.

A national census was conducted in 1961 and 1974. The 1974 census was the first in independent Bangladesh. The latter figure is based on census figures and incorporates estimates of deaths from the 1970 cyclone and from the Bangladesh liberation war. But it appears to be a conservative estimate as it does not take into account the 10 million who fled the repression of the Pakistani Army in 1970 and 1971, before an Indian military victory allowed them to return home. Most of the migrants returned; yet nearly a million (believed to be mostly Hindus) stayed in India, apparently blending into the countryside. All this adds up to an outflow of 6 million in the 23 years between 1951 and 1974.

In a more recent paper, Begum states that although statistics for migration are not available after 1974, there is no valid reason to suggest that migration ceased at that time. She adds that in fact there are indications that Bangladesh lost a substantial proportion of its population from 1974 to 1981, due to migration and famine.

Though Bangladesh persists in its proclamations that it has not illegal aliens in India, Bangladeshi communities have sprung up in New Delhi and Bombay. While the Government of India declares that there are about 100,000 Bangladeshi migrants in Delhi, intelligence estimates say the figure is actually closer to 200,000.

The Border Security Force that patrols the Indian side of the international frontier says that it detained more than 56,000 Bangladeshis trying to cross into West Bengal in 1990. Detentions and deportations of people held at the border in Assam and Tripura were far less, estimated at several hundred. "The rule of thumb in this game is that for every illegal immigrant caught, at least four get through, especially if they are Hindus," says one senior Indian diplomat, who knows the problem well. He states that the issue is raised at virtually every Indo-Bangladesh meeting of officials, diplomats and politicians. "But illegal migration remains the unfinished agenda of every dialogue, the unresolved issue. It is really a dialogue of the deaf : we tell Dhaka these people are coming in, Dhaka says they are not Bangladeshis, they are Indian smugglers or citizens returning after illegally visiting relatives or friends in Bangladesh."

This raises the question as to what is to be done.

Let me outline a series of steps which I believe can tackle the problem at its root and develop a road toward cooperative endeavour in the region, for it is only a regional approach that can work.

Migration will continue, especially from Bangladesh and Nepal. No wall, law or police force anywhere in the world has been able to stop it. People, like water, always find their level for survival. But if massive inflows are to be checked, then we have to find strategies to help Bangladesh and Nepal develop their economies and help curb the outflow of people. Otherwise there will be snowballing conflicts over land and other resources as nearly a billion Indians and nearly 200 million Bangladeshis will compete for jobs and land by the year 2020. Without policies on population, migration, flood and river control, we may see a clash of nationalities and border communities that will overshadow ethnic conflict elsewhere in the world. If we consider that pressure on natural resources and cultural/ethnic identity are the basis for conflict, then we must also accept that the trigger for change is in tackling these very issues.

Economic development, rooted in cooperation in water and other resource sharing, multilateral trade and assisting communities at the micro level, instead of imposing centrally-sponsored schemes on them, are the opportunities for change. Again, I would stress here that the sense of inclusion and participation of the local communities is critical in making programmes work rather than a paternalism that provokes bitterness.

Some steps are being taken in this direction with the adoption of a South Asia free trade zone by the member nations of SAARC. Indeed, the region as has been described here makes a coherent trading bloc - for it has time, tradition and geography on its side. But if SAARC is to be more meaningful, this eastern Himalayan stretch and its plains must become the focus of attention and cooperation, to transform the lives of millions of people.

Some specific strategies towards such a goal are

* Devise economic strategies within Bangladesh that will enable people to stay in their country rather than migrate. This would include developing markets and opportunities at home which can only come as part of a larger strategy that involves its neighbours.

* Strengthen existing constitutional safeguards for the small communities so that they can survive the inflow of migrants and the growth of larger domestic populations. In addition, they need to be trained in skills that will enable them to compete outside their enclaves.

* As many as 54 large, medium and small rivers flow into Bangladesh; all of them originate outside the country, giving it few alternatives in its regular battles against floods. One would suggest a network of small and medium dams as run of the river projects in parts of Nepal, Bhutan, Sikkim and Arunachal Pradesh to tap a fraction of the vast reserves of hydro energy that are going waste and creating flood havoc downstream.

* The easing of floods would open up new land for cultivation and harvesting, and ease some of the demographic pressures. It would also enable Bangladesh to get more water when needed. The tapping of the smaller streams would be a major source of river water during the dry months when farmers most need it.

* Sell the power within the region or export it to other parts of India and South east Asia. Energy hunger is destined to grow rapidly in the next few decades as industralisation and unshackled economies surge forward.

* Increase the open trade between the countries and communities by building better roads and other transport and communication facilities. Revive the water transport system that would generate employment, trade and better communication and decrease freight costs. Develop a series of inland ports that would cater to the revived river traffic and make Calcutta the hub of this river strategy as an inland port and not an international seaport, a role for which it is no longer suited but which Paradeep is better placed to play. It would also lessen the reliance on Farakka and remove a major thorn between the two countries.

* Give port and transit facilities to countries of the region and make legal travel easier.

* Develop local economic schemes with regard to handicraft and handloom development, marketing local products and improved

agriculture and water use strategies including better seed technologies, that will strengthen community-based economies.

* Develop education projects that would enable students and people from the new zone to learn about each other by teaching the languages, histories and traditions in educational institutions. We know so little about each other. It is perhaps easier to learn about the Chakmas at Harvard and Cambridge than in Calcutta or Shillong. It is time these information gaps are plugged so that dogmas are tackled and misunderstandings cleared.

* An information and communication network involving journalists and communicators of the region needs to be made broader and deeper. Journalists from the print, audio and visual media need to travel to each other's countries and states to understand the core issues. Without a change in attitudes, no policies, however laudable, will work.

* An international airport at Guwahati could be part of a methodical approach to improve regional infrastructure, giving industry and entrepreneurs opportunities to trade with Dhaka and also with the fast-growing economics of Southeast Asia.

Questions of identity will continue to be raised and resistance to Centre-driven changes will drag on for many years. But it is time for the people of this region, who have suffered long enough, to prepare themselves for new challenges and opportunities.

Yet, in closing, one cannot but recall the ringing words of Mahatma Gandhi to Bardoloi's emissaries in 1946, when they went to seek his support against placing Assam with Bengal in the Cabinet Mission's Plan:

"If Assam keeps quiet, it is finished. No one can force Assam to do what it does not want to do. It must stand independently as an autonomous unit. It is autonomous to a large extent today. It must become fully independent and autonomous. Whether you have that courage, grit and the gumption, I do not know. You alone can say that....

"You will have to forget petty jealousies and rivalries and overcome your weaknesses. Assam has as many weaknesses as it has strength, for I know my Assam.

"We look to the Congress and then feel that if we do not follow it slavishly something will go wrong with it. I have said that not only a province but even an individual can rebel against the Congress and by doing so save it assuming he is on the right. I have done so myself....

"I have given you all this time to steel your hearts, to give you courage. If you do not act correctly and now, Assam will be finished. Tell Bardoloi I do not want Assam to lose its soul. It must uphold it against the whole world. Else I will say that Assam had only manikin and no men."

13

Inter-state Disparities in Production and Productivity of Foodgrains

Atul Goswami
Archana Sharma

Inter-state disparities are measured either by using single indicators such as per capita state domestic product, percentage of people below poverty line, etc. or by combining a number of indicators into one composite index. Studies on inter-state disparities in India (Ganguli and Gupta 1976, Pal : 1975, Kantawala and Rao : 1992, Sharma : 1989, 1995, Datta and Jain : 1993, CMIE : 1994) suggest that there has been only a marginal reduction in inter-state disparities in the country over time. Moreover, the composition of the most developed and most backward regions has remained nearly the same. (Tables Al through A6 in Appendix), indicating that development programmes have not succeeded in enabling the backward regions to overcome their difficulties.

In the agricultural sector, inter-state disparities were not very high till the 1960's. But the 'new agricultural strategy', which relied heavily on the use of inputs such as improved seeds and chemical fertilizers, irrigated water, contributed to widening the disparities between regions in the sphere of agricultural production and productivity. A marked change was observed in the growth rates of foodgrains in the case of all the states in the post-green revolution period (Table A7 in Appendix). Many states which were having growth rates higher than the national average growth rate in the pre-green revolution period, experienced a deceleration in the growth rate in the post-green revolution period. Those states which performed better during the latter period were characterised by better infrastructure in respect of public irrigation, rural electrification, roads, literacy levels, land system, credit and marketing institutions and administrative capabilities, etc. (Rao: 1991). Variation in irrigation was identified as the most important factor contributing to inter-state variations in productivity of foodgrains. The green revolution succeeded in Punjab mainly because of the huge public investments in irrigation during the last 100 years, and its long experience with the canal colonies of Montgomery and Lyllpur (Krishnaji : 1975 Datta and Jain : 1994).

In the present study, we propose to look into the trend in inter-state disparities in agricultural productivity. For this purpose we compare production and the inter-state variations in per capita production and per hectare yield, with the help of coefficients of variation computed for annual averages corresponding to three triennia - viz.1970-73, 1980-83 and 1991-94.

The factors causing inter-state disparities in agricultural growth are well recognised. We examine the trend in the inter-state disparities in some of these factors, to have an idea as to whether any success has been achieved in removing the disparities.

The paper depends on secondary data collected from CMIE reports.

The results show that there has been. an. increasing trend in the inter-state disparities in per capita production as well as productivity (Table- 1).

Table 1
Inter-state coefficient of variation (per cent) in per capita production and per hectare yield of foodgrains : 1970-73 to 1991-94

	1970-73	*1980-83*	*1991-94*
Per Capita Production	54.71	72.76	88.99
Per hectare yield	36.62	39.91	42.74

Disparities in per capita production entails heavy expenditure on foodgrains for deficit states as they have to spend huge amounts on imports of foodgrains.

Irrigation continued to be an important factor in reducing inter-state disparities in foodgrains productivity as the coefficient of variation in productivity of foodgrains under irrigated land has been nearly 10 percentage points lower than productivity of foodgrains under irrigated land.(Table 2).

Table 2
Inter-state coefficients of variation (per cent) in productivity of foodgrains under irrigated areas and HYVs : 1990-91

	Irrigated	*Unirrigated*	*Overall Average*	*HYV*
Rice	28.59	38.02	38.72	36.65
Wheat	39.66	48.00	24.65	44.85

But productivity under HYV seeds showed higher inter-state disparities in the case of wheat although in the case of rice, disparities were lower for HYV seeds in comparison to the disparities in the overall average (Table 2). This may be because rice is cultivated mostly in rain-fed areas.

The inter-state disparities in irrigated area as percentage of state's cropped areas had declined over time. But this decline was mainly attributable to the reduction in disparities in irrigated area under wheat. The disparities in irrigated area under rice are still sharp. (Table 3). Worse still, there has been no absolute variation in net or gross irrigated area in Assam and Manipur between 1971-72 and 1991-92, whereas there has been a reduction in the irrigated area as percentage of total cropped area in Assam from 27.13 in 1971-72 to 21.04 in 1991-1992.

Inter-state disparities in fertilizer consumption has been so high that in 1994-95 fertilizer consumption per hectare of gross cropped area was only 9.5 kg. in Assam as against 174.7 kg. in Punjab and 457.3 kg. in Pondicherry. The trend in the inter-state disparities in fertilizer consumption has also been increasing. The inter- state coefficient of variation was 83.35 per cent in 1980-81, which increased to 128.0 in 1990-91; in 1994-95, it declined marginally but was still as high as 110 per cent.

Table 3
Inter-state coefficients of variation (per cent) in irrigated area

	1971-72	*1981-82*	*1991-92*
1. Irrigated area as percentage of state's cropped area	70.05	63.34	60.26
2. Irrigated area under rice	59.94	62.04	57.66
3. Irrigated area under wheat	39.30	28.15	14.90

Size of land holdings is also an important determinant of agricultural growth. Inter-state disparities in the average size of land holdings had also an increasing trend over time, with the coefficient of variation increasing to 71.28 per cent in 1990-91 compared to 61.48 per cent in 1970-71.

From the foregoing analysis we can come to the conclusion that the agricultural sector in India still shows sharp inter-state disparities and the disparities are widening over time.

Both quantitative and qualitative improvements in the infrastruc-tural facilities are an urgent necessity if inter-state disparities are to be reduced. In creating irrigation facilities, it has to be remembered that in flood-prone areas, the problem is not merely one of making water available but also of proper water management (Goswami :1989).

REFERENCES

Chattopadhyay, B and Moonis Raza. 1975. Regional Development : Analytical Framework and Indicators. *Indian Journal of Regional Science* Vol. VII No. 1.

Centre for Monitoring Indian Economy. 1994. *Basic Statistics Relating to States -1995. India's Agricultural Sector.*

Datta, K. K and T. L. Jain. 1994. A study on Inter—state variations in Rural Development. *Indian Journal of Agricultural Economics* Vol. 49 No. 1. Jan - March, 1994.

Ganguli, B. N. and D. B. Gupta. 1976. *Levels of Living in India : An Inter-state Profile,* S. Chand.

Goswaini, P.C. 1989. Modernising Assam's Agriculture in Goswami P. C. (ed.) 1989. *Agriculture in Assam,* Assam Institute of Development Studies, Guwahati.

Government of India : *Economic Survey*: 1994 - 95.

Kantawala, B. S. and A. S. Rao. 1992. Sectoral Development in India - An Inter-state Analysis. *IJRS* - Vol. XXIV No. 1 - 1992.

Krishnaji, N. 1975. Inter-Regional Disparities in Per Capita Production and Productivity of Food grain. A preliminary note on Trends. *Economic and Political Weekly.* Spl. No. Aug. 1975.

Pal., M. N. 1975. Regional Disparities in the Level of Development in India. *IJRS* Vol. II No. 1. 1975.

Rao, Y.V.K. 1991. *Growth and Inequality in Agriculture.* People's Publishing House.

Sharma, A. 1989. Levels of Living in Assam. 1955-1980. Unpublished Ph.D. thesis, Dibrugarh University.

Sharma, A, 1995. Inter-state Disparities in the Level of Development in India in B.J. Deb (ed.) 1995. *Regional Development in North-East India : Issues and Prospects.* Reliance Publishing House, New Delhi.

APPENDIX

Table A1
Rank of States in Terms of Composite Index and Infrastructural (Environment) Index of Levels of Living

States	*Ranks as per the composite index*			*Ranks as per the infrastructural index*		
	1955	*1960*	*1965*	*1955*	*1960*	*1965*
(1)	*(2)*	*(3)*	*(4)*	*(5)*	*(6)*	*(7)*
Andhra Pradesh	8	10	10	9	9	5
Assam	9	11	9	13	12	13
Bihar	14	15	15	14	15	15
Gujarat	11	8	8	7	6	6
Jammu & Kashmir	10	9	6	10	4	3
Kerala	4	7	5	8	8	8
Madhya Pradesh	12	12	12	12	14	11
Maharashtra	5	4	3	5	5	7
Karnataka	6	5	7	2	3	2
Orissa	15	14	13	11	11	12
Punjab	2	2	1	3	2	4
Rajasthan	7	6	11	6	10	10
Tamil Nadu	1	1	2	1	1	1
Uttar Pradesh	13	13	14	15	13	14
West Bengal	3	3	4	4	7	9

Source: Ganguli, B.N. and Gupta, D. B. 1976 : *Levels of Living in India : An Inter-state Profile* S. Chand. p. 116 and p. 137

Table A2
Most developed and most backward group of states in India : 1983-1984

Indices (1)	*Most Developed* (2)	*Most Backward* (3)
Composite with Environment*	1. Kerala	1. Assam
	2. Punjab	2. Bihar
	3. Himachal Pradesh	3. West Bengal
	4. Sikkim	4. Manipur
	5. Tamil Nadu	5. Madhya Pradesh
Composite without Environment*	1. Delhi	1. Manipur
	2. Chandigarh	2. West Bengal
	3. Pondicherry	3. Assam
	4. Kerala	4. Bihar
	5. Andaman & Nicobar Islands	5. Meghalaya
	6. Goa, Daman and Diu	6. Madhya Pradesh
	7. Himachal Pradesh	7. Karnataka
Environment *	1. Punjab	1. Assam
	2. Tamil Nadu	2. Bihar
	3. Kerala	3. Uttar Pradesh
	4. Karnataka	4. Madhya Pradesh
	5. Sikkim	5. Jammu and Kashmir

Note: * Environment stands for the infrastructural index.
Source: Sharma, A. 1989. 'Levels of Living in Assam 1955-1980, unpublished Ph.D. thesis, Dibrugarh University.

Table A3
Most Developed and Most Backward States in India

Most Developed	*Most Backward*
(1)	*(2)*
Maharashtra	Manipur
West Bengal	Tripura
Uttar Pradesh	Mizoram
Tamil Nadu	Nagaland
Andhra Pradesh	Meghalaya
Punjab	Assam

Source: Sharma, A. 1995. Inter-state disparities in the level of development in India : With particular reference to the N.E. Region in Deb (ed.).1995 *Regional Development in N.E. India* Reliance, New Delhi.

Table A4
Inter-state disparities 1970-73 — 1986-89 as per the composite Index constructed by Datta & Jain. *

States	*Ranks*	
	1970-73	*1986-89*
Andhra Pradesh	9	8
Assam	16	16
Bihar	11	11
Gujarat	8	10
Haryana	4	4
Himachal Pradesh	12	13
Karnataka	6	9
Kerala	3	2
Madhya Pradesh	14	14
Maharashtra	10	7
Orissa	15	15
Punjab	1	1
Rajasthan	13	12
Tamil Nadu	2	3
Uttar Pradesh	7	5
West Bengal	8	6
Coefficient of variation (per cent)	30.18	28.22

Source: Datta, K.K. and T. L. Jain. 1993, A Study of Inter-state Variations in Rural Development in India in *IJAE*. Vol. 49, No. 1 Jan-March 1994.

Table A5
Most Developed and Most Backward States as per CMIS's Index of Relative Development of Infrastructure

Year (1)	*Most Developed States* (2)	*Most Backward States* (3)
1980-81	1. Punjab	1. Tripura
	2. Haryana	2. Meghalaya
	3. Tamil Nadu	3. Jammu & Kashmir and Manipur
	4. Kerala	4. Nagaland
	5. West Bengal	5. Himachal Pradesh
	6. Gujarat	6. Orissa
	7. Maharashtra	7. Assam
1990-91	1. Punjab	1. Arunachal Pradesh
	2. Haryana	2. Mizoram
	3. Tamil Nadu	3. Tripura
	4. Kerala	4. Meghalaya
	5. Gujarat	5. Jammu & Kashmir
	6. West Bengal	6. Madhya Pradesh
	7. Maharashtra & Uttar Pradesh	7. Manipur
1992-93	1. Punjab	1. Arunachal Pradesh
	2. Goa	2. Mizoram & Tripura
	3. Haryana	3. Meghalaya
	4. Kerala	4. Jammu & Kashmir
	5. Tamil Nadu	5. Nagaland
	6. Gujarat	6. Madhya Pradesh
	7. West Bengal	7. Rajasthan

Source: CMIE : *Basic Statistics : States*. September, 1994. Table 5.1 - 1

Table A6
Most Developed and Most Backward States/U.T.s in India1980-81 to 1992-93 as per Per Capita State Domestic Product

Year (1)	*Most Developed* (2)	*Most Backward* (3)
1980-81	1. Delhi	1. Bihar
	2. Goa	2. Assam
	3. Punjab	3. Rajasthan
	4. Maharashtra	4. Orissa
	5. Haryana	5. Uttar Pradesh
	6. Gujarat	6. Mizoram
	7. Jammu & Kashmir	7. Tripura
1990-91	.. Delhi	1. Bihar
	2. Goa	2. Orissa
	3. Punjab	3. Tripura
	4. Haryana	4. Uttar Pradesh
	5. Maharashtra	5. Manipur
	6. Gujarat	6. Jammu & Kashmir
	7. Arunachal Pradesh	7. Assam
1992-93*	1. Punjab	1. Bihar
	2. Goa	2. Orissa
	3. Haryana	3. Jammu & Kashmir
	4. Maharashtra	4. Uttar Pradesh
	5. Arunachal Pradesh	5. Madhya Pradesh
	6. Karnataka	6. Rajasthan
	7. Tamil Nadu	7. Assam

**Note:* Data for Delhi, Himachal Pradesh, Manipur, Mizoram, Nagaland, Sikkim and Tripura are not included due to their non-availability.
Source: Government of India : Economic Survey, 1994-95

Table A7
Trend in Inter-state disparities in production and Productivity of foodgrains

States	*Trend in growth of foodgrains*	
	1961-70	*1971-85*
(1)	*(2)*	*(3)*
Andhra Pradesh	1.06	3.24
Assam	2.97	1.90
Bihar	0.35	0.55
Gujarat	3.65	3.44
Haryana	5.10	3.98
Himachal Pradesh	4.91	0.68
Jammu & Kashmir	6.57	2.30
Karnataka	3.86	1.43
Kerala	2.03	- 0.39
Madhya Pradesh	- 0.26	1.63
Maharashtra	- 0.09	5.97
Orissa	2.26	1.50
Punjab	9.09	5.91
Rajasthan	- 0.31	1.31
Tamil Nadu	0.71	0.71
Uttar Pradesh	2.38	3.93
West Bengal	2.83	0.46
All India	1.84	2.66

Source: Hanumantha Rao, C. H., Unstable Agriculture and Droughts as reproduced in Rao, Y. V. K. 1991 *Growth and Inequality in Agriculture*.

List of Contributors

1. K. N. Raj, Professor Emeritus, Centre for Development Studies, Thiruvananthapuram
2. K. K. George, Professor of Economics, Cochin University of Science and Technology, Kochi
3. Satish C. Jha, Ex-Chief Economist, Asian Development Bank
4. Neeraj Kaushal, Senior Editor, Economic Times, New Delhi
5. Srinath Baruah, Professor of Economics, Gauhati University, Guwahati
6. Jayanta Madhab, Chairman, NEDFi, Guwahati
7. G. Parthasarthy, Director, Institute of Development and Planning Studies, Visakhapatnam
8. Jayashree Anand, Senior Research Fellow, Institute of Development and Planning Studies, Visakhapatnam
9. C. V. R. Sankar, Lecturer in Statistics, Institute of Development and Planning Studies, Visakhapatnam
10. V. K. Ramachandran, Indira Gandhi Institute of Development Research, Bombay
11. Vikas Rawal, Indira Gandhi Institute of Development Research, Bombay
12. Madhura Swaminathan, Indira Gandhi Institute of Development Research, Bombay
13. Gunilla Sterner, Country Administrative Board of Stockholm, Sweden
14. Atul Sarma, Professor, Indian Statistical Institute, New Delhi
15. V. V. Bhanoji Rao, National University of Singapore

16. A. K. Neog, Indian Economic Services, New Delhi
17. Sanjoy Hazarika, Centre for Policy Research, New Delhi
18. Atul Goswami, Professor, Omeo Kumar Das Institute of Social Change and Development, Guwahati
19. Archana Sharma, Reader in Economics, Gauhati University, Guwahati